JAMES MERRILL

COLUMBIA INTRODUCTIONS TO

TWENTIETH-CENTURY

AMERICAN POETRY

JOHN UNTERECKER, GENERAL EDITOR

JAMES MERRILL

AN INTRODUCTION
TO THE POETRY

JUDITH MOFFETT

COLUMBIA UNIVERSITY PRESS
NEW YORK
1984

Library of Congress Cataloging in Publication Data

Moffett, Judith, 1942–
    James Merrill, an introduction to the poetry.

    (Columbia introductions to twentieth-century
American poetry)
    Bibliography: p.
    Includes index.
    1. Merrill, James Ingram—Criticism and interpretation.
I. Title. II. Series.
PS3525.E6645Z78 1983   811'.54   83-15022
ISBN 0-231-05210-3

Columbia University Press
New York   Guildford, Surrey
Copyright © 1984 Columbia University Press
All rights reserved

Printed in the United States of America

Clothbound editions of Columbia University Press books are
Smyth-sewn and printed on permanent and durable acid-free
paper.

COLUMBIA INTRODUCTIONS TO

TWENTIETH-CENTURY

AMERICAN POETRY

for Daniel Hoffman

Contents

JOHN UNTERECKER

Foreword

In the opening chapter of this perceptive and altogether helpful book on the poetry of James Merrill, Judith Moffett distinguishes two views of the tragic world in which we live—one that discovers "the surest path to wisdom is by insightful and sensitive penetrations," the other—Merrill's view—that concludes "in a tragic world the wise course is . . . to leave dark interiors alone." Merrill's mature view, she explains, "is that, all things considered, in a tragic world ambiguities are a blessing, and what we don't know can rarely hurt us as much as what we do know."

Merrill does, indeed, evade or avoid the final mysteries of life; his joy is in the surface of things: Beauty *is* skin deep, and if we look for it in subcutaneous flesh we're in for some very nasty surprises.

But I would like to propose—without invalidating any of Moffett's conclusions—an alternate world: one that seems to me more easily understood if we look at it as comic rather than tragic. Merrill does, after all, title a major collection *Divine Comedies;* and he manages to locate in contemporary notions of subatomic and cosmological physics a vaguely evolutionist "God" called Biology. His language—and, behind the language, his attitude toward being—seems to root itself in a world of process (where compassion is possible) rather than in a world of punishing moral and physical law. Were he to write an Oedipus, it might well end in analysis, insight, and freedom rather than in banishment, blindness and the enforced expiation of guilt.

There are, of course, an assortment of comic traditions in Western literature. Dante's is one of them, leading, as it does, toward a world of transcendent light. And in a moment I want to consider Merrill's and Dante's divine comedies as examples of systems, all "comic" in design and all offering a satisfaction that seems to me essentially aesthetic.

But for now I want to locate Merrill in a much simpler tradition, one of comic wit. Here are the writers of urbane literatures, writers of drawing-room poetry, fiction, plays that celebrate, dissect, or parody the virtues of the drawing room: good breeding, good manners, often good looks. These literatures resemble very high conversation—and if Auden comes first to mind (largely because Merrill uses him so conspicuously as a conversationalist in *The Changing Light at Sandover*), others in a tradition Merrill might call his own are such witty, eloquent writers of a high conversational style as Wilde, Lewis Carroll (and even more conspicuously, for those who know of him, punning Guy Wetmore Carryl), perhaps Edith Sitwell, certainly Byron, probably Sterne, perhaps Pope, and a whole crowd of sixteenth- and seventeenth-century figures, the most remarkable of whom is Shakespeare, punning his way through comedies, tragedies, sonnets, and songs.

What these writers share is a love of language *as* language: its manipulability and its capacity to charm us with a suavity that can sometimes pass for wisdom, indeed sometimes be wisdom.

If Merrill's kind of wit reminds me of Shakespeare's in the

more playful sonnets, his habit of breaking up narrative with intruded lyrics seems to me Byronic—as well as his habit of intruding chatty asides to the reader, digressions that more often than not wander off into footnotes on the poem he is writing or self-congratulatory parenthetical celebrations of a well-turned phrase—or episode.

Writers of this sort of a comic tradition, more preoccupied with syntax than sin, make true believers edgy. Literature, true believers feel, should be made of sterner stuff. Byron, Wilde, Gilbert (if not Sullivan), and certainly Merrill trouble serious souls who, especially when they are literary critics, dismiss this crowd as lightweight wits whose work amuses but does not seriously instruct, a tautology that makes the glum, if not gay, slightly less gloomy.

Merrill is a witty writer; many of his "comedies"—though often dealing with sad subjects—are genuinely funny.

The relationship between comedies, sad subjects, and funny situations gives me a chance to make my pitch for the special kind of pleasure Merrill's work offers—a pleasure I'm calling aesthetic—that we get from comedy and that we may not, in fact, always get from tragedy.

To develop this thesis, however, I need briefly to talk about the relationship between pathos—meaningless, unavoidable sadness—and tragedy. Arthur Miller once made the distinction very well: When a newspaper reports the "tragic" death of a man hit on the head by a collapsing building, it's talking of pathos, pure and simple. Such a death is sad, but it is not tragic. Tragedy involves both victim and audience in significant knowledge about a right way of living in the world. All the man walking under the unsafe building learns is that bricks can kill, and if the bricks hit fast enough he may not even learn that. The tragic hero, on the other hand—an Oedipus, say—learns that in defying the gods, he invites destruction.

Tragedy and pathos are, in fact, in most ways mutually exclusive. In both, we are moved to pity; but only tragedy can go one step beyond pity to engulf us in the kind of terror that leads to enlightenment. A "tragic" view of the universe consequently assumes that knowledge can be gained, that the universe is coherent enough, planned enough, to offer man lessons, even moral ones. Much of the pleasure tragedy offers seems to me therefore to be less aesthetic than moral; we feel good at the end of a tragedy because we have come to some understanding of man's place in an essentially rational universe.

Comedy is founded on a less anthropomorphic view of the nature of things. Its territory, like that of pathos, is distinctly mundane. Like pathos, its focus is on man and the accidents that befall him, though in comedy the bricks are made of sponge rubber.

It's one thing to recognize the nature of comedy, it's another to ask if there is a comic universe. Some say that's all we have. Current physics, at least, frequently suggests we're in one—not a universe of happy endings, perhaps, but a universe that does not end, a universe in process, a universe that allows for just enough erratic variation to account for the ups and downs of cosmic particles, for asteroid wobbles, for the charming mutations that permit evolved and evolving life—as well as cancer, for the not-quite-predictable flip-flop shiverings of ammonia molecules.

If the minute instabilities of things account for the evolving changes within process, process itself goes its merry way quite independently of man, affecting him, of course, but irrationally and amorally. A comic universe is one in which change—as well as accident—is always taking place but one in which man—short of trying to blow it and himself up—can do little or nothing about what is going on.

In such a universe—not chaotic, but hardly in any conventional sense moral—man feels very small. Such a universe is ideally suited for both comedy and for pathos. For if in the big system man is nothing (the gods, if there are gods, being no more than particles within atoms—or perhaps less yet, the "creator" merely an irritable vacuum that surges into a once-only explosively hot density from which everything is still being propelled), if man himself is accident caught up in both mundane and cosmic accidents, he can nevertheless invent, thanks to his own comic imagination, systems aesthetically more satisfying than the indifferent, faintly capricious one in which he is stuck. In an amoral universe, he is free to imagine a meaningful, infinitely moral one. His inventions sometimes take the form of cosmic comedies: universes *really* designed for men by men, systems that from man's point of view make, if not always "sane," then almost always adequate sense.

When Dante, using the best science and imagination of his time, engineered an aesthetically pleasing inferno and purgatorio, he accomplished a great deal—but his transformation of the paradiso into a hundred-petaled white rose with a pollen-dusted gold/godhead/sun center was sheer genius. Dante named his work a comedy, of course, not because it was either funny or aesthetically pleasing but because it really did have a happy ending: salvation was demonstrably "real" and saints, angels, cherubim, Christ, God, and Godhead were hierarchically arranged in their proper orders. But our own delight contemplating this structure—Dante's grand design for reality—is essentially aesthetic. It is a comic masterpiece because it is a man-made structure "better" than the inhumanly casual flow of which many of us now assume we and everything else are constituted.

System builders like Dante—and I include in the heap of them such recent writers as Blake of the prophetic books, Yeats of *A Vision*, and Merrill of the Sandover trilogy—are part of a long comic tradition that goes back at least as far as Plato.

Constructing from contemporary scientific (or antiscientific)

speculation of their own time and from fertile private imagina-
tions grand cosmic schemes, they make against most inhospita-
ble chaos significant designs, structures of mind that are elegant
and beautiful as the Eiffel tower.

Most of these comedians accommodate pathos nicely to their
schemes. (How sorry we are for Paolo and Francesca, whirling
around forever just millimeters from touch; and in the Sandover
trilogy how deeply we are moved by the brave and painful deaths
of loved, cheerful friends!)

Tragedy—that fated, willed, chosen, open-eyed defiance that
brings both Antigone and Lear to deaths we recognize as just
and desperate—tragedy seems far too cataclysmic for schemes
like Yeats's or Merrill's or even Dante's, schemes that please us
by their grace.

Superimposing his design on a universe that is indifferent
to man, the comic artificer constructs a new universe that is
beautiful (that white rose!) and that is shot through with human
feeling (Blake's Jerusalem! Merrill's ouija table surrounded by
loquacious angels and the transformed yet still transforming recent dead!)

But lurking in concordances and conference halls and class-
rooms, there is always the serious critic, Euclid in one hand and
the latest *Scientific American* in the other. Surely schemes con-
cocted from myth and metaphor, no matter how much they nod
toward Einstein and Bohr, and certainly schemes assembled via
a ouija board are, on the evidence of materials alone, invalid!
How can anyone, even the authors themselves, believe such
stuff?

This question grimly proposed by the serious critic is an
important one and it deserves a serious answer.

The answer, it seems to me, has to do both with our increasing awareness of the limits of knowledge and our growing
understanding of the ways by which we apprehend and syn-
thesize information. Among other ways of gaining information,

one of the most important seems to be our capacity to work from analogy—from primitive metaphors. And as far as the limits of knowledge go, we have fairly well established that—at least in detail—most of the "science" of the recent and ancient past is either inadequate or inaccurate. The true facts concerning astronomy, chemistry, physics, biology, and geology that I was taught in high school and college have been in the past quarter century so dramatically qualified as to seem distorted beyond belief. Similarly, in the social sciences, the bright determinism of the late nineteenth and early twentieth centuries seems now as peculiar as the notion that once kings exercized power and held tenure of office because of a heaven-ordained Divine Right.

What I am trying to suggest is that all systems, once they lose favor, are as metaphoric and mythic as the actions of discarded gods—and that our own systems will soon crumble into the metaphors from which they were made. We study failed systems and faiths with interest, pleased to speculate about the ways in which they must have satisfied certain fundamental human needs. Too often we forget that our own accurate analysis both of those failed systems and of "reality"—our best science and our most devoutly held faiths in any truths—are equally mythic and amusing. Every scrap of truth and fact that I believe in, including this statement of my current convictions, is bound, undoubtedly sooner or later, to be recognized as the invention— the unintended tissue of satisfying fiction—that it has always been, one that in its most convincing way satisfied for me an essential human need.

These human needs! Perhaps most essential of them all is the need for system itself—and though one system is certainly not as good as another, any believed-in system is unquestionably better than no system. Even rejected systems, if superficially coherent, are likely to make us feel good: in my earlier terms, to provide us authentic aesthetic satisfactions.

How else do we account for the crowds of us who study

our daily horoscopes, scientists and laymen alike, who love to have fortunes revealed by crystal balls, tea leaves, and lines on our palms? Believing none of it, I wait like the others for the facts of my life and the fate that awaits me to be exposed by an ingenious stranger.

And how else can I account for my own pleasure in trailing along after Merrill's galloping ouija-board cup or in keeping track of Yeats's wife's automatic writings that subsequently became groundwork for the two versions of *A Vision?*

But there it is. Yeats's wacky mix of the occult and of rational philosophy, of verified history and of the supernatural achieves, in spite of its weird roots, a logic of historical cycles no less "accurate" than Toynbee's and a classification of personalities quite as interesting and maybe even as fruitful as Freud's. Merrill's unlikely dialogues concerning the eternal verities delight not only for their affectionate commemoration of the living and the dead but also for their provisional and therefore (to me) responsible conclusions concerning the instability of both past and future.

All systems, I want to suggest, are or will become in varying degrees silly; many of the clarifications of all systems—outmoded, outdated, outrageous, or at present most passionately believed in—are for living men valid.

So, though it's easy to call Merrill and Yeats crackpot systematizers, it's equally easy, from an old-line Marxist point of view, to call such variant Christian systematizers as Dante and Milton even more crackpot. And skeptic antisystematizers find no difficulty in constructing systems that find Marx—let alone Freud, Darwin, Einstein, Blake, and Mary Baker Eddy—as crackpot as the rest of them. It's easy to discredit systematizers; it's infinitely harder to discredit what they make. Systems, aesthetically satisfying, please us inordinately because of their comic evasions of chaos.

As does, clearly, this ordered, integrated—why not say it?—tender and compassionate book. Judith Moffett, a poet in some ways very unlike James Merrill, insists that we see the whole structure of Merrill's work, insists that we recognize the way a witty technician evolves into a man risking wisdom, the way a very private—almost secretive—young man evolves into a mature artist whose life becomes the central organizing element in a poetry that sets out for us finally a most compelling diagram not just of "reality" but of being and becoming itself.

Preface

This study arrived at its present form by slow stages. The earliest draft was written with the assistance of research grants, both awarded in 1973, from the American Philosophical Society and the Pennsylvania State University, and I would like to thank these institutions here. A grant from the University of Pennsylvania Research Foundation paid for the preparation of this manuscript. My subject's forbearance and cooperation were exemplary, and I am grateful to him as well. Ted Irving read each chapter as I completed it; his shrewd criticism, suggestions, and unflagging encouragement have done more than I can well say for the book and for its author.

Merrill revised a number of his *First Poems* for the volume of selected work, *From the First Nine*. Since the revisions are in some cases radical, and since this is in part a study of his artistic development, I have chosen in nearly every instance to quote from the original versions of these early verses here.

Acknowledgments

All passages from *First Poems* and *The Seraglio*, by James Merrill, are quoted with the permission of the author. Quotations from the following works are reprinted here with the permission of Atheneum Publishers: *The Country of a Thousand Years of Peace*, Copyright © 1959; *Water Street*, Copyright © 1962; *The (Diblos) Notebook*, Copyright © 1965; *Nights and Days*, Copyright © 1966; *The Fire Screen*, Copyright © 1969; *Braving the Elements*, Copyright © 1972; *Divine Comedies*, Copyright © 1976; *Mirabell: Books of Number*, Copyright © 1978; *Scripts for the Pageant*, Copyright © 1980; and *The Changing Light at Sandover* (including *Coda: The Higher Keys*), Copyright © 1982; all Copyright by James Merrill.

The following complete poems appear in this book: the second and fourth sonnets from "The Broken Home" (*Nights and Days*), "Remora" (*The Fire Screen*), and "Yam" and the eighth poem in the sequence "In Nine Sleep Valley" (*Braving the Elements*); all are reproduced here with the permission of Atheneum Publishers.

Sections of this book first appeared, in a different form, in three publications. An essay review of *Divine Comedies* was published in *Poetry*, and much of the substance is reproduced here by permission. *The American Poetry Review* printed an essay review of *Mirabell: Books of Number*, most of which appears here. Parts of the chapter on *Scripts for the Pagent* are reprinted from *Shenandoah:* The Washington and Lee University Review, with the permission of the editor. My thanks to these magazines.

The illustration in chapter 7 for Merrill's poem "Yánnina" is taken from a postcard reproduction of a photograph of the painting "Kira Frossini's Drown"; the photograph is Copyright © Trimboli, Via Puccini, 67 Pescara, Italy.

CHAPTER 1

Introduction: Masking and Passion

"If man will strike, strike through the mask!"
—Ahab to Starbuck

The heart that leaps to the invitation of
sparkling appearances is the heart that would
itself perform as handsomely.
—John H. Finley, *Four Stages of Greek Thought*

"Manners are for me the touch of nature, an artifice in the very bloodstream."
—James Merrill in an interview

I

It is a commonplace of later nineteenth- and twentieth-century
thought that what is *real* can never be known with certainty.
Locked inside our senses, we perceive things and people as continually changing collections of sense data, and these unstable
appearances are all we can ever "know." It seems likely that the
less one has been led by religious or cultural conditioning to
expect meaning and truth of the world, the less distressing will
be the realization that certain meaning and absolute truth are not
to be had here, and that appearances are frequently pleasanter
than the things they conceal. Nineteenth-century writers like
Melville and Hawthorne, and Dostoyevsky in a somewhat dif-

ferent sense, were profoundly disturbed by the disparity between appearances and what lay behind them; the more deeply one penetrated in search of truth and knowledge, the more discomfiting, even horrifying, the truths discovered.

But the Impressionist painters and later writers such as Marcel Proust, Wallace Stevens, Vladimir Nabokov, and (usually) Henry James—less compelled to fuse their art with a sense of cosmic good and evil—have been sufficiently fascinated with the *processes* of perception and sufficiently content to render them in art without addressing unanswerable existential questions and accusations to a universe that seems indifferent if not malevolent. Ahab's mania for smashing through appearances to whatever realities lay behind them was suicidal; Ishmael, who saw as plainly as Ahab did but without Ahab's sense of personal outrage, survives, and is no more or less tragic than the next man.

In order to get on with his life, every thinking modern Ishmael must make some sort of provisional peace with the inscrutable nature of what he sees. *A* may acknowledge that to know the real and the true with certainty is never possible, yet still believe that *relative* truths are worth trying to attain—some things, after all, being demonstrably truer than others; *B* may conclude that where nothing is certain anything is possible, and feel no driving need to make the effort to know as much as may be known about what things and people are "really" like. *A* may be convinced that in a tragic world the surest path to wisdom is by insightful and sensitive penetrations, whereas *B* may feel as strongly that in a tragic world the wise course is to refrain from poking and prying, to leave dark interiors alone.

If *A* and *B* represent the poles of a dichotomy, then James Merrill—a poet who has based his most ambitious work on information dictated to him from somewhere by means of a Ouija board—is drawn, by temperament and experience and preference, to the latter pole. The whole body of his work makes it clear that knowing he cannot know has never tormented him long; even uncertainty about the source of the Ouija revelations was less important than continuing to receive them. His mature view is that, all things considered, in a tragic world ambiguities are a blessing, and what we don't know can rarely hurt us as much as what we do know.

Merrill's poetry has always been intensely visual. The strange imperative in an undergraduate poem of his called "The Green Eye" (somewhat revised from this version for the *Selected Poems*) expresses what might be described as a skeptical principle of seeing: "Come, child, and with your sunbeam gaze assign/ Green to the orchard as a metaphor/ For contemplation . . ./ A mosaic of all possible greens becomes/ A premise in your eye, . . ." Green is not here a quality of the orchard beheld but a color in the eye of the beholder, elaborated and qualified by greens remembered or imagined. Another early poem, "Periwinkles," describes a "blaze, that's mental": "You have seen at low tide on the rocky shore/ How everything around you sparkles, or/ Is made to when you think what went before." From Merrill's second book, *The Country of a Thousand Years of Peace*, comes a third supposition (in "The Locusts") that what we see can be more assigned than received: "You think first: This is no rain/ Of locusts, rather my own brain/ At work, whose preconceptions dye/ The whole world drab."

But—you think *first?* As Hannah Arendt has observed, doubts about the meaning, the essential reality, behind physical appearances are theoretical doubts raised by thought; by their nature they do not come "first," instinctively.

> That traditional hierarchy [that sets Being above Appearance] arises not from our ordinary experience with the world of appearances but, rather, from the not at all ordinary experience of the thinking ego. . . . The quest for meaning is "meaningless" to common sense and common-sense reasoning, because it is the

sixth sense's function to fit us into the world of appearances and make us at home in the world given by our five senses; there we are and no questions asked.[1]

In *Skepticism and Animal Faith*, George Santayana has also taxed with common sense the philosophical skeptics who insist on doubting, if not denying outright, that the evidence of their senses meaningfully describes the phenomenal world. "Children," he writes there, "insensibly accept all the suggestions of sense and language. . . . People are not naturally skeptics, wondering if a single one of their intellectual habits can be reasonably preserved. . . ."[2] Arendt goes further: "Since we live in an *appearing* world, is it not much more plausible that the relevant and the meaningful in this world of ours should be located precisely on the surface?"[3]

One wonders what Arendt and Santayana would have made of James Merrill; for the child, the young man, the persona of his early poems and point-of-view character of his novels, gives evidence of being, from a very early age, an instinctive skeptic disabused of innocence, perceiving the world, before he was old enough to conceptualize it thus, as artificial and unreliable.

An educated adult understands what Ahab means by saying that all visible objects are but as pasteboard masks, understands the ambiguous Henry James of *The Sacred Fount* and *The Turn of the Screw*, understands Nabokov's stating in his 1944 study of Gogol what novels like *Lolita*, *Pale Fire*, and *Look at the Harlequins!* say less directly: that "All reality is a mask" (and stating elsewhere that the word "reality" is meaningless without the quotes).[4] Howard Moss makes sense when he points out that Proust, by giving his own name to the narrator of *Remembrance of Things Past*, "begins the process of merging appearance and reality. . . . This doubling of names makes us aware that we are reading a novel that is, in some way, based on fact; it warns us simultaneously that appearances can be deceiving."[5]

But the premise that things are not what they seem is ordinarily considered for the first time, if ever, in required sophomore philosophy and taken much to heart only by the little fraction of students who take such things to heart; because what Arendt and Santayana have asserted is usually true: people do spontaneously accept the audible, visible, tactile world on faith; seeing is believing. But Merrill's *First Poems* don't read like those of a young person who has suddenly realized that what he sees may be illusory. They read, most of them, like the poems of a young person who has assumed for as long as he can remember that what he sees may be deceptive, cannot be trusted, may mercifully mask something fearsome. They seem either unaware of this assumption as an assumption, or aware of it in the unsurprised way in which one explains a principle one has operated in terms of all along without thinking. What distance, what absence of trust, there is between the viewer and the view in "Entrance from Sleep," published in *First Poems* (but not in *From the First Nine*):

> Upon the eye
> As dawn to the shade-embroidered fountain brings
> The young fern's wisdom, the first world takes shape
> Where shadow and light on a white ceiling meet;
> And the late garden builds its trellises
> And the machinery of light begins.

First Poems especially is full of writing as visually focussed as many Imagist poems, but with this difference: that while the Imagists may cherish the natural, physical thing-in-itself—Williams's red wheelbarrow and cold sweet plums—Merrill petrifies or freezes it and looks past it fixedly. His apparent subject, cameo or peacock or whatever, much too rigidly stands in for the real subject, a feeling or a thought that must be armor-plated before it can be expressed. Several reviewers, unable to imagine that any poet so evidently intelligent could have chosen to ground

his first two books so single-mindedly on metaphor without ar-
riving by the usual route, have called him a philosophical poet
and referred to his "philosophy of metaphor." But not until *Divine Comedies*, if then, could Merrill have been called philosophical in any sense at all.

His undergraduate honors thesis, completed at Amherst in
1947 when he was twenty, is a remarkably sophisticated analysis
of metaphor in Proust; but that Proust or Mallarmé or Stevens,
or anyone else, *taught* Merrill how to view the natural world as
a relative place, furnished with objects which stand for something other than themselves-as-absolute-states-of-being, cannot
be true. (That these writers confirmed a natural inclination of
his cannot, of course, be doubted.) In the Proust thesis Merrill
refers to the pre-Impressionist painters' "confidence in the reality of matter and a tradition of vision whereby grass was green
and shadows grey or black," and contrasts their beliefs with those
of the Impressionists, who

> came to realize that the sensuous experience of an object was
> infinitely variable, depending upon the light in which it was seen
> and other objects around it. And despite their desertion of the
> studio in favor of the open countryside, they discovered more
> and more that, in practice, no objective reality in the world about
> them could be revealed.

The Impressionists believed they were painting " 'the actual
impressions which objects make upon their vision,' instead of an
attribute residing inherently in the exterior world." Art rather
than philosophy, then, provided a reason for and a means of
framing in words the *idea* that reality is relative. But juvenile
poems published privately in a volume entitled *Jim's Book* when
Merrill was sixteen, well before college, are already deeply em-
bued with a *sense* of the trickiness of appearances.

The reaction of reviewers to the collection of static emblems of *First Poems*, as to the livelier ones of *The Country of a*

Thousand Years of Peace, must have shocked the young poet. It couldn't have been very pleasant to read again and again that his poems showed talent and intelligence but were cold. Peter Davison's comments are representative: in *The Country of a Thousand Years of Peace* Merrill, "more often than not, erects a chilly but ornamental barrier between the reader and the underlying feeling. These poems are brilliant, neurotic, subtly made, and extremely intelligent, but too often the terrifying shapes underlying his poems trick themselves out in elaborate and elegant masks." [6] The ornamental barrier was erected equally between the *poet* and the feeling; as Helen Vendler has written (in a review of a later book), "in Merrill's earliest poetry he stood at several removes from his own experience." [7] Whether because he acknowledged the justice of such objections, or simply got to be on easier terms with himself and the world as he grew older, or both, the whole shape of Merrill's development as a poet since *Water Street*—allowing for a sidestep here and there—has been away from the bloodlessly artificial and superficially decorative, and toward the expression of emotion entirely honest even when only partly visible. It seems likely that the guileless emotional openness of *The Changing Light at Sandover*, his Ouija trilogy, is a result of self-consciousness lost in the face of the large issues he was forced to deal with while writing this enormous and demanding work. The decorative impulse has persisted, but nobody could call the mature poetry cold; and where facts and details are still concealed, they are concealed for reasons other than fear.

2

The habit of not taking the natural world at face value has also persisted, though the trilogy wrought changes in this as in

so much else. Merrill's early poetry is full of nature, closely observed and accurately labeled, to which *as* nature he could not
deeply respond. He has speculated by hindsight that

> whether I truly liked nature or not, or liked her best when she
> most resembled artifice, I understood—especially as I approached
> maturity—that she provided images invaluable through being
> common currency. Anything in nature could not be wholly pri-
> vate or subjective. The most peculiar thoughts or feelings were
> "safe" [i.e., not expressions of one eccentric personality] the mo-
> ment they touched the base of whatever natural object or process
> one might choose in order to describe them.[8]

Merrill's later uses of nature imagery and emblems abandon the
static, polished swans and pelicans of *First Poems* for increasingly
supple, whimsical, interesting, and charming figures. But the
other dimensions of a setting, especially a natural setting, have
continued to be more important than its literal one, which masks
or mirrors—often intriguingly—the real life of a poem: its emotion. Merrill has said in an interview that "You hardly ever need
to *state* your feelings. The point is to feel and keep the eyes
open. Then what you feel is mimed back at you by the scene.
A room, a landscape. I'd go a step further. We don't *know* what
we feel until we see it distanced by this kind of translation."[9]

The room or landscape reveals to us whatever feelings we
project upon it; often it has no more intrinsic value than a movie
screen. Objets d'art might sometimes be excepted, and tasteful
interiors, but not tangled undergrowth, not wide open spaces
which overwhelm the single human sensibility. Merrill has natural feeling for the sea, and for mountain views, but to put even
these into his poems he typically domesticates them: wind-erod-
ing rock formations in the Southwest "Dwindle in the red wind
like ice in tea," for instance, in "Under Libra" (*Braving the Elements*).

In another interview Merrill once called Eugenio Montale

"*the* twentieth-century nature poet. Any word can lead you from the kitchen garden into really inhuman depths—if there are any of those left nowadays. The two natures were always one, but it takes an extraordinary poet to make us feel that, feel it in our spines."[10] Merrill would agree seriously with Stevens' ironic imagining of a world where "the deer and the dachshund are one"; dogs and kitchen gardens are nature in the same sense as mountain fastnesses, as "a sudden deepsea squid," as "the molten mineral heart of Earth."[11] Ancestrally, of course they are. But the wild grape and the wolf thrive in country, under conditions, which would kill the muscat grape and the Irish setter. As much as any urban human, tamed things depend on people. And not for survival alone. That they exist at all is a consequence of human interference with nature in the form of carefully controlled breeding. Those differences are not superficial ones; biologically we are more like fifteenth-century Iroquois, or Cro-Magnon cave-dwellers for that matter, than setters are like wolves or garden strawberries like wild ones. Merrill appreciates the connections which bring nature close to home, but nature in the wild, which needs to be taken on animal faith, does not register in his work.

Not surprisingly, then, nature appears there shrunken small, even toylike. Animals, vegetables, and minerals are given human characteristics or those of household artifacts; at first they were usually like gems. Proust's example may have shown the way: "Matter," says Merrill in his Proust thesis, "is spoken of as though it were personality, personality as though it were material." He will say "Autumn turns windy, huge,/ A clear vase of dry leaves vibrating on and on" in "A Renewal," letting *huge* and *vase* question and correct one another. In "16.IX.65" "The tiny fish . . ./ Lie in the boat, gasping and fanning themselves/ As if the day were warmer than the sea." Like an injured patient in analysis "The creek, a crystal tendon strained,/ Tossed on its couch, no longer freely associating/ Hawk with trout, or cloud with pebble white as cloud" in "McKane's Falls." *The Book of Ephraim* speaks of another "brook that running slips into a shawl/ Of crystal noise—at last, the waterfall," and of how "early light sweeps under a pink scatter/ Rug of cloud the solemn, diehard stars." And with a gesture he can turn glacial movement into an after-dinner scene; from "Under Libra: Weights and Measures":

> The stones of spring,
> Stale rolls or pellets rather, rounded
> By a gorgon's fingers, swept to the floor,
>
> Dragged south in crushing folds,
> Long dirty tablecloth of ice,
> Her feast ended, her intimates dispersed . . .

In these examples, chosen from hundreds and spanning the whole of Merrill's career, there is much charm and wit and, often, beauty; what it lacks is trust. The eyes Merrill simply cannot believe—very shortsighted eyes from a very early age, a fact which (as in James Joyce's case) may or may not be relevant—keep transforming, domesticating nature in the act and moment of viewing, and the effect is to disarm: wild things become little people amusingly disguised as fish or fly or bird, or even a grizzly who "Dies for pressing people to his heart." Galway Kinnell's great bleeding bear would shamble through that silvery snare as if it were a cobweb; Merrill, who relates to nature less directly, has made that limitation serve a different purpose.

The transformations may be most effective when done overtly, as in "The Green Eye," "Periwinkles," and "The Locusts" (quoted at the beginning of this essay), where the mind's ordered or suspected alterations of a scene in color and tone (green, blaze, drab) are explained, or when a natural scene is presented in the process of being changed into a painting, as in "16.IX.65" from *The Fire Screen*:

> Light downward strokes of yellow, green, and rust
> Render the almond grove. Trunk after trunk
> Tries to get right, in charcoal,
> The donkey's artless contrapposto.

Or presented as a book; "In Nine Sleep Valley," from *Braving the Elements*, describes Merrill's efforts to get in closer, truer visual touch with mountain landscapes:

> Trying to read in Nature's book
> The pages (canyon forest landslide lake)
> Turn as the road does, the stock characters
> Come and (marmot mallard moose)
> Go too quickly to believe in.

The emblems and symbolic objects characteristic of Merrill's books after *First Poems*—Van Eyck angel, etched tumblers, Willowware cup, little glass horse, bells from Isfahan—are much more his sort of thing; since they were already small, artificial products of highly developed cultures, perhaps he could more readily believe they are what they appear to be, care more for them in themselves, and let them carry the weight of metaphor without canceling them out *as* themselves; at any rate that has been the effect. Moreover, his sphinx and vampire, and much later his gigantic hot-eyed bats and hornless unicorn, are believable as his natural creatures never were.

It may be that not even attractive artifacts have always "felt" wholly real to Merrill as they do most of the time to others; in a 1972 review of two books by Francis Ponge, he says of W. C. Williams's famous statement about the primary importance of physical objects: "No thoughts, then, but in things? True enough, so long as the notorious phrase argues not for the suppression of thought but for its oneness with whatever in the world—pine woods, spider, cigarette—give rise to it. Turn the phrase around, you arrive no less at truth: no things but in thoughts." [12] Finally, one other element accounts for the artificial "feel" of the pine woods and spiders in Merrill's work: his characteristic style in prose and verse, itself poised, polished, tense—mannered at times, as some have said—to a degree that made it, for many years, a more suitable style for describing glass horses and vampires than live grizzlies.

Hannah Arendt observes that the world manifests itself "of its own accord"; this she calls *self-display*, which "has no choice but to show whatever properties a living being [or object] possesses." *Self-presentation*, however, "is distinguished from self-display by the active and conscious choice of the image shown."[13] In a world where all is necessarily appearance, phenomena can only spontaneously display themselves; people may choose between the spontaneity of objects and degrees of deceit. Any understanding of Merrill's poetry must begin with a grasping of the possibility that for him the physical world "out there" full of objects and creatures, the common-sense world we know through a lifetime of accumulating sense data and which we habitually call the real world or reality, was early a source of anxiety and has remained for better *and* worse a source of ambiguity and illusion. Taken as a whole, his work conveys the sense that what we see, and all we see, is the mask reality lurks behind; that reality is subjective; that indeed, for all we know, the Other World of Ouija may be equally real. Not until Mother Nature appears personified in *Scripts for the Pageant* does a modified attitude toward nature begin to emerge; and not until the hurricane in *Mirabell* is a natural force presented as violent, and more or less to actual scale.

That appearances could not be trusted, at first a source of fear, later became a source of comfort. Merrill's work conveys the further sense that for a long time he knowingly collaborated with illusion, placated and reinforced the mask worn by reality in the self-presentations of his poems. But, as his skills matured, he found ever more sophisticated and interesting solutions to the problem of how to protect himself without damaging his poetry. "Later on, it developed that the alternative to the brocaded coat didn't have to be nakedness—an ironic leotard, for instance, did just as well."[14] And irony proved to be only one sort of leotard. While it was necessary not to expose all the truth at once, fragmentary glimpses of personal truth might from time to time appear, only partially masked in complicated syntax, or in the laugh-clown-laugh effect, the thin glaze of "deadpan wit and surface detachment" (noted by David Kalstone in *Five Temperaments*) cast over a turmoil of passion or a welling of tears, or in self-deflating puns, or in something else. Finally, the self-presentations of *Divine Comedies* and the *Sandover* trilogy, as well as of a growing number of poems along the way, depart from factual truth not to deceive but to present the truthful self more engagingly or evocatively. After *Divine Comedies* Merrill never troubles to conceal his homosexuality. The JM-persona of the trilogy, in fact, is no longer *masked* in that armored, defensive sense at all; by this point masking and passion had ceased to be the foci of his concern. The nature of reality, the source and credibility of the Ouija board dictations, the riveting messages possibly of global, even cosmic, significance—such matters had given perspective to the difficulties of the personal life.

3

Merrill's sense of the perilous real and the safer apparent can be deduced from his strategies of presentation, from a style characterized at first by lacquered surfaces, coldness, and remoteness, later by irony and hermeticism. These are barriers between the poet and his readers. But a fascination with the way masking operates in human relations other than in the poet-reader relationship also is evident in the poems, sometimes taking the form of a literal or figurative mask or mirror. In certain poems it is also discussed *as* an idea, or a credo.

First Poems contains several literal masks. One, in "Variations: The Air is Sweetest That a Thistle Guards," is a "red-/ Chequered-lavender and bordered with seed pearls" mask worn at a ball by a lady called Jane. Merrill's nervous habit of encrusting his early poems with gems probably proceeded partly from the same instinct that produced Jane's mask: a sense that the concealing exterior ought not only to mask but to be beautiful, do its job partly through distraction. When Jane takes her mask off at midnight, as she was bound to, the disturbed poet wonders (in this original version, later revised):

> What barrier
> Holds up, what is not vulnerable? Down, down,
> Sand on a sunken crown
> Settles; but that shape is always there.
>
> Just as beneath her mask there is always Jane:
> She let it drop, we saw her jubilant smile,
> Thought, "Beauty is not so temperate, nor is pain,
> But that they burst the seal
> We stamp upon them."

Even a mask of stone (as in "Medusa") breaks down eventually; no mask's safety is permanent.

Literal masks appear in later books in the forms of the "thin gold mask" the world puts on as Proust transfigures it through his art (*Water Street*), the many shifting masks and disguises of "From the Cupola" and "The Thousand and Second Night" (*Nights and Days*), and the mummy-swaddlings of "The Friend of the Fourth Decade" (*The Fire Screen*). Merrill's first novel, *The Seraglio*—a veritable treatise on the subjects of personal concealment and the fear of being known—shows the young protagonist Francis accidentally kissing his father on his black sleeping-mask, and shows his father's face changed by heart medicine from hour to hour, so that none of his faces is the "real" one; in context these metaphors make up in effectiveness what they lack in subtlety.

A poem called "Mirror" in *The Country of a Thousand Years of Peace* first speculates at length upon the nature of reflection, important in all Merrill's books and brought to a sort of apotheosis in the trilogy, where the spirits can *see* their mediums only in the mirror propped like a third party at the table, and which must be symbolically broken at the end of the dictations. A mirror is a mask to hide behind, in which the viewer sees himself—his own needs, feelings, expectations—reflected back at him. Mirrors take the form of cupola panes in *Nights and Days*, the panes turned by moonlight into one-way mirrors, and in *The Book of Ephraim* they take many ingenious forms: sea-wet sandbar, phone-booth glass, bronze gong, wings of a plane, facets of a sapphire, a steam room's colored panes. All the books contain real mirrors as well. A mirror cannot be seen through, but shows the viewer to himself; Merrill's work, which long opposed insights into others, never opposes self-knowledge.

This poet has found inventive ways of showing how much he dislikes the idea of one person's violating, intruding upon, the inner life of another. The theme appears in every book, both novels and both plays included, and largely accounts for some of his most important pre-Ouija poetry. Two poems in *The Country of a Thousand Years of Peace* present dissection as a metaphor for obtaining knowledge by murder—present it with withering distaste for the coldblooded relish of the scientist who cries "Ha!" above a severed head: "this brow/ swaddles a tangleworld I must explore!/ Stout vein and swaying lobe/ Redden beneath my knives." *The Fire Screen* shows a hemonaut imprudently exploring the chambers of his lover's heart in "Part of the Vigil": "More than pleased" at what he finds scrawled on the walls of "sunlit outer galleries," and at "How alike we were! . . . I penetrated further," only to encounter increasingly alarming views, prior tenants, and empty cells, and to wonder finally in panic:

> Where was the terrace, the transparency
> So striking far away? In my fall I struck
> An iron surface (so! your heart was heavy)
> Hot through clothing. Snatched myself erect.
> Beneath, great valves were gasping, wheezing. What
> If all you know of me were down there, leaking
> Fluids at once abubble, pierced by fierce
> Impulsions of unfeeling, life, limb turning
> To burning cubes, to devil's dice, to ash—
> What if my effigy were down there? What,
> Dear god, if it were not!
> If it were nowhere in your heart!
> Here I turned back.

"You have to kill a thing to know it satisfactorily," says D. H. Lawrence in his essay on Poe, and warns us "above all things" not to try to know the man or woman one loves; "to know her mentally is to try to kill her." Merrill, obviously, is in sympathy with this; but the vulnerable and perishable masks throughout his work express his own conviction that, with the passing of time, lovers do inevitably come to know each other too well. Romantic love begins on both sides in sparkling appearances that must finally be seen through from both. When Merrill says "love" in a poem, what he ordinarily means is "passion," though loves of other kinds also appear in his work, even the rare love which survives the end of passion. But prior to the reconciliations and syntheses of *Divine Comedies*, erotic loves dominate passionless ones in the emotional landscape of his writing; and in a passionate relationship, objective knowledge is a destructive force.

The cumulative message of the love poems is this: love matters more than anything else; people are fundamentally unlovable; therefore since I want and need to love you I must contrive not to know you any better than I have to; for what I love is an appearance, a mask you wear or one I project upon you; and we must each do all we can not to see through the other's mask. Kindness, as much as self-interest, requires lover and beloved to guard one another vigilantly from difficult truths about themselves as long as possible. All Merrill's poetry, and all his novels and plays, convey a sense that the very first principle of good manners is to pretend reassuringly that appearances *are* realities, and that it's neither civil nor sensible to take any notice of, or call attention to, a misstep. "Manners for me are the touch of nature, an artifice in the very bloodstream," he said once. "They are as vital as all appearances, and if they deceive us they do so by mutual consent." [15] At the heart of the paradox that artifice is natural (and nature artificial) lies this fatalistic view of human love.

Love and family relations have been pointed to correctly, by Helen Vendler and others, as Merrill's best subjects, at the center of the life which has always been his true subject. They are what he has cared about most, returned to most frequently, and written about most effectively. And, often enough, most elusively; in addition to a natural instinct for concealment, and the desire to protect his friends, Merrill is a homosexual poet who for many years followed W. H. Auden's practice of addressing poems to a "you" of unspecified gender. This convention has blurred the focus of many love poems, though not all. It allowed Merrill to appear to be what he was really not, or at least not to appear to be what he really was: to make masks of his poems and novels and take advantage of another sort of masking device within them, that of displacement, as authorized by Proust and Christopher Isherwood. Homosexual characters appear in Merrill's novels, and in "After the Fire," but they are never narrators (when Francis, the point-of-view character in the first half of *The Seraglio*, embarks on what is implied to be a gay life-style, the narrator becomes omniscient and Francis is himself displaced).

That doomed love is, or has been, its central subject means

that before *Divine Comedies* Merrill's poetry had been given a tragic twist not all his wit and irony could mask; nor could a complete lack of self-pity make less poignant the resignation with which he says, from behind the mask of Proust, "And presently she rises. Though in pain/ You let her leave—the loved one always leaves." And yet the will not to see through the mask is matched in strength and tenacity everywhere in Merrill's work by the will not to give in to bitterness or despair when the mask breaks down, not to settle for the dark view of things. Rather than bewail the certainty that love doesn't last, he chooses to be grateful to masks for making intervals of love possible. Far from despised as a snare and a delusion, masks are the "sparkling appearances" to which the brave heart leaps in assent.

And when at last the mask does break down as it must, poetry-making, the perennial life preserver, will still be there. The last two pages of Merrill's thesis on Proustian metaphor show that he already understood, at twenty—perhaps, again, thanks to Proust's example—that art can heal, that metaphor can be "a way of making pain bearable." He illustrates the point by describing the difference between reading Proust and reading the relatively artless Dostoyevsky:

> In the latter we are shown human suffering in as unrelieved a form as is possible in a work of art. In Proust there is always a protecting surface of metaphor. It is as though we were skating upon a sheet of ice that had formed above a black torrent; we may skate with an assurance of safety, but the ice does not make the water beneath us less terrible. This use of metaphor may be, for the writer, a form of flight, but it is also a form of healing.

The image will return nearly twenty years later to be included in *The (Diblos) Notebook*, as part of a description of Orson/Orestes: "O. wore myth night & day like an unbecoming color. . . . Ah, but it made him so happy, made the ills that befell him bearable. Metaphor formed like ice between him and the world. Backwards, forwards, sideways, he glided, spiraling, curvetting. . . ." Appropriately it is Merrill's poem "For Proust" which makes what must be his own first poetic statement about how the tragedy built into the nature of things can be borne, supported, *affirmed* by art. Proust, in the poem, goes home bearing an encounter with his lover and writes about it—"What happened is becoming literature"—with the result, finally, that "The world will have put on a thin gold mask." That thin gold mask— the "sheet of ice" of the thesis made into an artifact—is Proust's art, or Merrill's, the shape and containment with which form gilds even tragic experience: for a creative act can only be an act of affirmation.

CHAPTER 2

Jim's Book, First Poems, The Country of a Thousand Years of Peace

I

When Merrill was at Lawrenceville School, near Princeton, his father arranged to surprise him by publishing privately some two dozen of his stories and poems in a collection entitled *Jim's Book*. These very youthful pieces, written when the author was fourteen, fifteen, and sixteen, are of chiefly paleontological interest, proof that the bejeweling effects of *First Poems*, and the fear of being seen through, were well established as early as that. But the assorted "juvenilia" preserved in this little book have an uncanny precocity. A sonnet, "Masquerade," dated June 1942, when Merrill was sixteen years and three months old, is anxious and precocious in equal parts:

> Just as the sky has donned her mask of black,
> Star-spangled satin, so each person here
> Is hid behind some make-believe veneer
> Of unreal cloth or paper. Now in back
> Of his disguise, prepared for the attack,
> Some unknown Harlequin comes sidling near

His lady; she in turn conceals her sneer
Or smile of favour: passions swell and slack.

I think I walk among them undisturbed
By those who smash their cymbals in my ears;
I tell myself that I am not perturbed
By smirking Columbines who weep false tears;
But all the while I know I see no sign
Of their true emotions as they study mine.

A minor liberty has been taken with the rhyme scheme of this otherwise strict Petrarchan sonnet's sestet; "favour" gets the British, or more exotic, spelling; and the last line has an awkward extra syllable. But any experienced writing teacher would instantly recognize this as the work of a sensitive youngster with an exceptional ear. Merrill was already beginning to see how some control could be exerted over troublesome feelings by giving them form—perhaps also to suspect that the pleasures of putting them into form made troublesome feelings worth the trouble.

Another privately printed book, *The Black Swan*, appeared in 1946; and everything in it worth keeping was reprinted in *First Poems* when Knopf brought that volume out in 1951. *First Poems* was widely reviewed and generally acknowledged to be an impressive debut—with reservations; Louise Bogan for one was quite ferocious about what she too quickly dismissed as the sort of poems any average graduate student could write, "frigid and dry as diagrams." [1]

Merrill had admired Elinor Wylie at school, and had written an essay about her beginning with a description of a diamond ("Supreme in the realm of gems . . . whose fire is alternately blue and white, and whose glitter proclaims the mastery of the cutter's work"). And in the army he had read Auden's *The Sea and the Mirror* and been "dazzled by the range of forms. . . . Certainly I was inspired to try some of these things myself." [2]

But the most salient source of the decorative elegance of *First Poems* is Wallace Stevens, and five or six poems from the book—of which only one, "The Green Eye," has survived into the volume of selected work—are thoroughly imbued with the spirit and style of Stevens, to the point of echoing his very cadences and phrasing: "whip/ In kitchen cups concupiscent curds" sounds plainly in "Describe in strings of light impossible curves"; "The air/ Is not so elemental, nor the earth/ So near" almost as plainly in "Beauty is not so temperate, nor is pain. . . ."[3]

Merrill's model was especially the Stevens of "Sunday Morning" and "The Comedian as the Letter C," of the cool, vividly colored, exotic, abstract, and polysyllabic vocabulary including such words as *foxed* (modifying "book") and *quotidian* and *fictive*—all of which occur in poems by Merrill; the Stevens who liked "artifact" birds (cockatoo, peacock, parrot) made of jewels and feathers, and the plural gerunds ("fresh transfigurings," "oracular rockings," "gawky flitterings") that will abundantly bedeck Merrill's own later poetry—there actually are some "flitterings from within" in *The Country of a Thousand Years of Peace.* When Merrill said in 1967 that "Stevens continues to persuade us of having had a private life, despite—or thanks to—all the bizarreness of his vocabulary and idiom,"[4] that was expert testimony; few know better how bizarre language can be made to mask strong feeling. The younger poet's work was the more formally restricted, but in all these matters of verbal style *First Poems* owes Stevens a great debt. Also, as we have seen, an interest in the processes of perception is common to both. But the special emotional qualities of *First Poems* are absent from *Harmonium* as the tough intellectual qualities are absent, even in amateurish form, from *First Poems.* The mature artistry is, of course, absent too.

These poems of Merrill's early twenties—he thought of them as "visual artifacts"—still sound precocious, more impressive for what they portend than for what they attain. From this distance the tremendous effort they make is touching, but even Richard Howard, who admires *First Poems* considerably, admits that "their shellac and jewelry make them seem . . . little more than machinery," and that the most immobilized conclude with "something elegiac and anguished, something decorative and heartbreaking."[5] Howard forgives this pose in view of Merrill's astonishing technical achievements.

A few poems offer something besides technique and are worth a closer look. "Variations: The Air is Sweetest That a Thistle Guards" has six parts, each in a different form and all linked by thistles or pearls. Most are typically elegiac, anguished, decorative, and heartbreaking, but the language of the sixth part is different: it is the most relaxed and least mannered in this book, and sounds most like a human voice. The unrhymed lines are metrically looser and vary in length, probably at this stage encouraging a naturalness the demands of the tighter forms made difficult to sustain. The passage is about Stendhal, "for whom love was/ So frankly the highest good":

> not love, great pearl
> That swells around a small unlovely need;
> Nor love whose fingers tie the bows of birth
> Upon the sorry present. Love merely as the best
> There is, and one would make the best of that . . .
>
> To say at the end, however we find it, good,
> Bad, or indifferent, it helps us, and the air
> Is sweetest there. The air is very sweet.

So is this voice, the voice of Merrill's future, figured with its graceful metaphor, pleasant double entendre, and freshly viewed cliché.

A much more typical poem, "The Parrot" (see the Appendix), represents in technical ways the better emblems (Howard's term) in this collection. Its stanza is a very formal one used several times in this book and in others. The poem's "message" is muddled—clarity of statement being a lesser priority than getting the stanza-units right—and the stiffness of the writing is only slightly relieved by a few inverted feet at the beginnings of lines and a few slant rhymes at their ends. It is just this sense of having enough control over a demanding form to fill it accurately, but not enough to play it flexibly and freely, that gives the "precocious" feel to many of the *First Poems*.

Masking is the subject of "The Parrot": a quasi-literal mask, the bird's head, its "haggard eye set in white crinkled paint," and our metaphorical masks of self-protection expressed—again—through the device of the costume ball, where everyone is masked but only until midnight. This parrot's mistress is a "spinster" who, we are told, has looked forward all her life to the stroke of twelve:

> Our revels now are ended, pretty Poll,
>   For midnight bells extol
> The individual face behind the mask.
> Each dancer seeks his partner to embrace
> As if he had seen deep into her soul
>   And gave what it dared ask,
>   While knowing but a woman's face.

But this is myth: the idea of "the Moment . . . When mask *did* matter least, and face *did* tell/ More than it knew of private riches" acquires "a sad irrelevance" as the spinster ages. Why? The poem tells us that under the masks of parrot and spinster are "Jungles" (passions? are they unacceptable?); that the parrot "destroys the personal" by parroting back mechanically what the spinster says with emotion; that the "human voice . . . is pretense/ Of gentleness and sense"; but these bits and pieces refuse to be tidied into a picture with all its appearances and realities clearly labeled, and the spinster's sadness remains unaccounted for in the stanzas which make as if to explain it. Does Merrill call the midnight bells "irrelevant" because aging wears the mask away? Or does he mean that age is itself a mask, and "the parrot masked always not young" a mirror-image of its owner? He seems divided between pity and disgust for both, insofar as feeling can be inferred at all from these ornate and clotted stanzas. Yet the parrot itself is somehow memorable, as an image of what is forever masked and impersonal but capable of sudden startling jungle squawks that threaten all our masks.

Most interesting of all Merrill's *First Poems* is "Transfigured Bird," a set of four variations on a theme designated by yolks or birds in delicate eggshells—a much more communicative metaphor for what appearances conceal. The first part opens: "That day the eggshell of appearance split/ . . . / A child fond of natural things discovered it." He carries it home, knowing that "What had been/ Inside was nimble and hungry and far away." In the fourth section the same child finds another egg in a symbolically thorny patch of bushes,

> Lifted it out, as children will, but stopped:
> He had thought to blow it clean, but there had broken
> From the cold shell his chilly fingers cupped
>
> The claw of the dead bird, clutching air, a token
> Of how there should be nothing cleanly for years to come,
> Nor godly, nor reasons found, nor prayers spoken.
>
> And though it was still early morning he went home
> And slept, and would not till nearly dusk be woken.

The eggshell of appearance, the exquisite, translucent, blue, natural thing, has turned out when looked at closely to be horrid.

This robin's-egg anecdote occurs in Frederick Buechner's autobiographical novel of childhood, *The Season's Difference*, dedicated to Merrill as *First Poems* is dedicated to Buechner. The two had been friends at Lawrenceville School, and Merrill appears in Buechner's novel as a fat boy named Rufus, who tells of finding the awful egg. This traumatic incident might well have cautioned anyone at a vulnerable age against a fondness for the unpredictable natural eggshells of appearance. The enameled Fabergé egg of part III, which splits to reveal its tiny golden mechanical rooster, is safer. (The little rooster is modeled on Yeats's nightingale of hammered gold and gold enameling; Merrill had read "Sailing to Byzantium" in the army, when, as he said once, "I couldn't wait to get out of nature myself."[6])

The eggshell motif is modulated through these "Variations" from clean-blown or hatched-out robin's eggs, to fertile "yolk of remembrance" hatching a "bird or cockatrice" wild-winged and golden-plumed, to the rich toy eggs, to birds of time and prophecy, to the image of God who will "prick a hole in either end of the sky/ And blow it clean away," to the egg cracked by the dead bird's claw. The unobtrusive terza rima continues right through the section breaks, and the last part resolves into the semblance of a sonnet by adding two terminal lines which repeat the rhyme-sounds of the final tercet (above). The fusing of a technically demanding verse form or forms with a theme approached from several directions like a musical theme, its different manifestations sparking back and forth between its several parts, will continue to be a hallmark of Merrill's best work.

Other traits already present in *First Poems* will characterize the mature poetry: intelligence, formal prosody, complex sentences kept straight with colons and semi-colons, a baroque sense of decor. His pleasure in stock characters (Spinster, Lovers) also persists, but over time these are joined by increasingly individualized ones; and from the first the Child—as in "Transfigured Bird"—was recognizeably the same child, himself. Qualities that make his later poetry peerlessly crafted are obvious from the beginning; those that make it emotionally powerful and moving, the refined gift for form as a buffering, enhancing vehicle for emotion rather than a defensive shield against it, are beyond him at this early stage.

2

They are still all but beyond him in *The Country of a Thousand Years of Peace*, but eight years' serious work is evident almost at a glance into this second book, published in 1959. (A chapbook-size collection of poems called *Short Stories* had been printed semiprivately in 1954, but nine of its ten poems are reprinted in this volume, the second edition of which marks the beginning of Merrill's long and happy association with Atheneum.) In their problematical aspects *First Poems* and *The Country of a Thousand Years of Peace* resemble one another, each having its share of ubiquitous jewel metaphors, hard surfaces, coolness, and mannered diction. And the new book has broken out in a pox of plural gerunds. But the static stiffness is gone—the sense that the *First Poems* didn't *dare* move, were all but visibly trembling with the strain of keeping up appearances—along with the utter humorlessness of youth taking itself seriously. During those years, from somewhere, came the confidence to start relaxing.

Eight years is a long time in a young writer's life, and some poems are more relaxed than others. In "The Octopus," an emblem poem that measures the distance traveled from "The Parrot" and its kind, Merrill's idiom is still rather affected. But the octopus moves, and for reasons which can with much less effort be untangled fairly well; interiors no longer obsessively repel attention:

> There are many monsters that a glassen surface
> Restrains. And none more sinister
> Than vision asleep in the eye's tight translucence.

> Rarely it seeks now to unloose
> Its diamonds. Having divined how drab a prison
> The purest mortal tissue is,
> Rarely it wakes.

This is the familiar visual theme, inventively expressed. Jaded vision sleeps in the eye like an octopus in its tank, waking now to swim toward only "lusters/ Extraordinary . . . / Till on glass rigid with his own seizure/ At length the sucking jewels freeze." (Who but Merrill would see the suction cups on an octopus's tentacles as *diamonds*, or make them *freeze* "at length" on the cold glass that invisibly keeps impulse and object apart?)

> the octopus
> From the gloom of its tank half-swimming half-drifting
> Toward anything fair, a handkerchief
> Or child's face dreaming near the glass, the writher
> Advances . . .
> the dreamer wakes and hungers. . . .
> His hands move clumsily in the first conventional
> Gestures of assent.

There is a suggestion of entranced complicity on the part of the fair prey, giving the eye's doomed intent to grasp what it cannot reach the tone of sexual possessiveness reinforced by ambiguous referents and pronouns: which is the dreamer? whose are the clumsy hands? The poem seems to say, or at least imply, that the sinister monster vision rarely pursues things anymore both because experience has shown that most apparent attractions aren't worth pursuing, and because the "glassen" tank restrains it when it goes after one that is. Sympathy for both vision and its object can be felt in this, but the weight of sympathy is with the object protected from those sucking arms by what vision, of its nature, cannot do.

These lines are more iambic than anything else, but compared to the forward-march of "The Parrot" they move with and against the basic grid of meter with confident freedom. The line lengths are uneven, and the usual rhymes—masculine and feminine endings alternating, the masculine line rhyming with the accented penultimate syllable of the feminine line: *sur*face with sinis*ter*, trans*luc*ence with un*loose*, and so on, a system learned from Auden's practice—form nearly invisible and inaudible couplets that force more discipline on the writer than response from the reader. Unpatterned internal rhyme and consonance, writher/wreath/wrath, Volutions/volition/evolve, tie things together more obviously and give the poem its heightened effect of artifice, of being hyper-crafted. Merrill is building prosodic muscle. Before he is finished, a poem's whole dimension of sound will move in fine-tuned response to his will.

A new forcefulness breaks through in "Salome," like "Laboratory Poem" an allegory of love's murderous nature. Its three parts are variations on this theme. Each is given three of those stanzas in which "The Parrot" was so stiffly caged, and one look is enough to show how much more freely John the Baptist, a mad dog, and a doctor in a lab are able to move within it:

> Our neighbor's little boy ran out to greet
>> The chow, his runaway pet,
> And was fearfully mauled. Breaking its mouth on fences
> Down the struck street the orange mad dog tore
> Until my father's pistol made of it
>> Pinks, reds, a thrash of senses
>> Outside the stationery store.

Merrill has by this point learned most of what there is to know about shifting accents and adding extra grace-note syllables. Like the octopus this dog is metaphorical, but he is quite a lot like a dog as well, and the language that tells about him sounds quite a lot like speech. Thematic crossfire between the three sections is fairly complex: Herod, "slavering" and "bitten to the bone" in I, prefigures both the mad chow and the boy he bites in II; in

III the boy's delirium brings on a doctor to dissect "prophetic heads . . . / Upon a platter." Each part is decoratively linked by water (baptism/hydrophobia/thirst). In III the beatitude summing up the point of all parts—"Whosoever faithfully/ Desires desire more than its object shall/ Find his right heaven, be he saint or brute"—connects the chief figures of I and II, as calling John a "shaggy saint" connects them in I. Merrill's mature poems will manage this sort of interweaving more and more dexterously and complexly.

Two poems in this book could be seen as responding to the accusations that those in his first were cold and lifeless. In "Dream (Escape from the Sculpture Museum) and Waking," the speaker worries about his own coldness and strangeness (a worry Merrill also confronted in his first novel about the same time). The dream locates him on the first floor of a museum full of marble statues; he himself may be one of them, though he says bravely that "for a long time now/ I have wanted to be more natural/ Than they. . . ." Two muffled figures, vaguely human, approach through a snowstorm beyond the window—another plate of cold glass—and "Cause me to stiffen in a show/ Of being human also," but they pass by without seeing him. Then the dream changes. The speaker is another sort of statue,

> mounted in a village common.
> A child calls. Early lamps and sunset
> Stream together down the snowman's
> Face and dazzle in his jet
> Eyes. He lives, but melts. I summon
> All my strength. I wake in a cold sweat.

The marble figures, like Yeats's nightingale, are imperishable but dead; the snowman "lives, but melts." The choices seem clear, yet equally chill. Waking, the dreamer remembers a conversation of the night before, when the lover now asleep beside him "called me cold, I said you were a child./ I said we must respect/ Each other's privacy. You smiled." The poem ends in fear of there being no alternatives to coldness and solitude, but not in resignation. If artfulness is all the affirmation here, to identify "cold sweat" with a melting snowman is certainly to make the most of limited possibilities. The diction is straightforward, the metrical choices made to convey quiet coolness rather than speed or energy. Emotion is the point of this poem; Merrill makes no effort to mask it from the reader by his manner. The sex of the lover, which *is* masked, doesn't matter in the least; the coldness masking dreamer from lover does—not here the merciful mask of love but the tragic one beneath, that always finally shows through.

"The Doodler" is less characteristic of Merrill's manner at this stage. It develops like an emblem poem, but the metaphor is an *act* instead of an object: doodling on a telephone pad during phone conversations with friends. (Merrill is in fact a great doodler, as many pages of his drafts in the collection at Washington University testify.) The writing is funny and high-spirited, free of the bitterness, fear, and self-doubt of other poems in this book. Contrasted with the chaste rhymes of "Dream . . . and Waking," some of these are almost wickedly cheerful: ikons/lichens, foretaste/artist, weevil/gravel; Merrill has learned to make the *kind* of words he rhymes on contribute to the emotional tone of a poem—to let them call attention to themselves, as here, or be functional but discreetly self-effacing, or anything in between. "The Doodler" is an early instance of the pentameter quatrains mentioned by the witty spirit of W. H. Auden in *Scripts for the Pageant*. Asked whether God has another name than Biology, Auden replies "I'VE HEARD THEM SPEAK OF 'ABBA' SOUNDS TO ME/ LIKE ONE OF JM'S FAVORITE RHYME SCHEMES." (See Mark 14:36.)

The poem's bounciness masks a serious subject—two serious subjects really, each a version of the other: the speaker's life, and his art. (Or three: Merrill once said "The Doodler" was "about God looking at his creatures,"[7] but every poem about the creative process probably participates in that ultimate metaphor.) As the life goes on—calls coming in, going out, relationships forming, developing, dissolving—images appear on the page by a semiconscious process with its own independent development, up from "certain abstract forms . . . / Stars, oblongs, or a baroque motif" to more ambitious works:

> Far, far behind already is that aeon
> Of pin-heads, bodies each a ragged weevil,
> Slit-mouthed and spider-leggéd, with eyes like gravel,
> Wavering under trees of purple crayon.
>
> Shapes never realized, were you dogs or chairs?
> That page is brittle now, if not long burned.
> This morning's little boy stands (I have learned
> To do feet) gazing down a flight of stairs.

With imperative confidence the poem ends: "Emerge, O sunbursts, garlands, creatures, men,/ Ever more lifelike out of the white void!" In this order, book by book, that is what they will do.

There are other poems in this book worth mentioning: "Voices from the Other World," for instance, Merrill's first poem about the world of the Ouija board and much the earlier of two premature rejections of that world in favor of this one; or "About the Phoenix," where the metaphor leads to a willful preferring of "not agony or resurrection, rather/ A mortal lull that followed either"—the kindly grateful interlude between crises when happiness is momentarily possible. Of greater importance are two that bracket the entire collection: the title poem, and "A Dedication."

The word *love* is very common in *First Poems*. But the best

Merrill could then do by way of expressing love directly was (in "Hour-Glass"): "You/ Are the kind gathering I most falter to"— which, with every allowance for the emblem, leaves a lot to be desired. The voice that speaks not only of but with love, undefended by the necessities of a rigid metaphor, speaks now for the first time in these two poems, in the aftershock of what Merrill has called, in a statement printed with "The Country of a Thousand Years of Peace" in the anthology *Poet's Choice*, his "first deeply-felt death":

> In 1950, at the beginning of nearly three years abroad, I went to Lausanne for an hour with my friend the Dutch poet Hans Lodeizen. . . . He had leukemia and died two weeks later, at twenty-six. It was my first deeply-felt death. I connected it with the spell of aimless living in Europe to which I was then committed and to which all those picturesque and novel sights corresponded painfully enough. As the inevitable verses took shape, strictness of form seemed at last beside the point; my material nevertheless allowed for a good deal of paring and polishing. . . . The poem still surprises me, as much by its clarification of what I was feeling, as by its foreknowledge of where I needed to go next, in my work.[8]

The poem begins with a sketchy suggestion of hospital routine and of life going on as usual in the city outside—appalling in such circumstances always—

> the toy city where
>
> The glittering neutrality
> Of clock and chocolate and lake and cloud
> Made every morning somewhat
> Less than you could bear;
>
> And makes me cry aloud
> At the old masters of disease
> Who dangling high above you on a hair
> The sword that, never falling, kills

> Would coax you still back from that starry land
> Under the world, which no one sees
> Without a death, its finish and sharp weight
> Flashing in his own hand.

Merrill pays as much attention as ever to the elements of his style. Rhyme, loosened from a pattern the reader can anticipate, still makes its closures in a way that beautifully mimes the brokenness of grief; and the rhymes are perfect—essentially monosyllabic, plain sounds, no half-rhymes or clever ones, arranged to fall most often on the trimeter lines, which in this sort of arrangement have the most force. It is a technical achievement of great sophistication, finer than anything he would publish for years thereafter. Nothing but the buffers of form without strictness are permitted to interfere between the emotion of poem and speaker and the reader.

As the poet himself understood, this risky business—clarification of feeling, no longer allowing strict formal stanzas to defend him against it—were "where I needed to go next, in my work." But the insight arrived earlier than his ability to follow it through. "The Country of a Thousand Years of Peace" was composed in 1950 or 1951, apart from minor revisions made years later just before the publication of the book whose title it bears, so most of the other poems in that book must have been written later. This fact makes the two about Hans Lodeizen all the more remarkable. In a number of others the writing is relaxed, but only the love poem "A Renewal" shares their tone of unmasked emotional authenticity to this degree.

The importance of the young Dutch poet to Merrill will be reaffirmed a quarter of a century after his death, when a crucial role in *The Book of Ephraim* is assigned to, or appropriated by, him. Read in the knowledge of this, the early poem's prescience is a little eerie. Certainly in his own mind Merrill has coaxed Hans back from that starry land under the world, which he himself has "seen" without a death, or at any rate without dying.

In general these first books herald a natural craftsman of great potential, but handicapped by fear of emotional expressiveness. This handicap might not have bothered a different sort of twentieth-century poet; Stevens and Eliot managed very well without talking openly about their feelings or their lives. But Merrill's poems were wholly without reference to public events or intellectual issues; even the convictions about perception which he shared with Stevens were for him more emotional than intellectual. His concern was with art and the personal life. Unless he could defeat, or compromise with, his own reluctance to risk exposure, he would never write effectively about the subject matter he seemed to care for most.

Happily, in *Water Street*—published next, in 1962—this enfeebling and occluding fear has been controlled, or outgrown, or has subsided of itself.

CHAPTER 3

Water Street

I

Whenever I'm asked to suggest one of Merrill's books to someone interested in getting to know his work, I name *Water Street*
or *Nights and Days*, supposing that the two before *Water Street*
would strike most people—at first—as too ornate and unfeeling
and those following *Nights and Days* as too formidable. In many
ways these two still seem the most appealing of his books—the
most approachable and likeable, if not the most imaginative, ambitious, or distinguished. Decoration in both concedes to deco-
rum, manner to manners. Discretion and reticence in both conceal only the sources of the emotion the poet no longer cares to
dissociate himself from. A reader new to Merrill can feel welcome there.

After the new simplicity and clarity of the writing—a great
relief—*Water Street* departs most strikingly from the earlier books
in the *voice* of its poems, often warm and nearly always personal.
The typical "I" or "we" of *The Country of a Thousand Years of
Peace* had the feel of a device, a conventional way to start talking;
Water Street speaks in the first person as though Merrill doesn't

mind if the edges of self and persona overlap. And they do overlap, many of the best poems drawing upon the particulars of the poet's life, his childhood, travels, writing, and general situation. "If I am host at last," he says in the book's final stanza, "it is of little more than my own past./ May others be at home in it"—a seminal epigraph for the whole future of his poetry. The great discovery of *Water Street* is that it was possible to make others at home in one's own past *within limits*, to talk like any good host about some personal concerns, while remaining discreet about details, and about other concerns. Merrill has learned that between the formal encrustations of *First Poems* and the excesses of unbuttoned confession, as between the flames and resurrections of the Phoenix, is a fruitful middle ground.

Despite the difficulty of much of his later writing, from this point forward Merrill's work is allied in various ways with that of the writers of so-called *confessional* poetry. The least artful and most outrageous of these have given such poetry a name so bad that a reviewer wishing to praise Merrill feels obliged to explain that his work, though autobiographical, shows "none of that urgency to reveal the untellable or unspeakable that we associate with the poetry we call 'confessional.' "[1] But the term as coined by the critic M. L. Rosenthal originally referred to poetry that—like Merrill's—deals with neurotic, distressing, sometimes humiliating and anguish-filled material, the "confessing" of which may have a therapeutic value for the writer and a cathartic value for the reader, and which achieves, beyond this, "formal realization and beauty through the impersonal use of its highly personal elements."[2] Rosenthal was describing the practice not of exhibitionists without talent but of serious poets capable of imposing formal restraints on such painful and volatile subject matter as divorce, periodic insanity, attempted suicide, alcoholism, and unorthodox sexuality. His book examines the work of Sylvia Plath, Allen Ginsberg, Theodore Roethke, John Berryman, and Anne Sexton, and pays particular attention to Robert Lowell's *Life Studies,* usually cited as the pioneering volume of the confessional "school," though Merrill himself believes that both he and Lowell were instructed first by W. D. Snodgrass's *Heart's Needle* (1959) in the handling of painful personal material in poetry.

By its nature this kind of poetry ignores T. S. Eliot's dictum (in his essay "Tradition and the Individual Talent") that "The progress of the artist is a continual self-sacrifice, a continual extinction of personality. . . . It is not in his personal emotions, the emotions provoked by particular events in his life, that the poet is in any way interesting or remarkable." Good "mainstream" confessional writing, like much other writing, demonstrates that personality, properly handled, can be as potent and proper a force in a poem as any other.

Moreover, at a special session on Confessional Poetry at the 1975 Modern Language Association Convention, the thesis was developed that the lives of poets like Lowell, Plath, and Berryman are also "exemplary," in the sense that lives haunted by madness and the death-wish are felt to exemplify the twentieth-century condition in an extreme form. Everyone is made sick by an insane world bent on nuclear suicide (this theory goes), but the artist, with his special sensitivities, has the least resistance; so that what weakens others kills him. But while the others are mutely going to pieces, the poet may *talk,* in dreadfully intimate detail, about the progress of his own collapse. By speaking so personally of private horrors, such a poet makes public "confession" on everyone's behalf. Afterwards, as like as not, he dies of our common social disease—not that by dying he can save anyone else from disease and death, but because death is the logical conclusion of the sickness unto death. Despite a tendency to romanticize the artist-as-tragic-misfit—a modern instance of an old tradition—this line of thought is not without a certain valid-ity, or so one is likely to allow upon considering the names listed in Rosenthal's Table of Contents.

Merrill, of course, is not *this* kind of confessional poet. He has never associated himself with politics or social causes, and has dealt with our specifically twentieth-century ailments—"the sickness of our time"—by concentrating on the personal life, the difficulties with family and vicissitudes of love which are timeless; and his poems of unhappiness, grief, and loss resolve characteristically into peace and beauty at the close. David Kalstone's simple term "autobiographical" fits better. As Kalstone explains in the introduction to his book *Five Temperaments:*

> American poetry of this period [the late 1950s and early 1960s] became increasingly available to autobiographical energies of *all* sorts, not simply to writing which was desperate and on the edge. It is easier to notice this development in the crisis mentality of "confessional" poems, and certainly their explicitness had a challenging effect on poets of every degree of frankness and reticence. . . . But we need not confuse the excitement of new subject matter with the special nature of these writings as *poems.*

Still, allowing for the differences, it remains true that like the best confessional poets Merrill has written openly about intensely painful family matters in poems held strictly to the highest standards of the art, poems which treat self-revelations exactly like any other material, and that this "impersonal use of its highly personal elements" distances and elevates the poetry beyond its origin in the life of a single man. Formlessness in this mode is deadly; but, because for Merrill the mask of artfulness is essential, the possibilities of self-revelation given in the idea of confessional poetry have served him well. The veiled and displaced autobiography he had found exemplified in Proust, synthesized with emotional immediacy like that of the best confessional poets' work, were to eventuate in those stories of his life masked and unmasked, varyingly intimate here in tone, there in

content, restrained while expressed through steadily increasing
powers and resources of style, which Kalstone labels "a kind of
autobiography in verse."

2

Kalstone singles out Merrill's reconsiderations of his childhood as "one of the things which makes his writing about himself so different from Robert Lowell's. A continuing access to
childhood memories and insights nourishes Merrill's verse; with
Lowell, the memories are most often terrifying and unavail-
ing."[3] Merrill's is a fairly thoroughly explored childhood. His
father was Charles Merrill, founder of the great brokerage firm—
powerful, emotional, wealthy, three times married; the full-length
portrait in his son's novel *The Seraglio* is consistent with glimpses
provided in the poems. His mother was the senior Merrill's second wife; they were divorced when their only child was twelve.
Many of Merrill's poems over the years since *Water Street*, as
well as *The Seraglio*, have struggled to understand and come to
terms with the powerful oedipal feelings nourished by this situation. Other poems build stories out of the details of life as a
poor little rich boy: nurse ("Mademoiselle") who taught him
French and German, cook and butler, splendid toys, terrors,
loneliness. His own childhood is a charmed subject for Merrill,
who seems unable not to write well about it.

"Transfigured Bird" gave us a quick early view, but childhood first opens as a field of exploration in *Water Street*, where
seven poems more or less obliquely address the question to
Memory: how did the boy I was become the man I am? "A
Vision of the Garden" takes a child's common experience for a
metaphor of the adult's: having drawn a face with his finger on
the frosted windowpane, the child looks through the wet lines
upon

> a winter garden so
> Heavy with snow its hedge of pine
>
> And sun so brilliant on the snow
> I breathed my pleasure out onto the chill pane
> Only to see its angel fade in mist.
> I was a child, I did not know
>
> That what I longed for would resist
> Neither what cold lines should my finger trace
> On colder grounds before I found anew
> In yours the features of that face
>
> Whose words whose looks alone undo
> Such frosts . . .

The extent to which Merrill had absorbed, and then found his own way past, the lesson of "The Snow Man" is plain. The Stevens affinities are still evident in the clarity and wintry essence of the scene, and in a turn of phrase or two, but the focus has shifted from perception toward the dynamics of human relations and the emblem poem become a love poem, its voice warmed and sweetened.

In the first of "Five Old Favorites," called (after Freud and Strauss) "A Dream of Old Vienna," three of the stock characters Merrill often prefers to "real" ones—Father, Mother, Child, the eternal triangle—assemble in what only seems to be an ordinary domestic setting. The mother, "Torn between conflicting libidos," wonders whether

> To wed the son when he has slain the father,
> Or thrust the brat *at once* into the damp . . . ?
> Such are the throbbing issues that enliven
> Many a cozy evening round the lamp.

—a lamp that luridly bathes the scene incarnadine, betraying the violent reality masked by surface calm. The first "favorite" makes its point through irony; the second, called "The Midnight Snack," plays upon a grown-up child's glee (no doubt universal) at sneakily getting away with a forbidden act. In this, a foreshortened sonnet, Father and Mother are somewhat more individualized as gas stove and refrigerator, blue pilot light of the one glaring but now helpless to prevent the nightly raid on the other: "It opens, the inviolate!/ Illumined as in dreams I take/ A glass of milk, a piece of cake . . ." The child is left out of the third old favorite, in which a mutually disaffected couple are translated (as the title tells) into "Sundown and Starlight," the husband still flushed, violent, voracious, the wife dressing in cool dark blue: "Men! Let him burn all night. She has other things to do/ Than care for him. She opens her jewel case." In none of these short pieces is identification with specific people insisted upon; the figures might stand in for any of thousands of parents and children, types in the family myth. All the same, when Merrill writes (in the second): "When I was little and he was riled/ It never entered my father's head/ Not to flare up, roar and turn red./ Mother kept cool and smiled," a first cartoon of his own parents is suggested in these emotional and temperamental polarities.

The villanelle "The World and the Child" uses its form to dramatize a child's discovery of what love is by its absence. He has been put to bed; a party is going on in the room below; his misery is like Marcel's, waiting through the long light evening for his mother's kiss:

> Letting his wisdom be the whole of love,
> The father tiptoes out, backwards. A gleam
> Falls on the child awake and wearied of . . .
>
> He lies awake in pain, he does not move,
> He will not call. The women, hearing him,
> Would let their wisdom be the whole of love.
>
> People have filled the room he lies above.
> Their talk, mild variation, chilling theme,
> Falls on the child. Awake and wearied of
>
> Mere pain, mere wisdom also, he would have
> All the world waking from its winter dream,

> Letting its wisdom be. The whole of love
> Falls on the child awake and wearied of.

By splitting the penultimate line where he does, Merrill converts the sadness of both repeated lines into a kind of triumph—emotional affirmation stage-managed by technical adroitness. We can recognize in this sensitive child, trapped with the rest of the world in a "winter dream," the poet who would later write about dreaming of himself as marble statue and melting snowman.

Last of this group, longest and most important, is "Scenes of Childhood." Two people here clearly identified as the poet and his mother, are watching a thirty-year-old home movie of themselves and the mother's two sisters:

> From the love seat's gloom
> A quiet chuckle escapes
> My white-haired mother
>
> To see in that final light
> A man's shadow mount
> Her dress. And now she is
> Advancing, sister-
> less, but followed by
> A fair child, or fury—
> Myself at four, in tears.
> I raise my fist,
>
> Strike, she kneels down. The man's
> Shadow afflicts us both.

At this point the film jams, and the shadow-man—the poet's father, behind the camera—is in effect deftly transmigrated into "Our headstrong old projector" that "Glares at the scene which promptly/ Catches fire," a little oedipal summary of what had happened all those years ago. The mother gone to bed, her son is left alone to "fade and cool" gradually and consider the perennial mystery of how time changed the woman and child in the just-destroyed film into the two who watched it burn. Clearly the man whose shadow fell upon them thirty years before, and whose other *Water Street* persona of gas-stove ready to "flare up, roar and turn red" connects him with the overheated projector, has had everything to do with the transformation.

This poem unreels in a setting alive with insect noise and presence: bugs in the movie, on the screen, in the antiquated projector's "racket," as "primal/ Figures jerky and blurred/ As lightning bugs" in the film (who make a firefly-metaphor for love outside the *present* house), and on and on: Father

> Whose microscope, now deep
> In purple velvet, first
> Showed me the skulls of flies,
> The fur, the flames
>
> Etching the jaws—father:
> Shrunken to our true size.
> Each morning, back of us,
> Fields wail and shimmer.
> To go out is to fall
> Under fresh spells, cool web
> And stinging song new-hatched
> Each day, all summer.

The ants-under-the-skin feel of all this small, mindless, kinetic life, the "minute galaxy" of starlike mosquitoes that will "Needle me back" from spiderweb and spells—almost another family setting (mother's cool trap, father's buzzing burning flybite)—give a peculiar telescoping scale to the significance of all this: the father/fly here under the microscope and the past miniaturized on film, against the stars which, riding above the fireflies and more constant, seem no less to mimic the configurations of Father, Mother, and grown-up Child "breathing/ In and out the sun/ And air I am.// The son and heir!" And additional possible reading of these lines should not be overlooked: that the cool web is the web of form—meter and rhyme, the "spell" of versified words—and the stinging song the poem caught within it.

The end of the poem, though grand-sounding, is inconclusive; Merrill is not yet ready or perhaps able to do more than say what he feels about a life-situation still being worked out as much in dreams as in poetry. But he is entirely in charge of his interlocking systems of images: insects, stars, fire, coolness, noon, night, dream, sleep; and in charge of the verse so that its short lines shift metrically, 3/3/3/2/3/3/3/2, rhyming on the two-stress lines only, so smoothly and almost insensibly that it has the feel of free verse mysteriously collected. Other touches positively identify this poem as Merrill's. His mother speaks "From the love seat's gloom": a figurative truth overlaid with a literal one. The double meaning of "spell" and the pun on "sun/ And air" are purest Merrill, as is the effortless way the verse describing even dead or stinging insects condenses lyrically. It was opera that showed this poet, at eleven or so, that even tragic passions may be beautifully expressed—that nothing, however ugly or unpleasant in life, need be so presented by art.

Merrill has spoken skeptically of "the splendors and miseries of writing"[4] as a fit topic for poetry, yet—drawn by the example of Proust—will return to it again and again. He combines this with the visual theme in "To a Butterfly," a companion piece of sorts to "The Doodler" but lacking the latter's panache. What sets out to be the familiar emblematic treatment of the butterfly abruptly breaks off in exasperation:

> soon four
> Dapper stained glass windows bore
> You up—ENOUGH.
>
> Goodness, how tired one grows
> Just looking through a prism:
> Allegory, symbolism.
> I've tried, Lord knows,
>
> To keep from seeing double,
> Blushed for whenever I did,

> Prayed like a boy my cheek be hid
> By manly stubble.

But "I am not yet," he admits, "Proof against rigmarole":

> The day you hover without any
> Tincture of soul,
>
> Red monarch, swallowtail,
> Will be the day my own
> Wiles gather dust. Each will have flown
> The other's jail.

All those early emblems are exposed in this confession. One wonders all the same how literally to accept it. Wanting not to deny the evidence of his eyes, to believe in rather than only "use" the natural thing he sees—a business viewed here as part of maturing, at least as an artist—is not very far from wanting to *be* natural. Both cut against the grain; Merrill was and on the whole would continue to be devoted to these "wiles" of artifice. In any case the disavowal seems not to have worked, since the distancing and diminishment of nature goes on, and a much later poem ("In Nine Sleep Valley") describes a similar, largely unsuccessful, effort to look trustingly upon a landscape. The point here is less what he did about what he knew than that he knew it: that to practice *on* himself artifice *about* himself was not his way.

3

The Country of a Thousand Years of Peace is a book of travel and life abroad, the very title placing its ideal emotional focus in Switzerland. *Water Street* is the street in Stonington, Connecticut where Merrill has lived for part of every year since 1954. Kalstone's chapter on Merrill is organized around the "improvised houses of survival and desire" in his work, which "—however real, solidly located and furnished—are also imagined as vulnerable houses of the spirit. . . . In the details he uses to conjure them up, there are always reminders of the particular kinds of exposure and emergency against which these domestic arrangements have been contrived."[5]

There is an emblem piece called "House" in Merrill's first book, but the theme *as* theme appears earliest in "An Urban Convalescence," the opening poem of *Water Street*. The poet, out for a walk after an illness, comes upon a demolition crew "tearing up part of my block/ And, chilled through, dazed and lonely" watches while he tries to call to mind this building he has lived so close to for a decade, now a heap of rubble: "Wait. Yes. Vaguely a presence rises/ Some five floors high, of shabby stone" with a stone garland over the lintel. Surprised both at his inability to remember the building better and at recalling the garland he cannot remember ever having seen, the poet shivers, suddenly

> Transfixed by a particular cheap engraving of garlands
> Bought for a few francs long ago,
> All calligraphic tendril and cross-hatched rondure,
> Ten years ago, and crumpled up to stanch
> Boughs dripping, whose white gestures filled a cab,
> And thought of neither then nor since.
> Also, to clasp them, the small, red-nailed hand
> Of no one I can place. Wait. No. Her name, her features
> Lie toppled underneath that year's fashions.
> The words she must have spoken, setting her face
> To fluttering like a veil, I cannot hear now,
> Let alone understand.
>
> So that I am already on the stair,
> As it were, of where I lived,
> When the whole structure shudders at my tread
> And soundlessly collapses. . . .

Of the two subjects developing here together, Memory is first: its surprising lapses and startling gifts, the garland-associations connecting the ten-years-lived-by present, abruptly vanishing, to the ten-years-vanished past, abruptly but imperfectly restored. All this is the method of Proust. The other subject is more personal: that things are torn down just as you think you know how to live among them, that the past has flashed back only to prove unusable save as a way of measuring how completely its structures have been demolished.

The poet displaces onto the scene, where "Wires and pipes, snapped off at the roots, quiver" like snapped nerves, the dread he carefully keeps out of his own voice:

> Well, that is what life does. I stare
> A moment longer, so. And presently
> The massive volume of the world
> Closes again.
>
> Upon that book I swear
> To abide by what it teaches:
> Gospels of ugliness and waste,
> Of towering voids, of soiled gusts,
> Of a shrieking to be faced
> Full into, eyes astream with cold—
>
> With cold?
> All right then. With self-knowledge.

Merrill said once in an interview that, having come this far, he had no idea how to finish the poem. Certainly it had to end elsewhere; this much grainy "reality," ugliness and waste, is not a gospel by which he ever lived before or since, if self-knowledge is. "Then," he says, "I had the idea of letting it go back to a more formal pattern at the end"[6]—in effect, to begin a new movement, like a musical movement, without a smooth transition. By restoring control to the poet, the quatrains that close the poem also—through the real magic of which creative work is sometimes capable—show him how to transcend the vision of destruction and loss he has sustained. He gathers the verses and builds a supportive structure of *them* that pushes the vision back, calling attention to the business of composition by using a phrase—"the sickness of our time"—and then immediately questioning the phrase. One other rescuer comes to hand,

> a pill
> They had told me not to take until much later.
>
> With the result that back into my imagination
> The city glides, like cities seen from the air,
> Mere smoke and sparkle to the passenger
> Having in mind another destination
>
> Which now is not that honey-slow descent
> Of the Champs-Elysées, her hand in his,
> But the dull need to make some kind of house
> Out of the life lived, out of the love spent.

That the ideals and values we learn when young no longer work in the world we have to live in later is a central theme in the autobiography of Henry Adams and the fiction of Faulkner, Fitzgerald, and the early Hemingway, and often seems to lead eventually to despair. Merrill can be desperate too, but his will not to despair ultimately is very strong. Again and again he fetches up against obstacles and then, in a burst of will, energy, and insight, surmounts them; it is impossible to imagine a first-person Merrill poem after *Water Street* ending "I have wasted my life" or "Daddy, daddy, you bastard, I'm through." At the end of "An Urban Convalescence" one cannot doubt that, given any luck at all, a house will be built out of a past and future of loving and living.

Before it coalesces into quatrains, this poem employs a loose line recurrently iambic and pentameter, rarely rhyming, very smooth and clear, even colloquial, the typical line of this book and the next. The comic and ironic touches are light, but keep what is after all a fairly grim meditation from bogging down in self-dramatization or self-pity, two sins Merrill virtually never commits. A crane's "jaws dribble rubble. An old man/ Laughs and curses in her brain,/ Bringing to mind the close of *The White Goddess*" [by Robert Graves, who wrote: "While an ignorant pale priest/ Rides the beast with a man's head/ To her long-omitted feast"]. Water in a glass is "no longer cordial, scarcely wet." And again a loveliness of description shimmers on the surfaces even of ugly things, taking them out of the world they refer to; Merrill doesn't try or care until much later to catch the feel of life ongoing, only a likeness transformed by his own willful view of things. If the transformations beautify, he never pretends otherwise. Because emotions at any rate are never beautified, if settings and objects are, there is no effect of sentimentalizing.

In the face of all this honesty, what is masked? Chiefly, the sources of the poet's intense unhappiness, of the state of mind that makes him see the fallen building as a metaphor for how we live. Amid the unknowable specific sorrows that would account for this is a general one that can be known by hindsight: in Paris, a girl's red-nailed hand clasped the flowering boughs in the cab filled with their "white gestures" (not "blossoms" but the active noun, just what Merrill *would* say). This classic image of Romance was part of a complex of attitudes, values, and expectations, his own and others', which had to collapse before his commitment to a homosexual life. Not a hint of this is present in the poem, nor is the knowledge necessary; but it brings the last two quatrains, quoted above, into acute focus.

If "An Urban Convalescence" reveals disaffection from a dwelling-place, the last poem, "A Tenancy," speaks of beginning to live in what one infers to be the house on Water Street which will become, like the house in Athens, a familiar presence in Merrill's later work and almost a character in the Ouija trilogy. Like the poem it balances, "A Tenancy" moves by looser verse through most of its length, then resolves into rhyming stanzas to conclude. The poem begins when a quality of light has triggered a meditation on the past—on snowbound rented rooms, scene of plans to confront the Real, and on the abandoning (again) of old fashions and youthful expectations:

> from within, ripples
> Of heat had begun visibly bearing up and away
> The bouquets and wreaths of a quarter century.
> Let them go, what did I want with them?
> It was time to change that wallpaper!

Years older, wiser, mortal, he rises now in his new house to admit three friends who stamp off what they hope to be the last spring snow. Like Magi, they come bearing gifts:

> One has brought violets in a pot;
> The second, wine; the best,
> His open, empty hand. Now in the room
> The sun is shining like a lamp.
> I put the flowers where I need them most
>
> And then, not asking why they come,
> Invite the visitors to sit.
> If I am host at last
> It is of little more than my own past.
> May others be at home in it.

Other parts of the poem, less clear than this, must be read and reread for an approximation of what Merrill means; he seems at such times to be talking, however beautifully, mostly to himself. Through all his work, indeed, talking in public to himself—or himself and a few friends—will be his one besetting sin. But nowhere is the poetry clearer than in *Water Street*, the friendliest and least exclusive of all his books. The "others" he invokes with its last words seem many and welcome, and he himself to have arrived somewhere, and to have settled, both into his work and into the life from which it will henceforth be inseparable.

CHAPTER 4

Nights and Days

I

In 1967 the National Book Award for poetry was given to a collection that achieved everything Merrill's early evidence of talent, and subsequent development, had seemed to promise. *Nights and Days* is the book of masking, of the disjunction between appearances and realities taken up as a major theme. The two very long poems at the beginning and end are suffused with this theme; the important shorter poems (and nearly every page, in fact) are touched by it as well, so that the book is unified by a minutely yet detachedly observed obsession. David Kalstone calls this "the classic Merrill volume—jaunty, penetrating and secure."[1] Thematic unity and voice, synthesized at the climax of Merrill's first terrific drive toward achievement in poetry, make this his one essential book in my view—though, as I will argue, *Divine Comedies* is the superior work.

Two good "action emblems"—"Violent Pastoral" and "Between Us"—and a neatly turned quasi-narrative called "Charles on Fire" would deserve more than passing mention had they appeared in a different book; but four important poems, three of them quite lengthy, outshine these and others so immoderately as to preempt all the space available here. Childhood and parents are again the subjects of "The Broken Home," a sequence of seven unorthodox sonnets—each linked to the rest by theme and imagery, yet for the most part self-contained—wherein the poet's feelings about his father and mother are further explored and expressed, gracefully masked as usual in mild irony and verbal wit, as in this second sonnet:

> My father, who had flown in World War I,
> Might have continued to invest his life
> In cloud banks well above Wall Street and wife.
> But the race was run below, and the point was to win.
>
> Too late now, I make out in his blue gaze
> (Through the smoked glass of being thirty-six)
> The soul eclipsed by twin black pupils, sex
> and business; time was money in those days.
>
> Each thirteenth year he married. When he died
> There were already several chilled wives
> In sable orbit—rings, cars, permanent waves.
> We'd felt him warming up for a green bride.
>
> He could afford it. He was "in his prime"
> At three score ten. But money was not time.

This clear, sane, civilized voice is the characteristic voice of *Nights and Days*. How does it work? The reader's attention is pulled in two directions: it registers the regret of a son whose father's "soul" was obscured by two consuming interests that could not be shared until "too late"; at the same time it is distracted and entertained by the devices of Merrill's style: the astronomical metaphor (eclipse, chilled wives in orbit), the double entendres (cloud banks, sable, rings), and the cliché "time is money" being stood on its head. This is not a complicated poem, but every touch counts, nothing strains, the sense is plain, the sonnet form, liberties and all, is flawlessly served, the reader is pleased; and the

sadness, which at first is less insistent than the wit, grows
stronger with each rereading, like the ominousness in Dickin-
son's "Because I could not stop for death."

The proportions of amusement and emotion are reversed in
the fourth sonnet:

> One afternoon, red, satyr-thighed
> Michael, the Irish setter, head
> Passionately lowered, led
> The child I was to a shut door. Inside
>
> Blinds beat sun from the bed.
> The green-gold room throbbed like a bruise.
> Under a sheet, clad in taboos
> Lay whom we sought, her hair undone, outspread,
>
> And of a blackness found, if ever now, in old
> Engravings where the acid bit.
> I must have needed to touch it
> Or the whiteness—was she dead?
> Her eyes flew open, startled strange and cold.
> The dog slumped to the floor. She reached for me. I fled.

Sexual language, often violent, describes this bedroom scene of
such deceptive simplicity—"passionately," "satyr-thighed," "beat
sun [son] from the bed," "throbbed like a bruise," "clad in ta-
boos," "outspread," "acid bit," and the flat terminal absoluteness
of "She reached for me. I fled." The comparative violence done
to the pentameters we expect seems appropriate. Because of her
context we know the woman must be the child's mother; otherwise she might be taken solely for the terrifying female principle
celebrated in a host of poems and myths, La Belle Dame Sans
Merci. Certainly this sonnet, which brilliantly reveals the contrasts between passive appearances and dreadful realities, reveals
as well this female principle in the clutching maternal figure on
the bed, against whom a child's sole defense is flight. Mother,

of course, represents Woman to all children; the point here is that Woman—even supine and probably asleep—terrifies this child who needs to find and touch her. The scene resolves as a paradigm for all the heterosexual material in Merrill's work: desire to open closed doors, to approach and touch the Sleeping Woman, is countermanded by fear of waking her innate deadliness and being made her captive.

The extent to which these parents continue to influence the grown-up child is plain ("Cool here in the graveyard of good and evil,/ They are even so to be honored and obeyed.// . . . Obeyed, at least, inversely"; "A child, a red dog roam the corridors/ Still, of the broken home"). But the note of relief at the end is unmistakable, and the last lines are illuminated by the quick final touch of lyric beauty that signals affirmation in Merrill's work:

> The real house became a boarding-school.
> Under the ballroom ceiling's allegory
> Someone at last may actually be allowed
> To learn something; or, from my window, cool
> With the unstiflement of the entire story,
> Watch a red setter stretch and sink in cloud.

To link this final image of a sunset with the child's familiar companion in trauma does more than unify the seven sonnets; it implies that in the "unstiflement of the entire story" is escape and salvation from what the story tells: the fundamental conviction of confessional poetry. The sonnets are framed by the window at which the first begins and the last ends, through which the broken home expels its "stifling" heat as the sun goes down. This progression from heat to coolness while a story is unstifled will come to characterize later poems of sexual anger and frustration on the way to their resolutions, especially in *Braving the Elements*.

2

"The Thousand and Second Night" is a long poem in five parts. The first, entitled "Rigor Vitae" and set in Istanbul, elaborates a comparison between Merrill's face, under freak attack by Bell's palsy, and the Hagia Sophia corrupted by latter-day alterations. The poem opens like a journal entry:

> Istanbul. 21 March. I woke today
> With an absurd complaint. The whole right half
> Of my face refuses to move.

In spite of this affliction, the poet goes out like a proper tourist to view the great church in its debased old age, and observes that

> .   The building, desperate for youth, has smeared
>   All over its original fine bones
>
>   Acres of ochre plaster. A diagram
>   Indicates how deep in the mudpack
>   The real facade is. I want *my* face back.

His own face is masked in the immobility of its disease, the "real facade" in a plaster mudpack. Hagia Sophia, the House of Heavenly Wisdom, is a "flameless void," her dome "Bald of mosaic, senile, floated/ In a gilt wash"—a thin gold mask; the poet feels in spite of himself "the usual, if no/ Longer flattering kinship" between this "transcendental skull" and his own, now void also—he says—of flame, faith, knowledge, "precious sensibility."

Later, back home in Athens and "cured," the poet admits to himself that though to all appearances he's as good as new, "Once you've cracked/ That so-called mirror of the soul,/ It is not readily, if at all, made whole," and that "Part of me has remained cold and withdrawn . . . not human." He remembers how a chatty Athenian, who *was* wholly human, had given him cause to reflect that in Greece "The stranger is a god in masquerade," unknown personally and only *therefore* perfect, the "perfect stranger" (to be encountered explicitly in *The Fire Screen* and implicitly in "From the Cupola" and elsewhere). Imperfections are revealed as knowledge and understanding make inroads into appearances.

"Strangers and beggars come from Zeus," runs the Homeric proverb. In a 1975 essay on Cavafy, Merrill refers to the Greek poet's "coldness"—emotional detachment—which

> comes through elsewhere as reticence imposed by an encounter with a god,
>
>> his hair black and perfumed
>> the people going by would gaze at him,
>> and one would ask the other if he knew him,
>> if he was a Greek from Syria, or a stranger.
>> But some who looked more carefully
>> would understand and step aside . . .
>
> Indeed, one way to sidestep any real perception of others is to make gods of them. But the ironic wind blows back and forth. The gods appeared to characters in Homer, disguised as a mortal friend or stranger. Put in terms acceptable nowadays, that was a stylized handling of those moments familiar to us all, when the stranger's idle word or the friend's sudden presence happens to strike deeply into our spirits. Moments at the opposite pole from indifference. . . .[2]

The poet's own apparent normality, in "The Thousand and Second Night," masks his inner coldness for a while. But the immobile, unrevealing half-face that seemed a half-mask in Istanbul now begins to strike the reader as truer than his "normal" face, itself a facade, like the "real facade" of the Hagia Sophia.

Merrill had accused himself of coldness before in poetry (in fiction also: Sandy, the Merrill-character in *The (Diblos) Notebook*, writes despairingly, "I am so cold to people,") and seems not ready to acquit himself yet. The cracked mirror is a flawed mask, and three good friends in three months' time see this well enough to complain of a change. "You were nice, James, before your trip. Or so/ I thought," say the friends. The poem claims they thought wrong. It was all an act the disease spoiled; and his promises to change, that in any case "never saved my face," were meaningless. The accusation in their eyes is rekindled in a dreamlike carnival scene:

> Among the dancers on the pier
> Glides one figure in a suit of bones,
> Whose savage grace alerts the chaperones.
>
> He picks you out from thousands. He intends
> Perhaps no mischief. Yet the dog-brown eyes
> In the chalk face that stiffens as it dries
> Pierce you with the eyes of those three friends.
> The mask begins to melt upon your face.
> A hush has fallen in the market place,
>
> And now the long adventure

Various ways of viewing this gliding figure suggest themselves. Is he Death, the breakdown of appearances due—like senile Hagia Sophia's—to the lapse of time which, through the experience it brought, has "bronzed and lined" his own mutable face? Surely he is not quite that, or simply that, though the poem's third section is full of intimations of mortality and the fifth can be read as an allegory of death. "The 'death-in-life and life-in-death' of Yeats'/ Byzantium" is mentioned at the end of the first section, the one subtitled "Rigor Vitae." While these hyphenated phrases could refer to old age, the indignity and obscenity of which has preyed upon Merrill's mind since *First Poems* and "The Parrot," they seem to express more strongly a young man's sense of insufficiently living his own life. The mask that "begins to melt upon your face" describes the way a face sags and grows wrinkled as it ages, also the corruption of the flesh after it dies (revealing that a face apparently beautiful was really all the time only a masked death's head). But the death is probably more metaphorical than literal: brutal reality that kills romantic illusion. It may well mean the death of one way of looking at a life, or at the world. And it may be—it almost certainly is—a message: To go on as you are going now will be the death of you.

More important than assigning this surreal passage a specific, limited meaning is noticing how the theme of masking—the disjunction between appearance and reality—has been modulated as a unifying factor through the poem, variously taking the forms of Merrill's paradoxical ailment, the plastered ironic facade, the "mask of platinum" acquired in the Turkish bath, the poet's appearance of normality contrasted to his real coldness, "The stranger is a god in masquerade," the attempt at face-saving promises to his friends, the "chalk face that stiffens as it dries," the carnival mask that melts (in an exchange with Death's stiffening chalk mask?), and the "face bronzed and lined" with living. Strikingly, and characteristically, the impact of the poem as a whole is affirmative; it expresses more joy, and gratitude to appearances for the pleasure they make possible, than horror at the skull beneath the skin, or the coldness a mask of niceness and courtesy conceals. It's in Section 4 of this poem that Merrill coins his best aphorism about what art can do with experience: "Form's what affirms."

Whatever other truths lie back of these masks, one can be identified with certainty. Sexual motifs crowd the poem, some obvious, some hidden in double entendres; Merrill allowed the poem to convey a sense of sexual distress and to let this resolve itself, along with whatever other shadowy stresses, in the final section. Part 3 opens with the accusations of the poet's three friends, which cause him to reflect:

These weren't young friends, what's more. Youth would explain
Part of it. I have kept somewhere a page
Written at sixteen to myself at twice that age,
Whom I accuse of having become the vain

Flippant unfeeling monster I now am—
To hear them talk—and exhorting me to recall
Starlight on an evening in late fall
1943, and the walk with M.,

To die in whose presence seemed the highest good.
I met M. and his new wife last New Year's.
We rued the cold war's tainted atmospheres
From a corner table. It was understood

Our war was over. We had made our peace
With—everything. The heads of animals
Gazed in forbearance from the velvet walls.
Great drifts of damask cleaned our lips of grease.

—another apparently peaceful scene described in terms of violence: the War, the cold war, the allusions to slaughter of animals for sport and food, the telltale traces of animal savagery
fastidiously removed. But what does it mean? What has caused
this sense of violent feelings now leashed in—and what has
leashed them, leaving the poet "a cold unfeeling monster"? (Not
so unfeeling: in the quatrain immediately following, when M.'s
wife—secure in her possession of M.—says "Let's be friends . . .
her clear look" is "returned in disbelief. I had a herd/ Of *friends.*
I wanted love, if love's the word/ On the foxed spine of the long-
mislaid book.")

The wartime fantasies (of heroism?) were directed at M.,
another boy, here however furnished with a wife to help indicate the distance from the time and self of the fantasies. Reading
further, we discover a half-comic, half-disquieting description of
pornographic postcards—"She strokes his handlebar who kneels/

To do for her what a dwarf does for him"—brought from Hamburg by "Great Uncle Alistair":

> We found the postcards after her divorce,
> I and Aunt Alix. She turned red with shame,
> Then white, then thoughtful. "Ah, they're all the same—
> Men, I mean." A pause. "Not you, of course."
>
> And then: "We'll burn them. Light the fire." I must
> Meanwhile have tucked a few into my shirt.
> I spent the night rekindling with expert
> Fingers—but that phase needn't be discussed. . . .

What pornographic postcards are doing in this poem may not be apparent at first, though the sections are sufficiently unlike, while yet being sufficiently linked thematically, for this one to seem no stranger than others. The contrast made by the romantic impulse to die in the presence of M. and the pictures of sex performed mechanically for money and the camera without love (a reference to "the monstrous pair" recalls that Merrill has called *himself* a "monster" on the previous page) begins to get us somewhere; but we need information concealed in the poem's language to make all this coherent.

"Ah, they're all the same—/ Men, I mean . . . Not you, of course," Aunt Alix has said. In one sense the poet immediately denies this judgment by putting the cards to their intended use, but in a narrower sense he means us to believe her. The facial palsy can be seen as a metaphor of sexual paralysis, a view encouraged by the secondary underlying sense of "Part of me has remained cold and withdrawn." A description of peacocks in the Royal Park in Athens carries the charge of the taxi scene in "An Urban Convalescence," though here it is more astringent:

> Peacocks
> Trailed by, hard gray feet mashing overripe

> But bitter oranges. I knew the type:
> Superb, male, raucous, unclean, Orthodox
>
> Ikon of appetite feathered to the eyes
> With the electric blue of days that will
> Not come again.

The word "Orthodox"—its sexual connotation partly masked by the Greek setting—connects forward to Aunt Alix's judgment and backward to the scene in Istanbul when, midway across the bridge between Hagia Sophia and the modern town—from "days that will/ Not come again" and the immobilizing present—a sense of all these contrasts strikes home:

> It is like a dream,
>
> The "death-in-life and life-in-death" of Yeats'
> Byzantium; and, if so, by the same token
> Alone in the sleepwalking scene, my flesh has woken
> And sailed for the fixed shore beyond the straits.

Merrill, who dearly loves a pun, and loves what William Empson calls "plurisignation" hardly less, could never put or keep double entendres this insistent in a poem by accident or mistake; he does quite certainly mean the *fixed* (repaired, made whole) shore beyond the *straights*, where his sexual flesh will wake from its solitary sleeping. And this in turn connects forward, to the maritime imagery at the end of Part 3:

> Tomorrow, if it is given me to conquer
> An old distrust of imaginary scenes,
> Scenes not lived through yet, the few final lines
> Will lie on the page and the whole ride at anchor.
>
> .   .   .
>
> Lost friends, my long ago
>
> Voyages, I bless you for sore
> Limbs and mouth kissed, face bronzed and lined,
> An earth held up, a text not wholly undermined
> By fluent passages of metaphor.

A summary might go like this: a young man with romantic ideas of love and sex encounters some obstacle to their fulfillment, which so troubles him that he is temporarily unable to relate to people satisfactorily at all. The impasse ends with a crisis, acceptance of the disillusioning factors, a more realistic view of sexual possibilities that allows him to give up "Orthodoxy" and seek his own version of sexual and spiritual fulfillment. To identify the obstacle in this case as homosexuality might be valid—the presence of M. in the poem would justify it—but would unnecessarily eliminate other sorts of romantic disillusionment also implied here (as they are in "An Urban Convalescence"), which give the poem the broader reference it seems to claim. In the mid-sixties, when "The Thousand and Second Night" was written, Merrill had no intention of being openly "confessional" about his sexual preference. Yet he managed to write about it covertly, and at the same time to make the poem satisfy readers to whom its entire sexual dimension—barring the postcards—would have been opaque. Read thus, the poem resisted paraphrase except in parts of parts, yet *felt* unified by the masking-theme and by the emotion engendered by whatever it was masking. For all its obscurities it did not cold-shoulder the reader.

The poem ends with Section 5, an exchange between Scheherazade, who eluded death each night by telling one more story, and the Sultan she told them to. Now she begs him to release her: "Your servant would refresh/ Her soul in that cold fountain which the flesh/ Knows not." The Sultan expresses his own desire "to go in search of joys/ Unembroidered by your high, soft voice,/ Along that stony path the senses pave." Of this duality David Kalstone writes:

> The very title of this volume refers to the interpenetration and inseparability of the days of raw experience and the nights of imaginative absorption and recall. It is in those late night mo-

ments that the poems discover the poet at his desk and perform
the ritual separations of poet from his poem. Such episodes . . .
seem to have their authentic emotional center in *Nights and Days*.
The close of "The Thousand and Second Night" was almost an
emblem of what poetry had come to mean for Merrill.[3]

In this context Kalstone calls the Sultan a "daytime spirit"; "It
is he to whom things happen, she who 'embroiders' what they
mean."[4]

Merrill, like Scheherazade, is telling stories to save his life.
In his case the stories also *are* his life, his autobiography; and
from this point on he will be found increasingly, like Proust,
beginning to tell the story at the very end of it, as well as inter-
rupting the forward flow of narrative to comment upon it, as in
this stanza describing and then questioning the Romantic View:

> Love. Warmth. Fist of sunlight at last
> Pounding emphatic on the gulf. High wails
> From your white ship: The heart prevails!
> Affirm it! Simple decency rides the blast!—
> Phrases that, quick to smell blood, lurk like sharks
> Within a style's transparent lights and darks.

Section 4 is a schoolroom spoof: a teacher is leading a discussion
of the very poem we are reading:

> Now if the class will turn back to this, er,
> Poem's first section—Istanbul—I shall take
> What little time is left today to make
> Some brief points. So. The rough pentameter
>
> Quatrains give way, you will observe, to three
> Interpolations, prose as well as verse.
> Does it come through how each in turn refers
> To mind, body, and soul (or memory)?
>
> It does? Good. No, I cannot say offhand
> Why this should be. I find it vaguely satis—
> Yes please? The poet quotes too much? Hm. That is
> One way to put it. . . .

And so on. In case it had *not* occurred to the reader that the passages in question refer to "mind, body, and soul (or memory)," he can now turn back and consider this suggestion, which also prepares him to see Scheherazade immediately as soul/memory and the Sultan as body. This amicably separating aged couple are, besides, some dream-version of Merrill's parents, and the Sultan image for his father—established in *The Seraglio*—will be seen again. Merrill identifies himself with Scheherazade the storyteller, but now also with the Sultan who divorces himself from her. At various levels this is a poem about the proper and possible relation of body to soul, experience to imagination, real to ideal, "what happened" to "literature," female to male (and female aspects of the self to male aspects): of days to nights in Kalstone's sense.

3

"Days of 1964," set in Athens, is a narrative poem, in predominantly iambic lines of no fixed length, about willful illusion in the spirit of *carpe diem*. Kyria [Mrs.] Kleo—who will reappear in "After the Fire" and again in "The Book of Ephraim" in volumes still unwritten at this point—is the focal figure; the other characters are the poet and a nameless lover. Kleo is the cleaning woman, but also a friend. Though she makes a convincingly human charlady, her main purpose in this poem is symbolic:

> How she loved
> You, me, loved us all, the bird, the cat!
> I think now she *was* love. She sighed and glistened
> All day with it, or pain, or both.
> (We did not notably communicate.)

Kleo does not communicate with, and therefore cannot "know" or "understand," the lovers; yet she loves them with such enthusiasm that Merrill identifies her *with* love: Aphrodite with aching legs, "copied in lard and horsehair," sighing with love *or* pain—these being hard to tell apart in Merrill's erotic world.

Scene briefly set and characters sketched in, the action can begin—or not action so much as a recounting of the memory of a memory, the narrator's, of having caught sight of Kleo beginning to climb the "steep hill" across the street—Lykabettos, a local trysting-site:

> Above a tight, skyblue sweater, her face
> Was painted. Yes. Her face was painted
> Clown-white, white of the moon by daylight,
> Lidded with pearl, mouth a poinsettia leaf,
> *Eat me, pay me*—the erotic mask
> Worn the world over by illusion
> To weddings of itself and simple need.
>
> Startled mute, we had stared—was love illusion?—
> And gone our ways.

Kleo is love; Kleo is tarted up in face paint. The narrator must take some sort of attitude toward the discovery that love's a whore—that her mask of paint is as true as her cleverer mask of domesticity—that just as love *is* pain, it *is* also illusion. A nightmarish interlude in a market ensues, where the disoriented poet is visited by frightening images now recognizable as homoerotic ("Self lost up soft clay paths, or found, foothold,/ Where the bud throbs awake/ The better to be nipped, self on its knees in mud—") and chiefly fears being duped, "taken, plucked." But presently he reconciles himself to this:

> Where I hid my face, your touch, quick, merciful,
> Blindfolded me. A god breathed from my lips.
> If that was illusion, I wanted it to last long;
> To dwell, for its daily pittance, with us there,
> Cleaning and watering, sighing with love or pain.
> I hoped it would climb when it needed to the heights

> Even of degradation, as I for one
> Seemed, those days, to be always climbing
> Into a world of wild
> Flowers, feasting, tears—or was I falling, legs
> Buckling, heights, depths,
> Into a pool of each night's rain?
> But you were everywhere beside me, masked,
> As who was not, in laughter, pain, and love.

The emotion of the poem, after that moment of panicky fear, resolves into acceptance of all these risks as a fair price for making the love-that-is-illusion last long. Acceptance, moreover, on love's own terms: if love sometimes needs to wear the mask of degradation, very well then; these lovers know how to see the humor in that. Love and pain were identified early in the poem; now Merrill has added laughter. All three are masks the poem's lovers have learned to wear gracefully.

The unnamed lover in "Days of 1964" is—as we know from later works, and from the clue provided in the title—a handsome young Greek called Strato. This poem celebrates the heyday of the relationship, as poems in later volumes have recorded its erosion, collapse, and hesitant recasting along new lines. They reflect also the power and slow eventual diminishment of the suffering Merrill endured on this account; for Strato was clearly the grand passion of his maturity. "Days of 1964" is the last poem in *Nights and Days*, a sign that the sexual conflicts and dilemmas confronted in "The Thousand and Second Night," which opens the book, are at the last resolved in this evocation of an intensely engaged-in and realized love affair. Merrill's feelings rather than the person who occasioned them are the poem's true subject—or rather these feelings abstracted and personified in Kleo—which accounts sufficiently for the genderless insubstantiality of the lover. "Days of 1964" is about the dependency of *all* love upon illusion, though the title is borrowed from Cavafy, who gave similar titles—Days of 1903, 1911, etc.—to his openly homosexual lyrics in praise of beautiful young men. The end of that particular inner conflict as a secret theme in Merrill's work appears quietly in the choice of this title. The 1,002 nights with which the book began have resolved into these passionate days of 1964; and a sense of emotional closure comes through strongly, even though a reader could not have been expected to identify the nature of the journey completed between its covers when *Nights and Days* was published in 1966.

<h1 style="text-align:center">4</h1>

Before beginning to unfold the intricate origami angel that is "From the Cupola," Merrill's most dazzling stylistic achievement to this point and considerably beyond, it may be useful to remember that *light* in his work has been the elemental power that *dispels* ignorance and kindly illusion, and drives knowledge, however unwelcome, home. When we say "I see" we mean "I understand." Early in *The Country of a Thousand Years of Peace*, the octopus drowsing in its tank is a startling metaphor for seeing: "There are many monsters that a glassen surface/ Restrains. And none more sinister/ Than vision. . . ." And the waking lover's eyes, at the end of "Dream (Escape from the Sculpture Museum) and Waking," "fill with the sunrise/ And close, because too much light stings. . . ." Merrill's play *The Immortal Husband* (1956), based on the myth of Aurora and Tithonus, casts light as its leading lady; Aurora is light in the sense that Kleo is love. As essential rosy-fingered dawn, Aurora might be expected to light up her surroundings. Merrill uses her instead as the antithesis of darkness—makes her recoil from darkness as an element which is everything she is not, refuse to dispel it: "I never see the hidden side of things. That must always be most unpleasant.

If people are unhappy, I don't want to know about it. I'll do anything—I'll even lie to them!—in order to keep them smiling. I can't bear to know what people do in the dark."⁵ Similar quotations could be drawn from the next two books of poetry. Not until "Yánnina," first published in 1972, is there any departure from this sense of light as a hostile force—always excepting candlelight, which is flattering and therefore masking.

Light in "From the Cupola" is *the* instrument of devastation. The poem uses the myth of Psyche and Eros to frame a modern fable. In the myth a beautiful mortal arouses the jealousy of the love goddess Aphrodite, who sends her son Eros to kill the girl, called Psyche. But Eros falls in love with Psyche, and instead spirits her away to a lavish palace where he comes to her under cover of darkness. Psyche longs, not unnaturally, to know what her new husband looks like; but this he will not permit. For a while she lives contentedly enough in these bizarre circumstances, but as their novelty wears off she begins to pine for her family. Eros accordingly arranges for her two older sisters to visit her. The sisters, envious of Psyche's splendid new household arrangement, taunt her with the suggestion that her husband is probably a hideous monster. Goaded on by them, one night after Eros is asleep Psyche lights a lamp and beholds not a monster but a god; but, bending close for a better look, she allows a drop of burning oil to fall on his bare shoulder. Awakening, Eros takes in the situation at a glance and vanishes.

All this is shadow background for the story Merrill is about to tell, or imply, or arrange to have told or implied to him. The myth, unlike the "story" of the poem, ends happily, with Psyche and Eros reunited. There are other discrepancies: Merrill's Psyche lives with her sisters in their own house, in present-day Stonington, Connecticut. Instead of a mysterious husband she has a mysterious pen pal: all communication between the two is written; the relationship begins and ends without closer contacts. *Her* merciless sisters also plague *her* with facts and truths, however, and she is desperately alone. She takes walks, washes windows, goes to drive-in movies, and digs parsnips, and in her Greek Revival house there are electric lights. And light—of sun, moon, lamp, star, candle—comes to seem the central element of Psyche's life, as it is the poem's central metaphor.

As in the myth, light is the source of knowledge. Psyche has been receiving love letters and gifts from someone whose name she doesn't recognize. Her correspondent is, of course, Eros, who may appear frequently in the poem, always winged and often mothered; Psyche calls him "my angel," her sister Alice, less infatuated, makes one reference to "the batwing offspring of her ladyship." Invariably, however, he is disguised, so nothing is certain. "The rare stranger I let pass with lowered eyes," says Psyche. "He also could be you." ("The stranger is a god in masquerade," said the narrator of "The Thousand and Second Night.")

To get the story told, Merrill uses the framing device of casting himself as sympathetic listener to a heartsick Psyche. At the outset he sketches, in his favorite envelope quatrains, the bewildering situation in which she finds herself, and at the same time hints at his private identification with her and with it: "That seed" of the first love letter

> Has since become a world of blossom and bark.
> The letters fill a drawer, the gifts a room.
> No hollow of your day is hidden from
> His warm concern. Still you are in the dark.
>
> Too much understanding petrifies.
> The early letters struck you as blackmail.
> You have them now by heart, a rosy veil
> Colors the phrase repaired to with shut eyes.
>
> Was the time always wrong for you to meet?—
> Not that he ever once proposed as much.

Your sisters joke about it. "It's too rich!
Somebody Up There loves you, Psyche sweet."

Tell me about him, then. Not a believer,
I'll hold my tongue while you, my dear, dictate.
Him I have known too little (or, of late,
Too well) to trust my own view of your lover.

After the introduction Psyche takes over—but the tale is anything but straightforward in the telling. Psyche is distraught,
her mind leaps and wanders. Even with the myth in mind, it's
often hard to see just how these details that sweep the reader
along by sheer lyric force advance her story. What they do first
is evoke the quality of a childhood in Florida, terrifying beneath
the masking surface beauty, as Psyche's fact-loving sister Alice,
to Psyche's dismay, insists:

> Any mirage if seen from a remote stand
> point is refreshing   Yes but dust and heat
> lie at its heart   Poor Psyche you forget
> That was a cruel impossible wonderland . . .

> Our orchid stucco house looked on greenshuttered

> stoic   But the sidewalk suffered most
> Like somebody I shall not name it lacked
> perspective   It failed absolutely to detect
> the root of all that evil   The clues it missed . . .

> Off to the beach   Us nurse in single file
> Those days we'd meet our neighbor veiled and hatted
> tanagra leading home out of the sun she hated
> a little boy with water wings   We'd smile

> then hold our breaths to pass a barricade
> of black smells rippling up from the soft hot
> brink of the mirage past which sidewalks could not
> follow   Ours stood there crumbling then obeyed

The veiled and hatted "tanagra"—a figurine found at an ancient
Greek town by that name—is Aphrodite, of course, with her

small winged son, making a typical appearance. Even in Psyche's childhood, as in everyone's, they were there—a part of all that muddled violence and unhappiness she would rather not remember.

The disjointed sections that follow this, in varied lyric forms and short stretches of prose, do less to develop a plot than to reveal and apotheosize Psyche's feelings of love and dread and, finally, of loss—the *psycho*logical plot of every love affair in Merrill's emotional world. All motifs in "From the Cupola"—lamp, mask, sidewalk (the Concrete), sisters, flower—are reinforced constantly. Light, because of Psyche's "lamp I smell in every other line" the most important, has been worked into this poem with such complexity that to trace out all its exfoliations here will not be possible. Psyche shuts her eyes repeatedly against the light. The cupola it is her task to clean is a lampshaped *look*-out, and "Even/ on sunless days the cupola is an oven" of lanternlike heat. Dutifully she polishes its windows, till by poem's end her listener can say "Thank you, Psyche. I should think those panes/ Were just about as clear as they can be." The effect of lamp- and window-cleaning is to see more clearly; living the story, Psyche works against her own real wish as if she cannot help herself. Re-living it in the telling she talks these punning "panes" clear to better pupose.

That the cupola is the poem's largest, most lethal, most unavoidable "lamp" is pointed up by parallel incidents. One comes only a few lines from the end. The poet mentions *his* lamp—his knowledge of Psyche's story, and his personal version of it, as well as the lamp in the study where he is about to begin the poem that will tell the story (fearing lest it smell too much of the lamp):

> From its rubbed brass a moth
> Hurtles in motes and tatters of itself
> —Be careful, tiny sister, drabbest sylph!—
> Drops, and is still.

Much earlier in her tale Psyche recounts, in breathtaking language, this:

> MIDNIGHT   I dream   I dream   The slow moon eludes
> one stilled cloud   Din of shimmerings   From across the Sound
> what may have begun as no more
> than a willow's sleepwalking outline quickens detaches
> comes to itself in the cupola
> panics from pane to pane and then impulsively
> surrendering fluttering by now the sixteenfold
> wings of the cherubim unclipped by faith or reason
> stands there my dream made whole
> over whose walls again
> a red vine black in moonlight crawls
> made habitable   Each cell of the concrete
> fills with sweet light   The wave breaks
> into tears   Come if its you   Step down
> to where I   Stop   For at your touch the dream
>
> cracks the angel tenses flees

The cherub who, mothlike, "panics from pane to pane" comes to Psyche, like Eros of the myth, by moonlight; but neither can endure, nor can the dream endure, touch. The "sweet light" that fills and transforms "each cell of the concrete"—the real, the hard and factual, as well as the building material—is shattered with the shattering of the dream, painfully lovely but doomed.

Somewhat more than halfway through the poem, Psyche and her sisters go to a drive-in movie. There it becomes obvious that a movie projector is just another lamp, destined by a ruthless nature to expose what would be better left concealed. In the next car sit "young Eros and his sweetheart"—the sweetheart's "mask of tears does not exactly fit"—watching while "The love goddess his mother overflows a screen/ sixty feet wide or seems to." Sickened, Psyche knows that the tear-jerker being projected before them is a fake. Psyche's awful sisters, who "fatten upon fact," inform her that by now this star

is on location in Djakarta where
tomorrow's sun illumines her
emoting in strange arms   It's all an act

Eros are you like her so false a naked glance
turns you into that slackjawed fleshproud youth
driving away   Was he your truth
Is it too late to study ignorance

More than anything else, Psyche differs from her mythical namesake in that she is not curious, that her sisters' taunts cannot goad her into the "torchlit hunts for truth" her listener himself foreswore at the beginning of the poem:

The point won't be to stage
One of our torchlit hunts for truth. Truth asks
Just this once to sleep with fiction, masks
Of tears and laughter on the moonstruck page;

To cauterize what babbles to be healed
Just this once not by candor. Here and now,
Psyche, I quench that iron lest it outglow
A hovering radiance your fingers shield.

—her lamp. Unswervingly, Psyche tries not to probe, not to unmask. Indeed, though her task of cleaning the cupola/lamp panes cannot be avoided, "wipe as I will" her features are superimposed by reflection on the landscape seen through them (just as Eros disguised as an angel *comes to himself* in the cupola: to his own reflection, made by moonlight, in the glass). Psyche tries to preserve herself from knowledge not—as in the myth—because that is Eros's pleasure or Aphrodite's, but because what she sees may be horrible. In the myth, that's why she wants to know; in the poem that's why she doesn't.

In the end, of course, she must. On the last morning Psyche's "task is done," and what she sees through sparkling panes this time is no dream-angel but, in an abandoned warehouse, "a face male old molepale in sun/ though blinded by the mullion's shadow": a glimpse of whom? Psyche, guessing, looks away; "When I look back/ the panic's over," but time is running out. On the next page, digging parsnips for her sisters' dinner under "spring's first real sun," Psyche makes a discovery and then a decision perhaps influenced by what she has seen:

> Two of the finest
> are tightly interlocked have grown that way   They lie
> united in the grave of sunny air
> as in their breathing living dark
> I look at them a long time
> mealy and soiled in one another's arms
> and blind full to the ivory marrow
> with tender blindness   Then I bury them
> once more in memory of us

The dark is breathing, living, safe; the sunshine is a grave. Love's heights of degradation, acknowledged in "Days of 1964," have their counterpart in these parsnips, "soiled in one another's arms." Blind as moles "to the ivory marrow/ with tender blindness," they suggest another reason for wing'd Cupid to be painted blind himself (and for Psyche's inability to *shut* her eyes tightly enough to keep a rosy glow from penetrating her lids: "Shut my eyes it does no good"). Truly blind and in the dark is where love happens, and there only. The parsnips relate ambiguously to that blinded "face male old molepale in sun," Psyche's final view of Eros as a creature which lives sightlessly underground.

At the beginning of "From the Cupola" we are told that Psyche has learned her love letters by heart, and now "a rosy veil/ Colors the phrase repaired to with shut eyes"; Merrill returns repeatedly, in this and other poems, to this image of sunlight turned beautiful by eyelids unable to exclude it altogether. Back home at evening and at poem's end, Psyche's sisters—as they do in myth—call to her to "light the lamp"—call several

times before she submits and lets light penetrate her closed eyelids once again:

> My hand is on the swtich   I have done this
> faithfully each night since the first
> Tonight I think will not be different
> Then soft light lights the room the furniture
> a blush invades even the dropped lid
> yes and I am here alone
> I and my flesh and blood

When Merrill tells himself in "Verse for Urania," three books
later, to "light a lamp," the phrase bristles with significance for
those who remember that the effect of lamp-lighting on Psyche
in "From the Cupola" was to show her that she is, as she expects
to be, alone; there is no lover here.

In the poem's finest lyric interlude the line "We see according to our lights" recurs as a refrain in every stanza but one.
This line answers Psyche's anguished question, a question that
lies at the innermost heart of this poem: "what of him the lover,"
she cries, "all eclipsed/ by sheer love?" Eclipsed, blotted out,
overshadowed: how can Eros measure up on his own merits to
the splendor of the abstract thing she feels for him? How can
the real suffice her craving for the ideal? Psyche's most willful
turning from the facts cannot blind her forever to this discrep-
ancy which continually menaces her, and even though she knows
better—earlier stanzas make this clear—she cannot keep from
putting the question any more than she can help cleaning the
cupola panes. Here Merrill, who has been listening patiently
and tenderly, breaks in, and in his own voice hushes and soothes
her:

> All our pyrotechnic flights
> Miss the sleeper in the pitch-dark breast.
> He is love:
> He is everyone's blind spot.
> We see according to our lights.

Like Merrill himself, Psyche must make do with this scant comfort; it is in the nature of things for love to end.

Finally the poet dismisses Psyche and turns his own light on, so as to begin transforming what happened into literature. The gesture—repeated in later poems—seems to say that while the Sturm und Drang are being experienced lamps should stay dark; afterwards, while recollecting them, is the time to turn on the light. Knowledge and understanding, necessary to the literature which is remembrance, only get in the way of the living which is action and passion; or, to use Kalstone's terms, the "days of raw experience" then give way to "the nights of imaginative absorption and recall."

To consider the style of "From the Cupola" in terms of its lamp/light imagery alone would be to miss the magnitude of Merrill's feat. The poem's other image-systems and themes have been cunningly linked and interrelated with this one and with each other, as when we are shown the *sisters* as children trotting in *tear*drop-punctured shoes the length of a *sidewalk* heavily shadowed by Aphrodite as coconut palm:

> *a towering mother*
> *smooth as stone and thousandbreasted though*
>
> *her milk was watery scant so much for love*
> *false like everything in that whole world*

False like everything. Though light, and Psyche's efforts not to know, have all been related obliquely to Merrill's masking theme, he also presents this theme more directly:

> Nights the last red
> wiped from my lips the harbor
> blinking out gem by gem how utterly
> we've been undressed
>
> You will not come
> to the porch at noon will you rustling your wings
> or masked as crone or youth
> The mouths behind our faces kiss

Or: ". . . Time, like Love, wears a mask in this story," as one of the poem's prose passages informs us. Or: the girl beside young Eros at the drive-in has on a poorly fitting tragic "mask of tears," the raindrop-spangled windshield. "Alice can weep at will," we are told. So, apparently, can the monstrous actors on the screen. It's all an act.

Merrill once described in an interview his own sense of the mix of knowns and unknowns in this poem:

> there are, let's see, three stories going. There's the story of Eros and Psyche which is, if not known, at least knowable to any reader. Then there is the contemporary situation of a New England village Psyche and her two nasty sisters and somebody writing love letters to her. And finally there is what I begin by describing as an unknowable situation, something I'm going to keep quiet about. But, in a way, the New England village situation is transparent enough to let us see the story of Eros and Psyche on one side of the glass and, perhaps, to guess at, to triangulate the third story, the untold one.[6]

With no details at all to build a case from, we understand perfectly that Psyche is Merrill's alter ego—*his* psyche, that her grief and distress are his, and that when he addresses her he speaks to the most interior part of himself out of another part able to view Psyche's situation detachedly, comprehend it, write it down as poetry. The emotions of the untold tale are so available, and the writing so luminous, as to make the secrecy of no account; it is arguable in fact that from this point onward Merrill will be at his best when he holds back something, if it's the right thing, and at his worst when he keeps the wrong secret or too many secrets altogether. Neither of the two long poems in *Nights and Days*, though often obscure, is injured in this way.

CHAPTER 5

The Fire Screen

[Gloriani:] ". . . There may be a great deal of interest in an ugly nose, my dear sir—especially if one has put it there."

"You mean there may be a great deal of character. Very likely," said Roderick, "but it's not the sort of character I care for. I care only for beauty of Type—there it is, if you want to know. That's as good a profession of faith as another."

—Henry James, *Roderick Hudson*

I

Three years after the transcendent realizations of *Nights and Days*, a new volume appeared to universally admiring and serious reviews. Only Richard Howard saw it at the time as "transitional," and only by hindsight would David Kalstone refer to it as a "strange, off-key book," though Merrill himself correctly suspected it of being the first that had failed to surpass its predecessors. *The Fire Screen* now seems less a misstep than a sidestep. If much in it is excellent, nothing quite equals the supreme achievements of those two long, complex poems in *Nights and Days;* if it enlarges the total number of Merrill's important poems, each previous book had done as much *and* had sharply raised the

standard of excellence. This volume, Merrill's fifth, is a pause
for regrouping rather than a quantum leap forward, a fact which
may tend to obscure its own real virtues and strengths.

The Fire Screen is primarily "about" Merrill's life in Greece
and the working out of his relationship with the Greek youth
Strato, and is therefore coupled to *Nights and Days* by the last
poem in that collection, "Days of 1964." Many poems address
the love affair directly, and emotions and concepts associated
with it occur in nearly all the rest, though Strato is never named
or otherwise identified as male, and all pronouns in the love
poems are first or second person. The joy and surrender of "Days
of 1964" dominate the first Strato poem, "To My Greek"; thereafter these feelings mingle increasingly with others—pain, anger, fear, despair, grief—and finally are supplanted by a will to
accept the loss as the affair runs a course whose outcome is
foreknown and inevitable: "The loved one always leaves." Poem
by poem the denouement unreels, while Merrill, his old belief
now tried and confirmed by fire, grapples with these feelings
lyrically, obliquely, ironically, in a variety of poetic forms and
styles.

Two interesting poems are extended metaphors with double meanings coordinated to the last detail, a game this poet
could enjoy and win even in the toils of heartbreak. In "To My
Greek," Strato and the Greek language cavort in lockstep, men-
aced (how seriously?) by their common rival "The mother
tongue." The tonal keynote is exhilaration, a dizzy joy that
thrusts caution aside in the excitement of discovering—and de-
ciding—how to communicate in the new language: "Let there be
no word/ For justice, grief, convention; *you* be convention—"

> each sunset yawned away,
> Hair in eyes, head bent above the strummed
> Lexicon, gets by heart about to fail
> This or that novel mode of being together
>
> Without conjunctions.

"Still," he says, "I fear for us." But the hostile incomprehension and jealousy of the mother tongue whose "automations and my mind are one" come to little more than an excuse for verbal wittiness here, and shadow the poem's exuberance only enough to give it definition. "Having chosen the way of little knowledge,// Trusted each to use the other/ Kindly except in moments of gross need," the lovers keep to their own rules so that illusion may be protected and the love last long.

"Remora" is an emblem poem, one of Merrill's best, far easier and surer of itself than "Octopus" but a lineal descendant even to the underwater setting:

> This life is deep and dense
> Beyond all seeing, yet one sees, in spite
> Of being littler, a degree or two
> Further than those one is attracted to.
>
> Pea-brained, myopic, often brutal,
> When chosen they have no defense—
> A sucking sore there on the belly's pewter—
> And where two go could be one's finer sense.
>
> Who now descends from a machine
> Plumed with bubbles, death in his right hand?
> Lunge, numbskull! One, two, three worlds boil.
> Thanks for the lift. There are other fish in the sea.
>
> Still on occasion as by oversight
> One lets be taken clinging fast
> In heavenly sunshine to the corpse a slight
> Tormented self, live, dapper, black-and-white.

Detail by detail, again the relationship and its metaphor turn together. A *remora* is a small fish that attaches itself to larger fish by means of its suction disc, a modified dorsal fin. "Pea-brained" and "numbskull" link *this* large fish to the "radiant dumbbell" of "To My Greek"; but nothing in "Remora" suggests a disarming radiance, and the poet appears here not as enthralled student but as cold-blooded parasite, his voice shifting between irony and cynicism until pain breaks through to soften the final lines.

The deus-ex-machina diver who descends on cue with his spear could be anyone or anything—time, knowledge, a rival— whose intervention destroys the point of their (here somewhat symbiotic) connection in the larger fish without destroying it in the smaller. The smaller should then sensibly turn loose and go in search of a viable partner; but to avoid the torments and humiliations which are the common fate of the jilted lover he must let go fast. A homoerotic reading, an uncomfortable, self-despising one, overlays line 7. One has here a sense of Strato's greater size and power compared to the "slight" and "dapper" poet, himself more intelligent, far-seeing, and sensitive, but helpless nonetheless. Merrill's watermark, the cleverly apt cliché, occurs in line 12; a characteristic mild contortion of sense and/or grammar offsets this obviousness in lines 8 and 13–15.

Between the emotional poles of these two poems are others, arranged to track the descending trajectory of the affair. "The Envoys" tells in two abbreviated sonnets how Strato would arbitrarily catch and then release the creatures of the world both shared. "Teach me, lizard, kitten, scarabee" the poet implores, resolving anecdote into metaphor in anticipation of what must happen. The scarab, or dung beetle (genus *Scarabaeus*, his bee-like qualities in flight enhanced by this whimsical form of his name), symbolized eternal life to the ancient Egyptians; Merrill imagines how the green beetle tied by Strato's thread will carry the tale, how "His brittle pharaohs in the vale of Hence/ Will hear who you are, who I am,/ And how you bound him close and set him free." Whether or not Merrill intends him to, Strato comes through this poem sounding, in truth, rather less like a charmer than a bully toward all his captives; so that the poem connects back to his attractiveness in "To My Greek" as well as forward to the flatter, colder designations ("often brutal") of "Remora."

Behind this group of some fifteen poems, by-product of his life's grandest passion, Merrill has placed another poem in which he appears to view *all* his passions with suspicion. "Matinees," a sequence of eight sonnets, invites comparison with "The Broken Home" both for its form and for the presence of the same precocious child—here introduced to what will prove a lifelong avocation, opera. "Matinees," though less substantial, makes a point the poet thought important. In a 1967 interview he had referred—half-jokingly?—to opera's corrupting influence on himself as an impressionable eleven-year-old; here again he says that the lesson he took from opera's seductive, melodramatic example "was to arrange for one's/ Own chills and fevers, passions and betrayals/ Chiefly in order to make song of them."

"Arrange"—however unconsciously—for his betrayal and abandonment by Strato, struggle in the wastes of grief for many months, in order to write "The Envoys" and "Another August" and "Flying from Byzantium"? Perhaps. The last-named poem, that in which the poet's sense of loss is most nakedly voiced ("But a near lightning sheets the brain./ I cannot take your hand for pain./ . . . / I love you still, I love you"), ends upon the same Proustian image that closes "From the Cupola": "Far off a young scribe turned a fresh/ Page, hesitated, dipped his pen." Yet in the actual experience of living, poetry is still as much a lifeboat as an iceberg. If pain makes metaphor possible, metaphor still, as always, makes pain bearable. And the chronic wound of this poet's history—the drama of parents, child, the broken home—was never within his power to arrange.

2

One response to such pain as that of losing Strato is to retreat behind a mask of anonymity. "The Friend of the Fourth Decade," an ingenious alter ego, declares that he is

> Tired of understanding what I hear,
> The tones, the overtones; of knowing
>
> Just what clammy twitchings thrive
> Under such cold flat stones
>
> As We-are-profoundly-honored-to-have-with-us
> Or This-street-has-been-torn-up-for-your-convenience. . . .
>
> I mean to learn, in the language of where I am going,
> Barely enough to ask for food and love.

Tired of understanding: the poet's sentiments exactly, just as the last lines quoted echo his exact strategy, pursued for identical reasons, in "To My Greek": "the way of little knowledge . . . The barest word be what I say in you." The friend goes on: he has discovered by accident—while soaking postcards for *his* friend, a stamp collector—that the ink floats off with the stamp, symbolically effacing his bond with the correspondent and with it the self to whom those cards were sent. He speaks of his profound relief at feeling this self "even by a grain dissolved/ Absolved I mean, recipient with writer,/ Of having cared and having ceased to care. . . ." Merrill's earlier alter ego, Psyche, hoarding not drowning her love letters from the mysterious admirer she shrinks from meeting, is not essentially different in her terror of too much understanding.

Intrigued and envious, the poet imitates his friend—"I heard oblivion's thin siren singing/ And bore it bravely"—only to find that an hour later he can still read the message on *his* mother's submerged postcard. He gives it up: "Certain things die only with oneself." Soon the friend contributes more cards to the collection (and his perverse bit to the selfhood of the recipient) from a far country where "Individual and type are one," where he is "reborn each day increasingly/ Conspicuous, increasingly unseen." The poem ends with a dream about this friend's success at ridding himself of all the details of cultural history and personal experience that, mummylike, have swathed him: unbandaged, handed a mirror, "his eyes darken in bewilderment—/ No, in joy—and his lips part/ To greet the perfect stranger." The cliché says exactly what Merrill means: to mar anyone's strangeness with knowledge is to ruin his perfection; "The stranger is a god in masquerade" but no one we *know* is perfect or godlike.

Sick of the misery and messiness of "personality," Merrill invokes the restful simplicity of type again in "Another August":

> Open the shutters. Let variation
> abandon the swallows one by one.
> How many summer dusks were needed
> to make that single skimming form!
> The very firefly kindles to its type.
> Here is each evening's lesson. First
> the hour, the setting. Only then
> the human being, his white shirtsleeve
> chalked among treetrunks, round a waist,
> or lifted in an entrance. Look for him.
> Be him.

To obey is as impossible as the friend's dream-divestment of culture and experience; what's meant is "Pretend to be him." After these lines comes the "Envoi for S.":

> Whom you saw mannerless and dull of heart,
> Easy to fool, impossible to hurt,
> I wore that fiction like a fine white shirt
> And asked no favor but to act the part.

—knowing all the while that the white shirt of "the human being," his costume of type, like any mask or fiction is doomed to fray thin.

The Fire Screen concludes with the longest poem Merrill had written at that time, a narrative in ballad stanzas called "The

Summer People." This light, ironic, flawlessly-written piece is pure entertainment, scarcely weighted anywhere by a "serious" thought. Though its nominal theme is decline—of friendship, of gracious living—the poem is too stylish and witty to be sad, or saddening. Four old friends spend their summers in a New England village on the skids (Stonington is the likely model). Rich, idle, bored to distraction, they are delighted to discover a new resident. "Interesting Jack Frost" has bought and refurbished the Baptist Church, and moved in with his white cat, Grimes, and his elderly Japanese manservant, Ken. "He's certainly attractive,/ To judge by the veneer," though nobody knows (or ever learns) a thing about him apart from the veneer: his splendid qualities as host, guest, and vastly amusing companion.

For several charmed summers Jack brings vitality and fun to this quartet, summers which were

> High-water marks of humor
> And humankindness, no
>
> Discord at cards, at picnics,
> Charades or musicales.
> Their faces bright with pleasure might
> Not have displeased Frans Hals.

The first year Jack stays on when the others leave, to their initial astonishment. "Whole nights, a tower window/ Threw light upon the storm," and the winter is spectacularly beautiful and cold. Each year thereafter, Nora, Margaret, Andrew, and Jane find themselves outstaying the season longer and longer. By this point in the tale, the reader has realized that there's a good deal more to Jack than meets the eye.

But in some manner the spell that binds his friends is a drain on Jack's resources. Eventually discord and distress break out among the group, and Grimes bites Margaret, who causes him to be destroyed.

> That same night, Grimes in ermine
> And coronet of ice
> Called [Jack] by name, cried vengeance,
> Twitching his long tail twice.

Jack flees the village forever. Tedium reclaims the deserted four-some; disease assaults the elms; Ken, left behind, descends into alcoholism and suicide. A decline suspended during Jack's residency now reassails the village, and a chemical plant—resisted for years—rises at last to spoil its attractiveness for the summer people, who decide to "get out for good." When Andrew takes one last look into Jack's tower room, he sees through one window the houses on Main Street "upright in defeat," and through the other how "Lights of the Chemical Plant/ Gloated over water." The past, when the village belonged to a full-time working class and the wealthy seasonal aristocracy, has been shouldered aside to make way for an industrial future: a miniature American allegory.

At the very moment Jack's magic charm is about to crack, Merrill interrupts the narrative to restate thematic concerns tailored even to this unlikely context. Perhaps, he says, his choice of form was wrong:

> For figures in a ballad
> Lend themselves to acts
> Passionate and simple.
> A bride weeps. A tree cracks.
>
> A young king, an old outlaw
> Whose temperament inclines
> To strife where breakers thunder
> Bleeds between the lines.
>
> But I have no such hero,
> No fearful deeds—unless
> We count their quiet performance
> By Time or Tenderness.

These two are the past masters
Of rime, tone, overtone.
They write upon our faces
Until the pen strikes bone.

Time passes softly, scarcely
Felt by me or you.
And then, at an odd moment,
Tenderness passes, too.

Yet "figures in a ballad" are, precisely, character types; and if Merrill has here no bride or king or outlaw he gives us equally serviceable (if less heroic) types: the Fey Sorcerer, the Familiar, the Houseboy. The four old friends, modeled on real people, are more individuated—Andrew, in fact, will reappear under his own name of Robert Morse in *Mirabell* and *Scripts for the Pageant*—but not much; each is still a recognizable leisure-class arts-gourmet-and-garden type. Merrill has told us again and again that Tenderness breaks down over Time. Here only the operative factor (knowledge/understanding) is missing, none being needed in a fairy tale. For these are summer people, fair weather friends. A wintry spirit enchants them; they have June in January for a time. But disenchantment dissolves their harmonious companionship and they scatter in pursuit of summer, to other climes and hemispheres.

Above all, "The Summer People" is a triumph of style. Quotation out of context does far less than adequate justice to the wit, charm, and perfect control with which these ballad stanzas invoke their emblematic settings with minimal touches and tell their tale in cartoon-strip vignettes, mindful every instant of the joke they play upon themselves by being a ballad at all:

[Nora] drove home from Caustic
Where Margaret caught her plane.

The windshield streamed in silence,
The wipers thrashed in vain.

October. Early twilights.
To the wharf came a blue
And silver haul of fish too small
For anything but glue.

The boatyard was a boneyard,
Bleached hull, moon-eaten chain.
The empty depot trembled
At the scream of a passing train.

Like the traditional ballad whose conventions this one both imitates and spoofs, setting as well as character is simplified to
highlit essentials; but nothing about the sensibility that imagined
"The Summer People" and found the formal means to frame it
is simple.

3

Two portraits of individual lives and characters cut ener-
getically across this book's bias in favor of type. *The Fire Screen*
is a volume characterized by a silken smoothness of line, though
predictable rhyme and regular meters are relatively scarce. But
in "Kostas Tympakianakis" the young Greek named in the title
tells his own story in a dramatic monologue of simple language,
designedly clumsy cadences, and couplets joined by the plainest
and least witty of rhymes:

I have other brothers, one whose face I broke
In a family quarrel, and that's no joke:
I'm small but strong, when I get mad I fight.
Seven hundred vines of his were mine by right . . .

The other portrait is of special interest for a different reason.
"Words for Maria," a poem merely pleasant and entertaining in

this book, turns out later to have been a crayon sketch of Maria Mitsotáki, *the* Maria, of the *Sandover* books. The poem uncannily prefigures the scene of the Ouija transcriptions by describing how a large mirror sat for ages in a chair in Maria's new flat, "Drinking the cool black teas of your appearances." Merrill portrays an extravagantly vivid character, though not everyone will find—or in life, evidently, did find—Maria as delightful and captivating as he clearly does:

> Unjeweled in black as ever comedienne
> Of mourning if not silent star of chic,
> You drift, September nightwind at your back,
> The half block from your flat to the Bon Goût,
> Collapse, order a black
> Espresso and my ouzo in that Greek
> Reserved for waiters, crane to see who's who
> Without removing your dark glasses, then,
> Too audibly: "Eh, Jimmy, qui sont ces deux strange men?"

The poet's affection emboldens him even to curiosity. Like the ancient headland of Greek earth masked by Maria's jasmines,

> About what went before
> Or lies beneath, how little one can glean.
> Girlhood, marriage, the war . . .
> I'd like once (not now, here comes Giulio)
> Really to hear—I mean—I didn't mean—
> You paint a smiling mouth to answer me:
> "Since when does L'Enfant care for archaeology?"

Since when indeed? An answer can be inferred: though erotic love must be guarded from understanding, asexual friendship is "safe." Like the four summer friends, these two "loved without desire." Self-dramatizing, but inwardly reserved, Maria is a creature after Merrill's own heart. "The muse of my off-days" comes across as histrionic, eccentric, even rude; but Merrill openly relishes the nutty behavior he pretends to chide her for, and is amused rather than perturbed when others criticize.

For Kostas the principle applies in reverse. There is here no question of passionate love; Kostas may freely tell about his family and his gritty experience, a life lived worlds away from the poet's and Maria's. (An *outer* life. In his 1975 essay discussing C. P. Cavafy's many poems of sexual attraction and release, Merrill speaks with assurance when he says that Cavafy is not "about to pretend interest in anything so conventional, so conjectural, as one more young man's inner life." [1] Not the destructiveness but the tiresomeness of such revelations is the point; nothing understanding could destroy is at stake here.) But honest affection for the speaker informs the selection and ordering of the colorful details that highlight Kostas' story—a story of such elemental Reality as to charge the last line's rhetorical question: "Who could have imagined such a life as mine?" One possibility, that Merrill imagined it, seems less likely—because less characteristic of him—than another: that he streamlines the story but gives it essentially as dictated, questioning or challenging or reaffirming his own long-ago choice for the life of the imagination, manner and mask, against the unmediated Real.

4

The poem to be discussed last is the one absolutely first-rate poem in a book of solid accomplishment. In a sense, "Mornings in a New House" is the title poem; the book is called by a phrase occurring halfway through, and the poem summarizes what Merrill has learned from experience which the entire book examines. Critics have recognized the importance of this poem from the first, the more sensitive reviewers singling it out for extended commentary, Kalstone focusing on the house metaphor, Richard Saez, in an important essay entitled "James Merrill's Oedipal Fire" (of which more in chapter 6), on its fire-and-mother imagery. Those sidelong references to his mother in "To My Greek" (the critical, uncomprehending mother tongue) and "The Friend of the Fourth Decade" (as author of a "Dearest Son" that has refused to dissolve in "holy water from the tap") aside, this is virtually our only encounter with the oedipal theme so conspicuous and compelling in *Water Street* and *Nights and Days*, and we meet the Sultan not at all.

In this book "To My Greek" was the first of a sequence of poems resulting from the affair with Strato. "Mornings in a New House" is the last. The new house is, of course, the metaphorical place where the poet, his love affair ended, has come to dwell; where "still at dawn the fire is lit/ By whom a cold man hardly cares." The account of what happens as the fire, anonymously kindled, catches and blazes high—gliding reflection, choking flue, slow stains and subsidings—can be read as a description of sexual arousal and resolution which is numbly impersonal, as different as possible from the electrostatic romps implied in "To My Greek." "The worst is over," we are told as the fire, "that tamed uprush," settles to its steady burning. Now between it and the poet "Habit arranges the fire screen"—a mask, a muffler, a quelling defense against the clawed brightness of the fire. What can it be, this screen that guards him?

> Crewel-work. His mother as a child
> Stitched giant birds and flowery trees
> To dwarf a house, *her* mother's—see the chimney's
> Puff of dull yarn! Still vaguely chilled,
>
> Guessing how even then her eight
> Years had foreknown him, nursed him, all,
> Sewn his first dress, sung to him, let him fall,
> Howled when his face chipped like a plate,
>
> He stands there wondering until red
> Infraradiance, wave on wave,
> So enters each plume-petal's crazy weave,
> Each worsted brick of the homestead,

That once more, deep indoors, blood's drawn,
The tiny needlewoman cries,
And to some faintest creaking shut of eyes
His pleasure and the doll's are one.

Saez has said that in this poem "oedipal and promethean fire fuse in the violent eroticism."[2] As in "The Broken Home," a seemingly static and harmless scene is elaborated in terms of such frightening violence, such suggestive multiple meanings, as to force a recognition of the emotional charge it carried for the "cold man" who views it thus. The fire screen is a crewel- [cruel-] work picture of another house, an old one, sewn by his mother as a child who dwarfs it with birds and trees. Even then, he imagines, his fate was prefigured in her caring for, and dropping and damaging, a sort of juju doll representing the real son she would someday bear. The imagery and intimations of witch-craft—a deadlier business here than in "The Summer People"—gather force as the fire burns and the "worsted" house shared by little mother and surrogate son becomes suffused with a sexual heat far more authentic and intense than the fire kindled in stanza one; and it reaches a climax in that furiously dense final stanza.

Circumstantial evidence assigns a primary meaning to this quatrain: the little girl, sewing on the doll's dress or the fire-screen picture, pricks her finger with her needle. But murkier secondary meanings lurk beneath. "Deep indoors," while refer-ring most obviously to the house stitched in yarn, refers also, and instantaneously, to the mother: deep inside *her*. The doll's molded eyelids creak shut with pleasure at the bloodletting, which is erotically toned and acquires suggestions of menstrua-tion, defloration, childbearing, and masochism, in varying de-grees of immediacy. We are told that the tiny needlewoman—evocative phrase!—cries (in pain? pleasure?) but not why. Does the passage imply a more general wounding of a deeply interior nature? A doll stuck with a sharp point? Whose blood has been drawn, and by whom? We can't be certain. Ambiguities abound, leaving the poem susceptible to a variety of readings, all simultaneously valid.

It should be helpful to consider a scene, uncannily similar even to its weird tininess, from *The Seraglio*. Francis, overwhelmed with guilt following a sexual escapade, hallucinates: it seemed

> that he was gazing into his mother's eyes as into a couple of spunsugar Easter eggs. Deep within the pupils a flowery scene of forgiveness was acted out. Growing tinier and tinier, "What did I do?" he piped, and let go of the needle. "Whatever you do, I shall love you," she replied, blood welling from her forefinger and staining her embroidery.[3]

The number of images and phrases repeated in each passage— "mother," "deep within," "flowery," "tinier," "needle," "blood," "embroidery" (see the discussion of the footnote, below)—cannot be coincidental. In some sense, I believe, it is precisely these feelings, these images, that are arranged between the poet and his own sexuality set ablaze—arranged not by him but by "habit"; those "automations" of the mother tongue which are one with his own mind. A kind of fatality seems to hold sway here, as if the—surely blameless—eight-year-old who would become the poet's mother is as truly helpless in her own mother's house as her son will be in hers to escape the foreknown relationship, its acts, emotions, terms, and consequences, before the time comes. The suffering hero of "Flying from Byzantium" kneels on the earth's crust and wishes for death: "Mother, I was vain, headstrong,/ Help me, I am coming back." Over and over, in small but certain ways, *The Fire Screen* confirms that the time for a definitive separation from this mother's messages and requirements, prejudices and heirlooms, is not yet. A screen of her making still stands habit-erected between the poet's self and his sexuality. And while that fire burns hot and high, the screen will stay in place.

A peculiarity of this poem, the first of two, is to include a footnote, this one recording Merrill's chagrined afterthoughts when the poem had been completed. The note refers to the fire screen itself, his use of the metaphor, which has been "All framework & embroidery rather than any slower looking into things. Fire screen—screen *of* fire. The Valkyries' baffle, pulsing at trance pitch, godgiven, elemental. Flames masking that cast-iron plaque—'contrecoeur' in French—which backs the hearth with charred Loves and Graces." He laments having "settled for the obvious" by showing the screen masking the flames, rather than making of flaming passion itself a mask for and defense against what lies at a still deeper level.

But the time was not yet. That Merrill could now imagine passion itself as the defense, however, indicates that he was right in more ways than one about the worst being over. "The worst," he said; but what had he imagined the worst to be? Losing Strato, no doubt; and more abstract evils beyond that: struggling with thwarted passion, for instance, and coping with objectless drives and desires. And beyond that? Something still too elusive to fuse with full poetic expression, existing in a tension between this actual poem of oedipal conflict and that other perception captured, after the fact, by the footnote. But *Braving the Elements* will take him farther, and *The Book of Ephraim* farther still.

CHAPTER 6

Braving the Elements

did I detect
In all that pain an element of play?
—"Chimes for Yahya," *Divine Comedies*

I

The development stalled in *The Fire Screen* could be seen to move forward again with the publication of Merrill's next book, after which he was awarded the Bollingen Prize by Yale "for his wit and delight in language, his exceptional craft." But *Braving the Elements* has its own oddity. Though plainly a more substantial achievement than its predecessor, it is less unified by theme, style, or story than any collection since *The Country of a Thousand Years of Peace*. In the new book Merrill seems to care less than ever before whether the love affairs he writes of be recognized as homosexual, and at the same time whether the sense of every poem be available at some level to a conscientious reader. The schizoid splitting produced by this simultaneous frankness and obscurity—both carried to unprecedented extremes—may have confused reviewers, who tended to focus on one group of poems or the other and evaluate the whole book accordingly. Helen Vendler in the *New York Times Book Review* (for instance) praised the new clarity of its "wonderful short narrative lyrics," mentioned that "secrecy and obliquity were Merrill's worst obstacles in his early verses; though his tone was usually clear, the occasion of the tone was impossibly veiled"[1]—but said nothing at all about the half-dozen or so outstanding examples of this very obstacle in *Braving the Elements* itself.

The few poems ("In Monument Valley," "Days of 1935," "Days of 1971," "Under Libra: Weights and Measures") in which lyric balances narrative, and significant content disclosed balances significant content withheld—the mode of Merrill's finest former and future work—are not always the finest in this book devoted to the poles of a dialectic rather than their fruitful synthesis. Like *The Fire Screen*, *Braving the Elements* is a collection of mostly transitional poetry; but the book makes clear that this transition is about to end.

The finest work found here is shorter, and less complexly organized, than "From the Cupola" or the long poems in Part I of *Divine Comedies;* and it tends to be more narrative than lyrical, or more lyrical than narrative, rather than exhibiting the qualities of both in roughly equal proportions. In "Up and Down" the familiar five-stressed envelope quatrains, though attentive to lyric effect, tell their two stories in straightforward fashion without the dazzling shortcuts and pyrotechnic leaps of Merrill's lyric style with all stops pulled (cf. "From the Cupola," "Lost in Translation," etc.). Two self-contained poems, each with its own title, are coupled under the joint title. Alike in length as well as form, they move—as "Up and Down" suggests—in opposite but complementary directions.

The first or "up" half, "Snow King Chair Lift," describes how the poet and a lover (not Strato) ride a ski lift to the top of a mountain in the American southwest one June. This modest adventure becomes a metaphor for the relationship. Having begun it somewhat nervously, the poet is surprised to find he's having fun, enjoys being swept upward by the shuddering "iron love seat" into "views/ Of several states and skies of several blues/ Promptly dismantled by the mover mist." A thunderstorm alarms the couple briefly (and Merrill turns it to precisely the account one expects: "how shall we avert/ Illuminations that electrocute!") but they arrive at the mountaintop safely and have a brief look at the view before riding back down:

> You merely said you liked it in that chill
> Lighthearted atmosphere (a crow for witness)
> And I, that words profaned the driven whiteness
> Of a new leaf. The rest was all downhill.
>
> Au fond each summit is a cul-de-sac.
> That day at least by not unprecedented
> Foresight, a Cozy Cabin had been rented.
> Before I led you to the next chair back
>
> And made my crude but educated guess
> At why the wind was laying hands on you
> (Something I no longer think to do)
> We gazed our little fills at boundlessness.

"The heart that leaps to the invitation of sparkling appearances," reads the poem's epigraph, "is the heart that would itself perform as handsomely." This time the poet takes the conscious, willed position that of course the affair will end, of course illuminations will perform their lethal office on sparkling appearances over time, and even now the lighthearted atmosphere is marred by a watchful crow; but why not jump at the chance for a diverting, if temporary, "lift"—escape from the "dark frames of mind" of lowland life? Painful feelings are absent from this poem, denied admittance indeed, as if Merrill were perfectly determined not to give way again to the pattern of his experience with Strato.

The ironic last line resists simple paraphrase: "little fills" sounds self-deprecating, as if the lovers were unequal to the immense vistas of the mountaintop, had pitifully small appetites, or capacities, for that much space and freedom, could see they were bound nowhere together ("each summit is a cul-de-sac") and see also that they were not bound together, that their bond was no boundless one—some of all this, perhaps. It was not a view they wished to take in long. The present tense of the ride up shifts to past when they have "reached the top and quit our throne," distancing ride and affair in time from the reader and from the poet who has "profaned the driven whiteness" of a fresh page to tell us all this. The expected puns, double entendres, and fresh clichés are scattered plentifully about, and the whole poem, with its powerful, enigmatic closure, is a handsomely turned out piece of work.

But "The Emerald," as the "down" poem of this pair, makes the expansive outlook of "Snow King Chair Lift" feel appropriately light-weight; and by coming second its inward contractedness is given the last word. Merrill has been summoned to be with his mother upon the sudden death of her second husband. At her request he drives her downtown, a single woman once again, and they descend together into the underworldly green depths of a bank's "inmost vault." Despite the agreeable weather and the narrator's pleasant voice, death is a palpable force all about them on this errand: the mother's precautions against skin cancer, the ghostly illusion of her youth restored, above all the tomblike vault where "palatial bronze gates shut like jaws" upon them. Her "face gone queerly lit, fair, young,/ Like faces of our dear ones who have died," the mother opens a safe deposit box containing jewelry given her by the poet's dead father. Wearing it, she becomes a "girl-bride jeweled in his grave." The last act of *Romeo and Juliet* is an inaudible backdrop to these proceedings.

What happens next strikes home with the force of myth. The mother hands her son a ring, the emerald of the title: "He gave/ Me this when you were born. Here, take it for—/ For when you marry. For your bride. It's yours." Extraordinary thoughts pass through the poet's mind; then

> I do not tell her, it would sound theatrical,
> *Indeed this green room's mine, my very life.*
> *We are each other's; there will be no wife;*
> *The little feet that patter here are metrical.*
>
> But onto her worn finger slip the ring.
> Wear it for me, I silently entreat,
> Until—until the time comes. Our eyes meet.
> The world beneath the world is brightening.

The acknowledgment, through this wedding-gesture, of *why* there will be no (other) wife, performed in the cool vault and without rousing the fiery feelings of "Mornings in a New House," measures the sea-change in Merrill's attitude toward this most imperative and problematical theme. Something is being put behind, worked through, and something else affirmed. That the affirmation has been a long time coming, and could not be consciously willed, is evident from Francis Tanning's desperate efforts to will it in *The Seraglio*, and the false feeling when the novel's conclusion insists upon his success. The closing here feels true.

How do the two poems combine to make a single statement? The title itself makes one, bluntly sexual. Against the green bedding of "The Emerald" it seems important to identify the lover in "Snow King Chair Lift" as male, perhaps as the Snow King himself, and so complete the message of the final quatrains. There will be no wife, nor any abiding passion; the reason for the former lies in the nature of the poet's own life circumstances, for the latter in the nature of life itself. Neither conclusion provokes Merrill now to reactions of despair, grief, rage, or lust; a new leaf has been turned. Mountain-top and vault are the cool settings appropriate to calmer emotional states. Each of the two excursions, though not unshadowed, is affirmative; wit and irony season the acceptance—*serenity* would still be too strong a word—prevailing in both poems; and if "The little feet that patter here are metrical" is almost *too* clever for its sober context, its place among Merrill's most memorable lines is secure.

Resignation, if less plainly affirmative, is no less definite in the finely wrought lyric "In Monument Valley." It begins with the narrator's memory of his last horseback ride "One spring twilight during a lull in the war." His mount is a mare; horse and rider move harmoniously through a fertile, lilac-scented atmosphere abounding in living creatures. "Yet here I sit among the crazy shapes things take"—in Monument Valley, Arizona, where wind-erosion has sculpted the bare sandstone grotesquely:

> Wasp-waisted to a fault by long abrasion
> The "Three Sisters" howl. "Hell's Gate" yawns wide.
> I'm eating something in the cool Hertz car
>
> When the shadow falls. There has come to my door
> As to death's this creature stunted, cinder-eyed,
> Tottering still half in trust, half in fear of man—
> Dear god, a horse. I offer my apple core
>
> But she is past hunger, she lets it roll in the sand,
> And I, I raise my window and drive on.
> About the ancient bond between her kind and mine
> Little more to speak of can be done.

The most available sense of this "ancient bond" is that between horse and (only recently motorized) man. But a more interesting drama lies back of this one, embedded in the other carefully established contrasts: fertility vs. aridity, lilac-star-and-swarming-stillnesses vs. howling and hellishness, past vs. present, and especially the contrast between the two horses, the "buoyant sorrel mare" of memory vs. this "stunted, cinder-eyed,/ Tottering" and seemingly dying animal. The images Merrill has used to build up the two scenes, when looked at more closely, begin to suggest another ancient bond—the sexual bond between women and men—and a more personal and meaningful way of reading the poem.

The mare of memory "moved as if not displeased" by his weight through a scene of burgeoning fecundity, meadow and lilac and lake. Monument Valley, where the tottering horse appears, is figured with vaguely female, obscurely threatening shapes: "The Three Sisters" howling as Psyche and her weird sisters never dared, "Hell's Gate" yawning like the *vagina dentata* itself. This decrepit animal could not support a rider. Being "past hunger" she rejects his apple core: an inverted replay of the temptation scene in an Eden which is no garden spot, with parts reversed, a different outcome, and players and props the worse for wear. This sexual reading turns entirely upon Merrill's having decided to make both horses mares, yet seems compelling in a book where "There will be no wife" is uttered with the same finality, the same coolness of voice and place, as the final sentence of "In Monument Valley." "An Urban Convalescence" (in *Water Street*) employed the same contrasts of remembered and present reality through the garland image, to speak of the dissolution of the same sexual bond; but this poem lacks the vivid distress of the earlier one: the "Hertz" are cooler now.

Merrill has not, here—particularly while evoking the farm—held nature off or diminished it through comparisons to anything small, artificial, or inoffensive (though he often does so in describing the Southwest):

> Stillnesses were swarming inward from the evening star
> Or outward from the buoyant sorrel mare
>
> Who moved as if not displeased by the weight upon her.
> Meadows received us, heady with unseen lilac.

Brief, polyphonic lives abounded everywhere.
With one accord we circled the small lake.

A device of the style is to imply and suggest without graphic precision: "the weight upon her" instead of "my weight upon her back"; "Brief polyphonic lives" rather than "spring peepers and cicadas"; "heady with unseen lilac." No meadow is distinguished from another; and "Meadows received us" gracefully reinforces the rider's sense of being smoothly and effortlessly borne forward, an almost dreamlike progress through the twilit landscape. Only the small lake is given—with no detail—as "seen"; other senses—smell, hearing, motion-and-weight—record the main impressions of the ride. It is by this uncharacteristic shift away from the visual that the passage achieves its extraordinary effect of a sensuous bliss almost infantile: suggestion of a young creature carried by a larger, stronger one, to their mutual pleasure, through sensations of sweetness, of lulling stillness, of life behaving for that moment exactly as the rider wills. In Monument Valley, if he is middle-aged, the mare is elderly and their bond broken; he can drive away and leave her, not without regret but free. Free in a sense that does not, perhaps, preclude the scene in the bank vault; for the more these poems are read in the light of one another, the more akin they feel.

The longest poem in *Braving the Elements,* and one of the most attractive, is another literary anti-ballad. "Days of 1935" is both less "perfect" and more important than "The Summer People"—that is, its success is more of substance than of style, and it is not so inclined to joke with its form through parodic mimicry. A less traditional variety of ballad-stanza—three tetrameter lines and a trimeter line, rhyming abab—was chosen for it, a tighter and tenser stanza unit than the tetrameter-trimeter xaxa of "The Summer People." The title, on the Cavafy model, alerts us to the possibility of finding a homosexual love-interest in the poem; but the date unexpectedly locates its events in the poet's childhood. This is the first poem of Merrill's since "The Broken Home" to mine his childhood, invariably a strong subject both because of its intrinsic human-interest value and because it taps the oedipal tensions that have most consistently absorbed him and energized his best writing. Of all the poems in *Braving the Elements*, this one most closely approaches an ideal balance of revelation and concealment, narrative and lyric, even though the ballad-form precludes inventive formal modulations.

"Days of 1935" takes the form of a serial bedtime fantasy spun by the poor little rich boy of "The Broken Home" and "The World and the Child." Stimulated by newspaper accounts of the Lindbergh baby's kidnapping, he thought it "entirely plausible/ For my turn to come soon." But the kidnappers his fancy conjures up, a couple of tough customers named [Pretty Boy?] Floyd and Jean [Harlow?] who "Lived in what my parents meant/ By sin," never for a moment frighten him and his resistance ("my toothprints on [Floyd's] hand,/ Indenture of a kiss") is a sham: these are the very surrogate parents of his dreams. Not because they are kinder to him than his real parents or love him more (they aren't and don't) but because he likes—loves and covets, really—the way they *are* with one another and with him: rough, vulgar, mannerless, blunt, everything his parents have taught him not to be. "To me they hardly spoke, just watched/ Or gave directions in dumb show." Their grammar is atrocious; when it suits him to, Floyd knocks Jean about; their lurid melodrama holds the nine-year-old protagonist rapt. Yet he gives the story a sad, realistic ending: the captors are caught in their turn and the child restored to his parents and his boring home life. He even finds himself complicitous in bringing Floyd and Jean to justice.

The sexual precocity suggested by the title is present from the poem's first page, where the child figures the theft of himself as a sort of elopement, making

> sheer imagination ride
> Off with us in its old jalopy,
> Trailing bedclothes like a bride
> Timorous but happy.

The gangsters are comically stylized, Jean with rosebud mouth and platinum spit curls, Floyd "lean, sallow, lantern-jawed" and furnished with a pistol. The boy's own parents represent these extremes of the Masculine and Feminine as ably; the differences are those of style. A newspaper photo evokes the stove/refrigerator polarities of "Five Old Favorites."

> My mother gloved,
> Hatted, bepearled, chin deep in fur.
> Dad glowering—was it true he loved
> Others beside her?
>
> Eerie, speaking likenesses.
> One positively heard her mild
> Voice temper some slow burn of his,
> "Not before the child."

By thrilling contrast, there's very little Floyd and Jean won't do "before the child":

> Sometimes as if I were not there
> He put his lips against her neck.
> Her head lolled sideways, just like Claire
> Coe in "Tehuantepec."
>
> Then both would send me looks so heaped
> With a lazy, scornful mirth,
> *This* was growing up, I hoped,
> The first flushed fruits of earth.
>
> One night I woke to hear the room
> Filled with crickets—no, bedsprings.
> My eyes dilated in the gloom,
> My ears made out things.
>
> Jean: The kid, he's still awake . . .
> Floyd: Time he learned . . . Oh baby . . . God . . .

> Their prone tango, for my sake,
> Grew intense and proud.

After this the fantasy takes the predictable turn. The boy adores Jean and the way she watches him, loves entertaining her all one afternoon with fairy tales, identifies himself with her in fact: "I stared at her—*she* was the child!" And it is Jean's place he takes, by having her catch cold so Floyd will join him on the rag rug where he sleeps:

> Time stopped. His arm somnambulist
> Had circled me, warm, salt as blood.
> Mine was the future in his fist
> To get at if I could,
>
> While his heart beat like a drum
> And *Oh baby* faint and hoarse
> Echoed from within his dream . . .
> The next day Jean was worse

What he wants, of course, is to stay with his kidnappers forever; what *they* want is his father's money. At the point where ransom seems inevitable, then, the two must be captured and punished; when Floyd's voice calls "Jean,/ Baby, we've been double-crossed!" it's the betrayed child (Baby) himself who has pulled that string. "Rescued" from randy, offhand Floyd and Jean, sent home to faked wood paneling, manicured lawns, and parents "out partying," he speaks from the witness box:

> "You I adored I now accuse . . ."
> Would imagination dare
> Follow that sentence like a fuse
> Sizzling toward the Chair?
>
> See their bodies raw and swollen
> Sagging in a skein of smoke?

The charge he presses is not spelled out. Though clues are provided in several semicoherent asides, this is the "concealment" introduced to balance the "revelations" of title and rag-rug Sleepwalking Scene. We can guess his most burning accusation: Floyd and Jean have snatched him off into their lives, shown him how to be happy, and then let his parents take him away from them again. The happiness-lesson is an illumination that electrocutes *them* (to borrow a phrase from "Snow King Chair Lift"). Moreover the paradigm set thus is one the poet will be condemned to repeat for many years. "Where does it end?" he wonders, thinking how often, in a grown-up affair, one lover or another has "driven" the same child

> till his mother's Grade
> A controls took charge, or handsome
> Provisions which his father made
> Served once again as ransom,
>
> Driven your captive far enough
> For the swift needle on the gauge
> To stitch with delicate kid stuff
> His shoddy middle age.

His mother's "controls" are multiplex, and we know something about the forceful forms they have assumed from "To My Greek," "Mornings in a New House," and other poems. We know much less as yet about his father's "handsome provisions," but the cliché is meant to exploit the sexual value of "handsome" behind the surface one of "opulent." These provisions cannot be specified; but every guess about them aims at a newly developing dimension of this by now familiar psychological territory. *The Seraglio*'s version of the oedipal conflict, probably reflecting Merrill's own immature understanding of the situation, was that his parents' divorce made Francis "the man" in his mother's house, fierce feelings of protectiveness and responsibility reinforcing his natural oedipal feelings to an excruciating degree. Later, to become aware of sexual attraction to any woman was unbearable; it was as if he too, like his father, were guilty of betraying her. The novel implies that Francis turned to men by default; and until now the "family" poems have tended to draw their narrow bead on an erotically charged mother-son relationship, behind which the father glowers but from which he is excluded, having chosen to exclude himself. "Days of 1935" is the first poem to suggest something else: that "the father," in the tolerable disguise of Floyd, has been in some sense *essentially and always* erotically attractive in his own right, and that sexual dynamics within the family are less straightforward than young Francis had imagined. (That thought had surfaced earlier in Merrill's second novel, *The (Diblos) Notebook*, published in 1965.)

Father and mother, then, are the fixed points of return from Merrill's "driven" forays into erotic adventure. In internalized ways obscure to us, and perhaps often also to him, they always reclaim him; yet repeatedly he is stolen away for one more doomed, brief interlude of joy. "That life was fiction in disguise" is a truth the kidnapped child knows well. His fantasy disguises, while it reveals, his present situation and his future one. Its unconscious sources cannot contrive a way to let Floyd keep him there, but "I/ will relive some things he did/ Until I die, until I die."

2

Those things were relived perhaps most intensely with Strato. The lead poem in *Braving the Elements*, "After the Fire," refers directly back to *The Fire Screen*—to failing passion and "Mornings in a New House"—and reaches still farther back to "Days of 1964": Athens, the adored lover, the housekeeper/whore/love goddess Kyria Kleo. In those days Kleo would putter about the house "Cleaning and watering, sighing with love or pain," or "climb . . . to the heights/ Even of degradation." She served the poem's purposes, which were frankly symbolic; there was no need to make a rounded character of her, even had Merrill been interested in portraiture then. But by these days of c. 1970 Kleo is only a housekeeper again, with troubles of her own that lend her a certain substance. "After the Fire" is furnished with seminaturalistic pictures of two people formerly identified only as Kleo's "pious mother" and "wastrel son"—a memorably awful pair, probably exaggerated, but strongly individualized despite their labels and "type" characteristics.

The Fire Screen records the end of the affair with Strato over which Kleo had presided. Now after an absence the poet has returned to the scene of all that happiness, and the experience is painful. Minor damage done by a small fire, which had broken out while he was away, has been repaired; but the new paint lends quiet emphasis to changes of a more profound sort:

> The walls' original oldfashioned colors,
> Cendre de rose, warm flaking ivory—
> Colors last seen as by that lover's ghost
> Stumbling downstairs wound in a sheet of flame—
> Are hidden now forever but not lost
> Beneath this quiet sensible light gray.

This is the gray of ash, cooling now.

The just-arrived poet has nothing better to do now than listen to Kleo's own tale of woe: "Her old mother has gone off the deep end." The yiayia (grandmother), nearly ninety, passes her days vilifying her daughter and grandson Panayioti: "Our entire neighborhood now knows/ As if they hadn't years before/ That he is a *Degenerate!* a *Thieving/ Faggot!* just as Kleo is a *Whore!*" The yiayia's accurate but "terrible gift of hindsight"—for we did glimpse a plump Kleo painted for business in 1964, and there were days when " 'Noti' cruised the Naval Hospital,/ Slim then, with teased hair"—sharpens the poet's own painful sense of a treasurable, if "degenerate," past painted over by time.

"Kleo goes on. The yiayia's warm,/ What can it mean?" In Merrill's pattern of burning passion and ash-cool aftermath, it means the yiayia inhabits and experiences the present as if it still *were* the past, taking past truths for present ones. This "little leaden oven-rosy witch" here assumes the muse-role played by Kleo in "Days of 1964," while the active sexual "degradation" of that past is displaced from Kleo onto Panayioti. Now, Merrill reflects,

> he must be forty,
> Age at which degeneration takes
> Too much of one's time and strength and money.
> My eyes brim with past evenings in this hall,
> Gravy-spattered cloth, candles minutely
> Guttering in the love-blinded gaze.

It is his own degeneration he is thinking of; by means of this juxtaposing Panayioti is made to seem a grotesque parody of himself.

And sure enough, when the poet calls on the Greek family, Kleo—a weeping background figure—lets him in, but Panayioti loudly fills the foreground, welcoming the guest with "anaconda arms" and Greek-accented French:

> "Ah Monsieur Tzim, bon zour et bon retour!
> Excuse mon déshabillé. Toute la nuit
> Z'ai décoré l'église pour la fête
> Et fait l'amour, le prêtre et moi,
> Dans une alcove derrière la Sainte Imaze. . . .
>
> Huge, powerful, bland, he rolls his eyes and r's.
> Glints of copper wreathe his porcelain brow
> Like the old-time fuses here, that blow so readily.
> I seem to know that crimson robe,
> And on his big fat feet—my slippers, ruined.
> Still, not to complicate affairs,
> Remembering also the gift of thumb-sized garnet
> Bruises he clasped around Aleko's throat,
> I beam with gratitude.

The fuses that "blow so readily" (and perhaps the "derrière" as well) poke fun at Kleo's unsavory son, who—though plainly still a thieving faggot—has lost his looks and cruises the Naval Hospital no more. "P caused the fire" the poet thinks—P for Passion? for faggotry gone to blowsy seed? Merrill seems here to invite the reader's conditioned aversion to Panayioti's repellent manner, which he makes too excessive to overlook or excuse. The Enfant Chic in *The (Diblos) Notebook* is a less dangerous but equally preposterous queen, who similarly functions to displace from the narrator and his protagonist excessive behavior that the straight world associates with, and finds distasteful in, the gay world. Both sketches are drawn with too much wicked wit and relish not to be important. To the extent that Merrill has projected onto Panayioti (like himself, a middle-aged homosexual son) qualities of "queer" style he himself finds unappealing, Panayioti can be taken partly as an alter ego—bearing in mind that the worst traits we see in him, dishonesty and brutality, have been assigned several times to Strato.

For the lovingly preserved masks and illusions of "Days of 1964" are gone now, and with them the love and joy they permitted when degradation meant love as well, and both meant Kleo—now thin, old, "Lips chill as the fallen dusk." Yet the yiayia will not or cannot take this in. "A strange car stops outside?/ She cackles *Here's the client! Paint your face,/ Putana!* to her daughter moistening/ With tears the shirt she irons." For all the senile old woman can see, degeneration is *now* the stylish family enterprise it used to be; and when she abruptly includes the poet in her skewed view of all this by recognizing him, he willingly embraces the view and the yiayia herself:

> I mean to ask whose feast it is today
> But the room brightens, the yiayia skrieks my name—
> *It's Tzimi! He's returned!*
> —And with that she returns to human form,
> The snuffed-out candle-ends grow tall and shine,

> Dead flames encircle us, which cannot harm,
> The table's spread, she croons, and I
> Am kneeling pressed to her old burning frame.

The feast, it seems, is his own. Merrill exploits the church-motif introduced through Panayioti's antics to summon up a scene of religious adoration: candles, table, Sainte Image turned human, figure kneeling in worshipful submission. The affirmation wrought here at poem's end, by the usual means of elevated language and lyric intensity, is of the past and the lost love. Only much farther into this book does grief cease to attend the loss, and reconciliation with the lover become possible, in "Strato in Plaster."

This poem bears an epigraph in Greek which translates "Breast of marble, heart of potato." Here at last is Strato in the flesh—rather more of him in fact than in 1964, when the Apollo at Olympia had seemed a fair likeness. "Joy breeds in the beautiful blind gaze,/ The marble mouth and breastbone," muses the poet, looking at a picture of the statue, then at his altered friend, who has turned up in Athens out of the blue one day to attend his sister's wedding, "in plaster from wrist to bicep." The broken elbow, and cast, supply convenient emblems for the broken relationship:

> Three winters. Trowels of frigid white
> Choke the sugar-celled original
> That once stayed warm all night with its own sun.
> The god in him is a remembered one.
> Inflexibility through which twinges shoot
> Like stars, the fracture's too complex,
> Too long unmended, for us to be friends.
> I, he hazards, have made other friends.
> The more reason, then, to part like friends.
>
> Today at least a cloud of rice and petals
> Aimed at others will envelop him.

The connection of the fractured relationship and the wedding is ironic, for the likeness to Eros has gone the way of the likeness to Apollo.

This sketch of Strato is not flattering. Merrill shows the self-importance, pride, resentment, spite, and vanity dwelling in a heart of potato no longer masked by a marble breast; and the brutality implied in "The Envoys" and "Remora" is made explicit now:

> At present he is living far from home,
> Builder by day and autocrat by dark,
> Athenian among peasants. Fine Athenian
> Whose wife learns acquiescence blow by blow.
> That strikes a nerve. "I haven't married her!
> Am I a fool to marry before thirty?
> Who trusts a woman anyhow?"

Physical changes in Strato merely point to more troubling perceptions. "Those extra kilos, that moustache,/ Lies found out and letters left unanswered" all are part of the same calamitous breakdown of sparkling appearances that finally divided the two. The extra kilos cover the broken but remembered beauty like plaster, as the present covers the past and gray paint the old warm rose and ivory.

Yet despite everything Strato's eyes still sparkle, he retains his cheeky attractiveness, his animal vitality, even an appreciation of his own outrageousness—and this despite a life, as Merrill imagines it, grotesquely distorted by poverty:

> Three winters, playing backgammon
> At the cafe for stakes that pierce the heart,
> One cigarette or dram of burning mud,
> And never losing ("dice are in my blood")—
> Marika sleeping, her cheeks ice,
> Where oil smoke sickens and a chicken's cough
> Wakes the child who dashes to the floor
> Any red elixir *he* might pour—

In fact, what we are given here is that rarest thing in Merrill's work, a balanced portrait, "good" and "bad" qualities all held together in one steady gaze of assessment. Before this, only "Words for Maria" had accorded anyone such rounded treatment of his/her own reality—the clear view that passion flees from and is destroyed by, but not affection. Erratic rhyme— mud/blood, sickens/chicken's, inflexibility/complex—and a second-nature orientation toward the pentameter in *Merrill's* blood, from which he rarely wanders far, bind "Strato in Plaster" together by means almost invisible; it's easy to miss the rhyme, especially the internal rhyme, entirely. "After the Fire" is cast in the same formal mold, and both conclude symphonically, the narrative shifting to a heightened intensity of regularized meter, terminal rhymes ordered for lyric emphasis, and a reverberant final line or image. (See the last strophe of "After the Fire," above.)

And despite predictions that the fracture between the poet and Strato can never heal, "Days of 1971" finds the two companionably driving across Europe together, Strato's attentiveness and the trip itself exemplifying the second clause of what Merrill wryly calls "Proust's Law":

> (b) Only when time has slain desire
> Is his wish granted to a smiling ghost
> Neither harmed nor warmed, now, by the fire.

There is a cross-reference in "Days of 1935" to this book's third poem permeated by the absence or presence of Strato: "Grown up, he thinks how S, T, you/ . . . Taking the wheel (cf. those "Days/ Of 1971") / Have driven. . . ." S stands for Strato, to whom Merrill can say in 1971: "Well, you were a handsome devil once./ Take the wheel. You're still a fair chauffeur." But their pleasant ten-sonnet travelogue requires no further comment here. By 1971 the fruitful tensions have passed out of this subject, it seems, leaving little to celebrate or exorcise.

3

"After the Fire" is the first long poem in *Braving the Elements*, "Days of 1971" the last. The lover whose presence/absence dominates the book is not Strato, however, but his successor, Merrill's companion on the ski lift. Poems in which this companion appears or figures are loosely grouped in the middle of the book and set in the vicinity of New Mexico. The first of these, "In Nine Sleep Valley," again recalls the driving-metaphor; it's the summer of 1968, and the two are touring somewhere in the American Southwest. The title is borrowed from the Indian name for a real place, but the "valley" here is a figurative one it takes nine sleeps to cross, and the poem accordingly has nine parts, each in a different form.

None of the exuberance of the earlier Strato poems can be felt in these. The older, wiser voice that speaks these verses is trying chiefly to keep itself steady so as not to cause alarm, aware that this loved one too will certainly leave, hoping to forestall the event even while sensing its approach:

> The beauty I mean to press fading
> Between these lines is yours, and the misleading
> Sweetness, leaves and portals of a body
> Ajar, cool, nodding at the wheel already.

That the poet asks no more than to be misled is an old story, now told and told again in new terrain: roaming the mountain sagebrush; exploring one abandoned cabin after another; cutting the enigmatically smiling lover's hair, when the shroudlike drape forces a recognition that

> Blind, untrimmed,
> Sheeted with cold, such rot and tangle must
> In time be our affair.
>
> But should you smile as those who doubt the novice
> Hands they entrust their beautiful heads to,

> I want to show you how the clumsiest love
> Transfigures if you let it, if you dare.
>
> There was a day when beauty, death and love
> Were coiled together in one crowning glory.
> Shears in hand, we parted the dark waves . . .
> Look at me, dear one. There.

One death is Robert Kennedy's; his funeral is mentioned in part
2, the "Eye-searing water/ Onion or headline or your fine print
drew" in part 4. But no public grief could touch Merrill deeply
at this stage; the private drama, "beyond history," absorbed him
fully, and all tears "Dried in a wink" in the arid Southwest.

Tension thickens or thins the poet's voice at times—crowd-
ing out punctuation, making it hard to follow him—but the
impression of his holding himself together by these words comes
through clearly, as does most of what they say. The best poem
of the group is atypical of it in tone:

> Geode,[2] the troll's melon
> Rind of crystals velvet smoke meat blue
> Formed far away under fantastic
> Pressures, then cloven in two
> By the taciturn rock shop man, twins now forever
>
> Will they hunger for each other
> When one goes north and one goes east?
>
> I expect minerals never do.
> Enough for them was a feast
> Of flaws, the molten start and glacial sleep,
> The parting kiss.
>
> Still face to face in halfmoonlight
> Sparkling comes easy to the Gemini.
>
> Centimeters deep yawns the abyss.

This pluperfect emblem of lovers separated by distance and
threatened by internal irregularities, and of their relationship

"Formed far away under fantastic/ Pressures," developing through a "molten start" toward "glacial sleep," needs little explicating. By now, readers of this study should recognize easily Merrill's unmistakable touches of language and technique, distortion of scale, ironic twinning of *sparkling* and *abyss* (in the case of a geode, it is the "abyss" itself that sparkles!), deft control of both aspects of the metaphor, use of "halfmoonlight" both as a reference to the shape of the geode's cut halves and as a timing/setting device, and so on. (They should even, briefly, entertain a doubt about where to stop: for instance, could "Jim 'n' I" possibly be hidden in Gemini? Such questions in Merrill's case are never foolish; the unturned stone could be the very one with the live bait beneath it.)

Another feature of this poem, less ubiquitous yet entirely characteristic of his work, shows in the exquisite compression of the final line: a glaze of wit that compels admiration yet by its very cleverness seems to undercut the emotional credibility of the poet, as if no one seriously in fear of a shattering loss would, or at least decently ought to, be capable of writing such a line. The geode poem (like "The Emerald") is a mild example of the phenomenon; "Syrinx" goes to riskier lengths. "The great god Pan" once chased a maiden called Syrinx into a river, where she turned into a reed; Pan cut several reeds forthwith, including Syrinx, and made his pipes of them. Kalstone has analyzed this latest mythological metaphor with a keen appreciation for how the language "walks a tightrope of ingenuity and feeling," and mentions particularly the poem's "most outrageous example" of emotion distracted by wit in the lines: "Who puts his mouth to me/ Draws out the scale of love and dread—/ O ramify, sole antidote!"—

The musician's breath or the lover's kiss, and then the high tragedienne's apostrophe, which, on a second glance, taking in the enjambment ("d—/ O"), we see disintegrate magically into the musical scale. This is precisely the action the poem repeats over and over: a human gesture, then the witty afflatus and effort of words. . . .

The "scale of love and dread": D/O RA-MI-FY- SOLE [L]A(N)-TI-DO(TE)! Yet the burden of "Syrinx" too is loss:

> Some formula not relevant any more
> To flower children might express it yet
>
> Like $\sqrt{\left(\dfrac{x}{y}\right)^n} = 1$
>
> —Or equals zero, one forgets—
>
> The y standing for you, dear friend, at least
> Until that hour he reaches for me, then
>
> Leaves me cold, the great god Pain
> Letting me slide back into my scarred case

The formula becomes an ideogram of love-making which we are invited to decode: a game, similar to that mairzy-doats-like musical scale. Such puzzle-setting may indeed strike one as outrageous, inappropriate, even offensive in a "serious" poem. Yet Merrill must be conceded his own style of playing the panpipes—even at moments when cleverness and virtuosity seem to him the best way for Art to make Pain bearable, and even though his highest art may always be that in which such witty puns and verbal high jinks do not unbalance the emotion of the poem or call it into question. "A pity about that lowest form of humor," he wrote in a review published the same year, 1972, as *Braving the Elements:*

> It is suffered, by and large, with groans of aversion, as though one had done an unseemly thing in adult society, like slipping a hand up the hostess's dress. Indeed, the punster has touched, and knows it if only for being so promptly shamed, upon a secret, fecund place in language herself. The pun's *objet trouvé* aspect cheapens it further—why? A Freudian slip is taken seriously: it betrays its maker's hidden wish. The pun (or the rhyme, for that matter) "merely" betrays the hidden wish of words.[3]

Nor is every pun a joke. With an impulse James Joyce would appreciate, "Syrinx" concludes by confessing she can no longer

stop the four winds racing overhead
Nought
Waste   Eased
Sought

—this to be read cruciform-fashion (in keeping with the signature—"X my mark"—given earlier as hers, and the X of the formula) but starting anywhere.

4

In another emblem, "Willowware Cup," sheer appealingness replaces the cutting edge of wit, though this poem too concerns the loss of the same southwestern lover. Freely interpreting the blue and white Willowware pattern, Merrill projects himself into it, a father signaling "Feebly, as from flypaper, minding less and less" as "gnatsized lovers" sail away. For his friend the relationship has proved "more trouble to mend than to replace." As he does in "Snow King Chair Lift," the poet accepts the situation without anguish or recrimination:

> You are far away. The leaves tell what they tell.
>
> But this lone, chipped vessel, if it fills,
> Fills for you with something warm and clear.

But there are other emblems in this volume, other vessels, that fill for this lost lover with language as opaque as the mud of the speaking "Banks of a Stream Where Creatures Bathe":

> Giving of my very
> Self, I've seen you
> Clouded by the gift.

> You want diversions
> Deeply pure, is that it?
> Trust me. I keep trying
> Not to break down.

This small group of poems, and a few others, are set apart by their intense hermeticism. To varying degrees they represent the only important failure in Merrill's long career, a failure not of ability but of attitude. For without extrinsic information, and/or more work than they repay, it is very hard to understand these poems on any level; nor are they so effective lyrically that the level of ready verbal sense seems unimportant. An impression of pent-up sexual rage, in the New Mexico cluster, does gradually soak in. Patterned images in the most accessible poems centered on that affair, "Snow King Chair Lift" and "In Nine Sleep Valley," recur in the murkier ones: images of dry heat and wet coolness, of youth and age, of purity, and—for the first time—many phallic images of erection, ejaculation, detumescence. In general, clarity of expression in these poems seems directly correlated with violence of feeling: the more obscure the poem, the more aggressive its tone. It looks as though the calm acceptances of "Willowware Cup" may have been gained at the expense of sharply splitting off "bad" feelings toward this lover's character and conduct from "good" ones; so that while love and acceptance of loss could be expressed plainly, rage and resentment—the dark side of the approved feelings—must be denied or concealed. A poet interested in concealing a powerful emotion, however, had better not write anything; the emotion will be the one thing impossible to hide. Aware of this, but unable to deny these feelings expression, Merrill fell back on the solution lamented by Helen Vendler in the review already quoted: that of veiling the occasion, since the tone must in any case be clear. "Yam" is the angriest poem in the New Mexico group, and the most obscure:

Rind and resurrection, hell and seed,
Fire-folia, hotbeds of a casserole
Divinely humble, it awaits your need.
Its message, taken in by you,

Deep reds obliterate. Be glad they do.
Go now by upward stages, fortified,
Where an imaginary line is being
Drawn past which you do not melt, you suffer

Pure form's utter discontent, white waste
And wintry grazing, flocks of white
But with no shepherd-sage, no flute, no phrases;
Parchment frozen, howling pricksong, mute

Periods that flash and stun—
Hit on the head, who brought you to this pass?
Valleys far below are spouting
Baby slogans and green gripes of spring,

Clogged pools, the floating yen . . .
You feel someone take leave, at once
Transfiguring, transfigured. A voice grunts
MATTER YOU MERELY DO I AM

Which lies on snow in dark ideogram
—Or as a later commentary words it,
One-night's-meat-another-morning's-mass-
Against-inhuman-odds-I-celebrate.

The imagery here and elsewhere suggests reasons for such elegant, howling pricksongs as this: that the lover came to view
their association as "impure" in some sense ("you suffer/ Pure
form's utter discontent, white waste . . ." plus the scatological
possibilities of the poem's end), and that the age difference between them was a problem. But all the poem really tells, and
tells but gradually over time, is the violence of its anger.

Merrill withheld "Yam" and "Under Mars," the angriest and
most hermetic of the New Mexico group, from the *Selected Poems.*
Those he reprinted are "The Black Mesa," "Banks of a Stream

Where Creatures Bathe," "Under Libra: Weights and Measures," and "Flèche d'Or."

Two other poems in the book are governed by the same images as these, though not focused narrowly on the relationship. "18 West 11th Street" is the centerpiece of a review essay by Richard Saez—"James Merrill's Oedipal Fire" (*Parnassus*, 3, Fall/Winter 1974)—referred to in the previous chapter. Saez's reading of this long, extremely difficult poem is sensible and penetrating, and he would not agree that the poem itself is fatally weakened by obscurity. In my view, "Yam" and "18 West 11th Street" illustrate the point made by W. K. Wimsatt and Cleanth Brooks, in *Modern Criticism:* that if an artist treats material which is "really private and eccentric, its expression might have value for the artist himself and might provide an interesting case-study for the psychologist, but it would cease to be a work of art." I have said that cleverness—whistling in the burying-ground—is not a capital offense against the reader. But not to care whether one communicates effectively, in some way, with one's genuinely committed average reader may arguably be the one capital crime a good writer can commit.[4]

The other poem, "Dreams About Clothes," gives the book its title:

> Tell me something, Art.
> You know what it's like
> Awake in your dry hell
> Of volatile synthetic solvents.
> Won't you help us brave the elements
> Once more, of terror, anger, love?
> Seeing there's no end to wear and tear
> Upon the lawless heart,
> Won't you as well forgive
> Whoever settles for the immaterial?
> Don't you care how we live?

Like the yam casserole's, a dry cleaner's hellish heat. "Arturo's Valet Service" contracts neatly to serve the metaphor—is where Art works and lives, mending the wear and tear, applying its special solvents to stubborn spots. To make what sense one can of this poem means interpreting the several dreams about clothes that compose it, and also interpreting Merrill's own implicit interpretations. In the first, a recurrent dream, a man (the poet's father, evidently) is being fitted by a tailor for another dark suit. Merrill wonders "in fact" what to do with his dead father's clothes: give them away? "Take them to the shrink until they fit?/ . . . or just let them be,/ Still holding sway above me?" No answer to the problem comes, a problem not unlike one faced by Francis Tanning:

> The years in which to acquire from his father an image of mature behavior had passed Francis by, taking this opportunity with them. He had spent them under his mother's roof. The long trousers, his first pair cut from the cloth of superior poise, had been tried on, as it were, with no mirror handy. *She* thought he looked well enough; he was forever made to feel his responsibilities as "man of the house." He emptied ashtrays and mixed drinks. He sat at the head of her table while she told of conflicts in which he took no part.[5]

The passage encourages an oedipal reading of what is either a second dream or a continuation of the first:

> Sure enough, a waterfront
> Glides into place on small, oiled waves.
> Taverns are glittering and the heavens have cleared.
> (Far inland lie the crossroads,
> Oxcart overturned, graybeard
> Lamented by his slaves.)
> From whom did I inherit these shirtsleeves
> And ancient, sexy jeans?
> Fingers of a woman I am with

Tease through holes made by the myth.
Bad music starts in 6/8 time.
I order drinks and dinners. I'm
Being taken, her smile means,
Once more to the cleaners.

No more than the business suits inherited from his father are these sexy jeans comfortable on him. The "woman I am with" behaves seductively, pokes her fingers though the punning mythholes, makes him feel threatened and exploited—feelings Francis might well recognize.

Next comes a wet dream during an August thunderstorm in which Merrill's father, as Prospero, is the virile and intimidating wizard who calls up tempests at the stock exchange and/or at home "Until the lightning twinkling of an eye/ Dissolved his corporation. . . ." After this volatile dissolution (divorce? or death?) "Relief poured through me shining wet,/ Lining of purest silver" to the storm-cloud. Finally a winged being, probably Eros, appears disguised as the old-clothes man. "Snow melts at the touch of his bare feet." Love has been melting snow since *Water Street* and "A Vision of the Garden" (or failing to, as in "Yam"), but there's no reason to insist on this identity; the figure might equally well be *Merrill*'s old [-clothes] man, winged like the virtuous dead, or both or neither.

Hot, cold, wet, and dry recombine so that the dry heat at Arturo's establishment opposes and complements the cool wetness of the thunderstorm dream: Art's cleansing cauldron; the purity of sexual release. Since Art's task is to make pain bearable, he/it is properly a *dry* cleaner in a scheme where wetness is repeatedly associated with release (in life) and "parchment" both with sexual refusal and the blank page waiting to receive the poem. But there is no point in trying to fix firm meanings to the elements of the dreams; it would take many pages to account for everything they might mean, since Merrill chose to limit them so slightly. A "real" dream, of course, is fluid and elusive, hard to seize firmly, hard to interpret with confidence, and the dream-format invites an impressionistic treatment of one cryptic, oddly disquieting image that gives way to another and then another.

It is probably safe to say this much: that "Dreams about Clothes" obliquely addresses, along with whatever else, the poet's difficulties about replacing and identifying with his father, and recognizes that the dream-problem of what to do about the father's clothes—his shape, his identity, "the man they made"—is an oedipal problem, as well as one of sexual identity. Again, Art's volatile, synthetic solution is the one that works. Only Art—the past life recollected, redeemed, mended and affirmed by form and metaphor—can finally say *Peace, be still!* to this triad of tempestuous elements. All three have been pacified in "Strato in Plaster"; "No syllable of certain grand tirades/ One spent the worst part of a fall composing" comes to Merrill's mind when he says goodbye to Strato. If Anger still chokes a handful of other poems in *Braving the Elements*, one triumph of *Divine Comedies* will be to have braved that element fully and faced it down.

CHAPTER 7

Divine Comedies, Part I

I

In 1974, Merrill collected and published a batch of 59 poems written between 1947 and 1972. The publisher was a small press, Temple Bar. A prefatory note accounts for the exclusion of these poems from the books we know: some "gave blood to others and were thrust aside for their pains," others "went a flighty route their maker chose not to call his own." They have some curiosity value, and the *Selected Poems* reprints a few, chiefly those with symbolic or thematic links to the *Sandover* trilogy. Two from the Strato era, "The Pardoner's Tale" and "Hourglass II," add effectively to the picture of that time. But more than anything else, in the context of what follows and precedes it, *The Yellow Pages* gives the impression that corners are being swept and drawers emptied out, a period of growth and change being brought to a close, by means of this satisfactory dispensation of the oddments and culls of Merrill's whole career up to that time. Two years later the lessons of the transition had crystallized in *Divine Comedies*, a stunning book, still his best single volume by every measure of poetic attainment, except that for sheer lyric power volumes II and III of the trilogy occasionally outshine even this. It was awarded the Pulitzer Prize.

Part II of *Divine Comedies, The Book of Ephraim* (destined to become volume I of the as yet undreamed-of trilogy), inevitably overshadows the nine more conventional poems of part I. Five of these, however, are quintessential Merrill narrative/lyrics, any one of which would stand out brilliantly in a book of still more conventional work. Merrill's poems have been getting longer and longer with each volume, but the *average* length of those in this quintet is seven pages, high even by his own standard. And all are so closely related in theme, style, structure, method, everything but actual subject, that the discussion ensuing here will take two of the most important—"Lost in Translation" and "Yánnina"—to stand for the group. There are no stylistic or thematic surprises among them; Merrill's way of writing, and his concerns, are what they always were. Nevertheless the book is one of startling departures of the sort that could follow from his having lived to be nearly fifty. Certain persistent needs and fears have loosened their grip now, and his technical prowess is fully mature, enabling him to sustain poem after densely textured poem at length with no loss of pressure.

Some general observations about this group may be useful at the outset. Each poem begins by narrating a scene from Merrill's own life past or present, waking or sleeping, in the present tense. He is a central actor in the scene, though in every case he shares the stage with others. The narrative progresses until broken, smoothly or abruptly, by a shift to another time-frame, setting, or mode of discourse. Shifts are sometimes marked by a change in formal organization or a section break with a new number; sometimes (especially in "Yánnina") they amount to no more than a pause for a musing interpolation. Other shifts in time and place may occur as the poem moves ahead, also subtler changes of voice, from narrative to meditative to lyric; so that in general the poems can be said to move in and out of focus as clear, particularized narration gives place to speculation or assertion which is relatively dense, cryptic, and abstract. Each shift serves to gather in new elements to be worked into the shaping pattern. And in each poem the line of thought woven through these details of experience leads to a final lyric affirmation so well-written that any might serve to illustrate poetic closure of this, symphonic, sort.

The poems are brought through their individual developments partly by Merrill's discovery of order and pattern within the apparently random events and particulars of his life. "Chimes for Yahya," for instance, begins as a doorbell rings, to be followed immediately by the clanging churchbells of Athens that sound like a locomotive bell. Their clanging calls to mind a childhood memory of traveling south by train for Christmas; then the "train of thought" carries him on to Isfahan, where he acquired the string of bells (now hanging beside him on his terrace in Athens) to be rung at poem's end. The mandarin suit and pipe he wore that Christmas morning as a child blur into the peasant costume he dons and the opium he smokes as Yahya's guest. The birth of the Christmas child is grotesquely parodied in Isfahan at a mock childbirth, the poet and another American visitor "Staring like solemn oxen from a stall/ Upon the mystery." These actual events (and the symbolic purposes such concepts as "train" and "drug" readily lend themselves to) chime together like Merrill's fortuitous rhymes: elements afloat in life or language, waiting for someone with the skill to perfect their meanings by recognizing and aligning them.

The familiar themes recur, but all are handled now in ways reflecting the maturity that has finally allowed some of the old tensions to be resolved. For those who have followed Merrill's work from the beginning, the most affecting resolutions are sexual and familial. Nativity scenes in "Chimes for Yahya" and

"Verse for Urania" dramatize a conviction that the part of his life governed by passion is finished, and a new age begun. By these lights he beseeches his new goddaughter—god-child, Child *of* God, Christmas Child, and the one child ever to be "his"—to let her mother

> help me to conceive
> That fixed, imaginary, starless pole
> Of the ecliptic which this one we steer by
> Circles, a notch each time the old bring golden
> Gifts to the newborn child, whose age begins. . . .
>
> Meanwhile, à propos of ages,
> Let this one of mine you usher in
> Bending still above your crib enthralled,
>
> Godchild, be lightly taken, life and limb,
> By rosy-fingered flexings as by flame.
> Who else would linger so, crooning your name,
> But second childhood.

Now passion's flames are banked; and, Aurora-like, the real baby announces the dawn of a day the poet thinks to pass taking life (and love) easy, as Yeats recommended. In "Chimes for Yahya" we learn that Merrill's "animal nature" was once a large sloppy dog, rambunctious, ecstatic, "off the leash at last/ Or out of the manger at least. . . ." The poem's other dog-in-the-manger is the centerpiece of that spoof on the Christmas crèche, in which Yahya's (possibly homosexual) male servant pretends to labor and give birth to"—*not* a wriggling white/ Puppy!" This puppy sexuality grows up to lead its master a merry chase, but it cannot romp forever.

> Times, too, it turned on me, or on another—
> Squawks, feathers—until the rolled-up *Times*
> Imposed obedience. Now by its own scale
> Older than I am, stodgy, apprehensive
> For all I know, of what must soon . . .
> Yet trustful, setting blurred sights on me still.

Finally, the tortuous sexual dream-imagery of "The Will," with its funereal ibis (latest, after swan and peacock, in Merrill's flock of phallic plumed serpents), dissolves at the poem's close into a wedding scene: a young couple exchanging vows somewhere in flower-fragrant sunshine.

Because he has largely succeeded in putting these wishes and fantasies—passion, youth, vows, children of his own—behind him, Merrill can stand aside without too much regret or bitterness now, blessing his goddaughter, her family, and the newlyweds, being touched and blessed by them. "Lost in Translation" and "Yánnina" cover between them all the common concerns of this group of five poems: love and family, time and memory, procreation, aging, and art.

2

"Lost in Translation" seems at first to be less about lostness or translation, in any of their senses, than about puzzles: those large pictures made up of many little pieces or clues, most of which mean nothing until the correct relationships between them have been discovered. As the poem will say, puzzle pieces are "Like incoherent faces in a crowd,/ Each with its scrap of highly colored/ Evidence the Law must piece together." The opening narrative evokes, in tight verse paragraphs and sure touches, a summer of Merrill's childhood, c.1935 (one of his marionettes plays "Gunmoll Jean"). He and his beloved governess, called Mademoiselle, pass quiet days in one another's company, days productively devoted to his care, education, and entertainment—to which end "the puzzle which keeps never coming" has been ordered from a shop in New York:

> A summer without parents is the puzzle,
> Or should be. But the boy, day after day,
> Writes in his Line-a-Day *No puzzle.*

Merrill explains in parentheses—he uses parentheses for all intrusions from the distant future—that "reading Valéry the other evening" had started him thinking about these days by a process of association that traveled from Valéry's poem "Palme," to a Rilke translation of it he seems to remember (each urging *patience* in one of the two languages he first learned from Mademoiselle), to Mademoiselle's coaxing *him* to wait patiently for the puzzle to come.

Already, three dozen lines into the poem, the first layer of detail and metaphor has been deftly laid in place. The card table waiting to receive the puzzle, "tense oasis of green felt," furnishes a life felt as a "Mirage arisen from time's trickling sands," and links with the reference to the Valéry poem about a palm tree in the desert: metaphor for days which, though they seem empty and valueless, "Have avid roots that delve/ To work deep in the waste." In Merrill's English:

> Patience and still patience,
> Patience beneath the blue!
> Each atom of the silence
> Knows what it ripens to.
> The happy shock will come:
> A dove alighting, some
> Gentlest nudge, the breeze,
> A woman's touch—before
> You know it, the downpour
> Has brought you to your knees.[1]

These very days of childhood, described here, will be more fruitful for good or ill than anyone suspects. The desert imagery all prefigures the puzzle's picture when it finally comes; and Mademoiselle's "watch that also waited/ Pinned to her heart, poor gold, throws up its hands—/ No puzzle!" connects her to the hourglass with its trickling desert sands, while the reference to her "French hopes, her German fears" foreshadows the translation metaphor. These linkages, the strongest element of Merrill's mature style, are everywhere, but so effortlessly made that one is at a loss, after reading one of these late poems for the first time, to account for its powerfully felt unity.

The interpolation about Rilke, almost murmured within parentheses, breaks the mood of static dailiness less than the arrival of the puzzle. Some of its "thousand hand-sawn,/ Sandal-scented pieces" are cut in shapes familiar to the inveterate doer of puzzles:

> Witch on broomstick, ostrich, hourglass,
> Even (surely not just in retrospect)
> An inchling, innocently branching palm.
> These can be put aside, made stories of

as Merrill has done in book after book: the Threatening Female; the most clownish Plumed Serpent (whose reaction to a dangerous view is to hide its eyes); Time. And we have seen the shadow-hurling Palm, "*a towering mother/ smooth as stone and thousandbreasted though/ her milk was watery scant so much for love,*" in "From the Cupola." The pieces are spread out and the work of putting them together scarcely begun, Mademoiselle doing borders as befits her (still secret) heritage, when the poem is broken into by a less gentle parenthetical aside from the future.

The poet has remembered an occasion when a medium performed a standard parlor trick: identifying an object in a closed box which everyone but the medium saw placed there. Merrill implies that he was present personally. His paraphrase of what the medium said about the hidden object grows darker and darker, the first difficult passage in a hitherto clear and charming tale:

> "But hidden here is a freak fragment
> Of a pattern complex in appearance only.
> What it seems to show is superficial
> Next to that long-term lamination
> Of hazard and craft, the karma that has

> Made it matter in the first place.
> Plywood. Piece of a puzzle." Applause
> Acknowledged by an opening of lids
> Upon the thing itself. A sudden dread—
> But to go back. All this lay years ahead.

The most common reaction of a reader is probably to skip this knotty bit and get back to the story. Words like "appearance" and "superficial," and "opening of lids"—of eye and box—"Upon the thing itself," followed by the sudden dread which can only be the poet's, are signals not to be missed by those who have followed Merrill's poetry from the first. But signals to what end? The puzzle piece of laminated plywood is treated like an emblem, but is very resistant to explication. No more than an ostrich has this poet chosen in the past to open his lids upon a dreaded view; but the list of nouns that give no purchase or traction defeats the wish to grasp firmly the sense of the sentence beginning "What it seems to show . . .," which—if understood—might help account for the dread. In effect, the lid stays closed upon this part of the story; we will have to come back to it.

The boy and Mademoiselle again begin to put the puzzle together, she working on the straight-edge pieces and he on those that will make up the picture's center. "By suppertime two ragged wooden clouds/ Have formed." Clouds on the horizon of this blue day? One shows "a Sheik with beard/ And flashing sword hilt"; in the other

> Most of a dark-eyed woman veiled in mauve
> Is being helped down from her camel (kneeling)
> By a small backward-looking slave or page-boy
> (Her son, thinks Mademoiselle mistakenly)
> Whose feet have not been found.

Merrill's father has appeared in his work in the guise of Eastern potentate often enough to be identified here once again as head of the quasi-family group assembling in the puzzle picture, still only half unpuzzled. As he and the woman are left to "gaze from cloud to cloud/ With marked if undecipherable feeling," the poem breaks again to show the boy (while Mademoiselle bathes) reading her letter to a curé in Alsace: "cette innocente mère,/ Ce pauvre enfant, que deviendront-ils?" This puzzle, like the other, is left incomplete, the feeling marked but undeciphered; what can she mean? What threat can be veiled in all this lazy summer pleasure? By this point the boy has become "I" explicitly, as he was implicitly all along; and, because the two preceding sections have awarded him no pronouns at all, the switch is unobtrusive.

The rest of this strophe retreats within parentheses again, as the grown-up poet tells us something he learned from Mademoiselle's nephew, long after these days of the "Fearful incuriosity of childhood": that she is French by marriage only; her mother was English, her father Prussian, a fact she told no one. Like a Faulkner character, Lucas Beauchamp or Charles Bon, Mademoiselle "With 1939 about to shake/ This world . . ./ To its foundations, kept, though signed in blood,/ Her peace a shameful secret to the end." In fact, it appears from material Merrill has published elsewhere that Mademoiselle's English parent was her *father;* the sexes have been switched, the better to make her situation parallel with that of the "pauvre enfant" in her charge, whose father, if anyone, was the powerful and cruel parent by her lights and his own. And it was the American Edmund Fanning (1769–1841; called "the Pathfinder of the Pacific") and not "the great explorer Speke," as the poem claims, who was her ancestor (what better name to associate with a governess engaged to teach languages, after all?). The poem tampers lightly with these facts to make its own point: that, like Mademoiselle, this child will be a "peace" signed in blood between warring parents.

"Schlaf wohl, chéri." Mademoiselle kisses him goodnight in

her two languages; the poem breaks—into Rubaiyyat quatrains which simulate a dream, but not a child's dream: vocabulary, diction, and content all are those of the sophisticated adult now openly translating the symbols of the puzzle into the emotional realities of the child's life, and translating those indecipherable feelings into verse:

> Kef easing Boredom, and iced syrups, thirst,
> In guessed-at glooms old wives who know the worst
> Outsweat that virile fiction of the New:
> "Insh'Allah, he will tire" "—or kill her first!" . . .
>
> While, thick as Thebes whose presently complete
> Gates close behind them, Houri and Afreet
> Both claim the Page. He wonders whom to serve,
> And what his duties are, and where his feet,
>
> And if we'll find, as some before us did,
> That piece of Distance deep in which lies hid
> Your tiny apex sugary with sun,
> Eternal Triangle, Great Pyramid!

The real puzzle revolves about these figures: temptress and demon; old wives resentful of the interloper; Eternal Triangle of parents and son; the custody battle for the Page—of writing, too—presented as though a whole set of troubling choices were his to make (who to be like? sympathize with? blame? choose?). The dream-sequence dissolves into another summer day and the finishing of the puzzle; and another break carries us and the two puzzle-doers back, into the accentuals dominating the narrative, and the dailiness now prickling everywhere with meaning behind its least detail. We watch "Mademoiselle sketching/ Costumes for a coming harem drama/ To star the goosegirl"—a marionette who also plays the destroyer Guinevere and Gunmoll Jean, and will stand in now for the New Wife. They dismantle the puzzle: "a populace/ Unstitched of its attachments rattles down," like so many coconuts from a desert palm, or so many relationships disentangled. "Power went to pieces as the witch/ Slithered easily from Virtue's gown." Pregnant lines! The story ends on this familiar note of ominousness beneath a superficial calm, and with a sense that now perhaps a meaning may be coaxed from that dense passage several pages back. What but the layered emotional truths of the parents' marriage as revealed in the "dream," or in the poem, could that "long-term lamination of hazard and craft" be, beside which the puzzle-picture— man, woman, boy—(or any piece of it) is superficial? Or: what could it be but the total meaning of the parents' absence, next to which the walks, lessons, marionettes, or puzzles of these summer days are superficial? Does Merrill believe that these deep truths are *simpler* than the "pattern complex in appearance only"? That "appearance," surfaces, are more complicated than deeper truths, the crystallized ice above the black water, sparkling appearances which the "Fearful incuriosity of childhood" instinctively dreads to question? Perhaps there is no knowing. Past a certain point, these intricate passages are not meant to be translated plainly—one way they allow art to imitate life.

The final section is long and needs to be read thoughtfully. Merrill is wrapping up his story here by meditating on how memory translates the personal past into the present, and how time itself translates objects and people as it bears them forward:

> Before the puzzle was boxed and readdressed
> To the puzzle shop in the mid-Sixties,
> Something tells me that one piece contrived
> To stay in the boy's pocket. How do I know?
> I know because so many later puzzles
> Had missing pieces—Maggie Teyte's high notes
> Gone at the war's end, end of the vogue for collies,
> A house torn down; and hadn't Mademoiselle
> Kept back her pitiful bit of truth as well?
> I've spent the last days, furthermore,
> Ransacking Athens for that translation of "Palme."

Has he imagined it? No; four lines are printed as this poem's epigraph, the ones about the seemingly empty days whose roots are drinking deep between the stones, like the summer days of his childhood when divorce was about to change his life forever. Thus nourished, what sort of tree can grow? Rilke's translation is the metaphor; Merrill remembers how much of the "sun-ripe original" French Rilke sacrificed "In order to render its under-lying sense./ . . ./ What Pains, what monolithic Truths/ Shadow stanza to stanza's symmetrical/ Rhyme-rutted pavement." The passage calls up "From the Cupola" again, its *"shadow that a royal palm hurled/ onto the sidewalk"* so violently. But now—French to German, sun to shadow, youth to age—"the warm Romance" cools down,

> The owlet umlaut peeps and hoots
> Above the open vowel. And after rain
> A deep reverberation fills with stars.
>
> Lost is it, buried? One more missing piece?
>
> But nothing's lost. Or else: all is translation
> And every bit of us is lost in it
> (Or found—I wander through the ruin of S
> Now and then, wondering at the peacefulness)
> And in that loss a self-effacing tree,
> Color of context, imperceptibly
> Rustling with its angel, turns the waste
> To shade and fiber, milk and memory.

Color of context: of people and events acted upon by others, pointless to blame or resent. We know who S is: a capital in the ruin, itself—be it noted—a place of cool Romance, like the Par-thenon by moonlight. But to assign identities to this self-effacing tree and its angel (who is also Valéry's) would be pointless. What matters is the serenity of the closure, drawing upon the Valéry poem for its image of how ordinary days rooted in wastes of desert draw up water to an imperceptible ripening, until the lightest touch—for instance, a casual reading of Valéry—dislodges a downpour of milky fruit: this time, this poem.

3

"Yánnina" is the most even-textured of the five narratives. Its whole tale is told in erratically rhyming eight-line stanzas, most of whose lines have five stresses (though some have six and some four, Merrill's way, frequently, of varying a basic pentameter scheme). Stanza by relaxed stanza the story unreels, the few shifts in time, place, and mode of discourse unobtrusively effected. A smooth flow suits the poem's deceptive drowsiness, though a lot is happening beneath the dreamy surface. Yánnina is a town in Turkey, where the ruler Ali Pasha (1741–1822) lived and died. Byron visited Ali there in 1809, Edward Lear described the place in 1848. Now a third poet has come to see it, and he can hardly keep his eyes open. Nor can anyone else. Tradesmen mentioned in the first stanza are "Somnambulists"; a magician's assistant fated to be sawed in two is napping; an old Turk at the water's edge has slept there "since, oh, 1913."

> And in the dark gray water sleeps
> One who said no to Ali. Kiosks all over town
> Sell that postcard, "Kyra Frossíni's Drown,"
> Showing her, eyeballs white as mothballs, trussed
> Beneath the bulging moon of Ali's lust.
> A devil (turban and moustache and sword)
> Chucks the pious matron overboard—
> Wait—Heaven help us—SPLASH!

> The torch smokes on the prow. Too late.
> (A picture deeply felt, if in technique slapdash.)
> Wherefore the Lion of Epirus, feared
> By Greek and Turk alike, tore his black beard
> When to barred casements rose the song

> Broken from bubbles rising all night long:
> "A ton of sugar pour, oh pour into the lake
> To sweeten it for poor, for poor Frossíni's sake."*

Frossíni may be sleeping still, but the reader now must cease to; and indeed, as if to compensate for the fact that so little "happens" in it, the language of the whole poem is consistently more lyrical, more compressed, and generally more difficult, than the language of "Lost in Translation."

Merrill's comically breezy description of what was after all an actual execution, a historical event, can be explained in part by the footnote—there are two in this poem—from William Plomer's *The Diamond of Jánnina:*

> *Time was kind to the reputation of this woman who had been unfaithful to her husband, vain, and grasping. She came to be regarded as a Christian martyr and even as an early heroine in the struggle for Greek independence. She has been celebrated in legend, in poetry, in popular songs and historical fiction, and surrounded with the glamour which so often attaches to women whose love affairs have been of an intense nature and have involved men of political or historical importance.

(One popular song is the one quoted, "A ton of sugar . . . ," translated more or less literally from a pamphlet—*Get to Know Yánnina*—that Merrill picked up in the town.) This piece of local color brings in two important themes: that of the faithless wife, and the more familiar one of time and memory—in this case, how historical fact is distorted by popular imagination on its way to becoming legend. According to Plomer, Frossíni had been sleeping with Ali's son Mukhtar, whose jealous wife set her father-in-law on a course of vengeance. But "For me, that 'popular view' is of unquestionably higher value than the 'facts' unearthed by Plomer," Merrill writes, extolling "the refreshment, the liberation of these truths founded on dream and instinct! *More of them!*" [2] The popular view is the mask worn by history; he is perfectly consistent to praise it.

Yánnina: Kira Frossíni's Drown

With the fifth stanza, the poem gently shifts. The poet addresses, for the first time, someone within the poem: a newly wakened traveling companion. Immediately the narration loses clarity, as if it had wandered out of the sun into a dimly lit passageway; from this point forward the reader will have to put much of the story together for himself. It seems that Frossíni's tale has a different import for the friend than for the poet. The former's response is represented by his choice of muddy, bitter coffee to drink, while the latter cheerfully quaffs brandy "with a fine/ White sandy bottom"—two versions of lake water, the brandy prefigured by the mythical Frossíni's song.

This difference established but unexplained, the poem shifts again as the two venture forth at twilight to see sights that seem freighted everywhere with private meaning. "Two paths that cross and cross" in a public garden trace the X of a signature, or kiss, or the unknown factor in an equation—trace it over and over, as people neurotically repeat the lessons of childhood "long after school." The garden's flowers are named, their blushes blending into an "unashamed/ Chorus out of *Ignoramus Rex:*/ 'What shall the heart learn, that already knows/ Its place by water and its time by sun?' " Ignorance seems to apply first to the provincial populace among the flowers; but behind that hovers something more personal, veiled hints of not being ashamed of the heart's fatal fealty to ignorance—in fact, a version of the oldest Merrill theme. Where is all this leading, and what does it have to do with Frossíni? No heart's passion is at evident issue here. Yet all around them marriageable girls are moving; and, to marry them,

> Look at those radiant young males.
> Their morning-glory nature neon blue
> Wilts here on the provincial vine. Where did it lead,
> The race, the radiance? To oblivion
> Dissembled by a sac of sparse black seed.

These young people, gaudy as the orthodox Greek peacocks of "The Thousand and Second Night" or Strato in his village, will come to nothing; their fresh early promise will be unfulfilled, their morning glory wilt by afternoon, despite the dissembling appearance of fruitfulness. And the morning glory, though beautiful, is a strangling weed. This appraisal of waste seems related to the bitterness of several stanzas back; what these tourists see is overlaid continually by the "meaning" of the feelings they carry with them. The dour mood is the companion's, but Merrill's own view is sympathetically affected. The shadow play they see next has no immediate relevance to their situation, but we can expect some metaphorical application to justify its inclusion soon in an increasingly meaning-burdened, increasingly mysterious, narrative.

Now, halfway along, the tale shifts to the future tense to tell what the two will see the following day: "The cottage tumbling down, where soldiers killed/ Ali." There, they will view a more skillful (and "historical") painting of Ali sleeping "In a dark lady's lap. Vassilikí," who presumably never said no. And now at last a light breaks:

> Your grimiest ragamuffin comes to want
> Two loves, two versions of the Feminine:
>
> One virginal and tense, brief as a bubble,
> One flesh and bone—gone up no less in smoke
> Where giant spits revolving try their rusty treble,
> Sheep's eyes pop, and death-wish ravens croak.

The two kinds of women, the virtuous and dark ladies, are the same as those so vividly described and theorized about by Leslie Fiedler in *Love and Death in the American Novel*. The theorizing here is presumably on the silent companion's account, and provides a glimmer of insight into the nature and source of his bitterness. "Bubble" is Frossíni's word; we know she is believed to be virtuous. Vassilikí must represent the other sort: a sexually compliant, somewhat maternal, but also rather Gothic and witchlike, smoked-flesh-and-bone, devouring or devourable woman (does she turn the spit or turn upon it?). The companion's problems have to do with women, then? Bubble is to smoke as brandy is to bitter, smoking coffee; "Grounds of our footnote infiltrate the treat,/ Mud-vile to your lips, crystal-sweet to mine!"—the footnote being Plomer's about Frossíni's translation from faithlessness to martyrdom by myth. The poet is clearly comfortable with this double character, able to dismiss her vain and grasping side as unimportant; his companion, it seems, cannot.

So far, the secret story has been all this companion's. That Merrill has a personal stake in it somewhere only now becomes apparent. After a smooth transition he mentions, with a casualness another footnote will belie, that

> Byron has visited. He likes
> The luxe, and overlooks the heads on pikes;
> Finds Ali "Very kind . . . indeed, a father . . ."*
>
> Funny, that is how I think of Ali.
> On the one hand, the power and the gory
> Details, pigeon-blood rages and retali-
> ations, gouts of fate that crust his story;
> And on the other, charm, the whimsically
> Meek brow, its motives all ab ulteriori,
> The flower-blue gaze twining to choke proportion,
> Having made one more pretty face's fortune.

The Jekyll-and-Hyde versions of his father match the two versions of the Feminine and—to carry through the theme of pairings—the Frossínis of history and myth, and the two companions with their different negative capabilities. In a Merrill poem, a pasha with two women would suggest the poet's father even were the identification not made aloud; but in this poem Merrill is as forthcoming about his father as he is reticent about his friend. This second asterisked footnote identifies Byron's words ("Letter to his mother, November 12, 1809"), then quotes Plomer again:

> "even allowing for Oriental effusiveness, it seems doubtful whether [Ali's] interest in Byron was exactly as paternal as he pretended, for a father does not give his son sweets twenty times a day and beg him to visit him at night. It is worth remarking that Ali was a judge of character and a connoisseur of beauty, whether male or female, and that the like of Byron, and Byron at twenty-one, is not often seen."

The quotation, like the scene in which child and gangster sleep in one another's arms, makes a clear statement of Merrill's feelings about his father. Since it cannot be free-standing in this tightly woven story, we must look for ways in which it parallels and reinforces other, probably less overt, feelings and acts. Ali is cast both as father and as would-be lover to Byron, traveling in Turkish Greece just after his love affair at Cambridge with the choirboy John Edleston was painfully concluded. That the poet might find himself assuming Ali's role toward his companion, under similar circumstances, is a possibility worth considering, particularly if some relationship of the companion's has been broken off (by faithlessness? shattering of an illusion?) after a promising beginning, like the "morning glory" of the young people in Yánnina. That this reading fits many particulars of the poem *proves* nothing, of course; Merrill has seen to it that the factual evidence is too slight to give any one version that fits the facts an edge over any other. In fact, random "fittings" of all sorts are everywhere. In *The Book of Ephraim* Merrill will offer the theory that "Somewhere a Father Figure shakes his rod/ At sons who have not sired a child." His own family's "race" has led, through him, to oblivion, as much as any provincial Turk's; his father's "flower-blue gaze twining to choke proportion" uner-

ringly links the poet and "those radiant young males" of Yánnina descended in some racial sense from Ali himself.

Back to the narrative present now, but only for a sentence
at a time; as the poem nears its end, Merrill's interpolations grow
longer and more insistent, with the urgency of his wish to persuade the friend that his unnamed sorrow need not cripple his
life forever. And something else is also being said, or alluded
to—at this point by the first of several references to age, to "This
or that old timer on his knees" at the monastery nearby, "Asking
the candlelight for skill to hold/ The figures flush against the
screen's mild glare." This "old timer" is at once a supplicating
monk (Father Time?), a shadow-play manipulator—and the poet,
who is himself paradoxically one of the figures being held, since
the play, which is to become the poem, is the one he and his
companion, two shadows, are acting now. And so to bed. "The
lights wink out along the lake./ Weeks later, in this study gone
opaque,/ They are relit. See through me. See me through." The
"study" is both a place to write and a piece of writing, "Yánnina": the story "gone opaque" with concealments felt to be essential. The lights come on in the study as he writes, and in the
poem as Yánnina is evoked on paper once again. This poem,
and all but one other in the group of five—"Verse for Urania"
and "The Will" especially—is partly about translating the experience lived into literature, recollecting it in tranquility, accounting for the attendant losses and gains.

For Merrill to say "See through me" to anyone for any reason—even, as here, in his mask of shadow-play puppet—is no
small event. The words are addressed to the friend; and into the
final three stanzas, which follow directly, he throws all his per-
suasive strength. The rhetoric is hard to follow, like other opaque
statements to the friend which hide as much as they communicate to us. What does come through, besides affection, tends to
confirm the guess that the companion, soon to part from *him*,

has probably parted company before this with someone else, and will now be living alone—not, the poet thinks, a good idea. What's needed is a change of attitude.

> That the last hour be learned again
> By riper selves, couldn't you doff this green
> Incorruptible, the might-have-been,
>
> And arm in arm with me dare the magician's tent?
> It's hung with asterisks.

So is the poem, itself a sort of magician's tent in which—as in this one they visit—deaths and rebirths are transacted, and the Sleeping Woman from Stanza One sawed skillfully in half:

> (Done by mirrors? Just one woman? Two? . . .)
>
> Then to a general exhalation heals
>
> Like anybody's life, bubble and smoke
> In afterthought, whose elements converge,
> Glory of windless mornings that the barge
> (Two barges, one reflected, a quicksilver joke)
> Kept scissoring and mending as it steered
> The old man outward and away,
> Amber mouthpiece of a narghilé
> Buried in his by then snow white beard.

Though every bit of what follows here should be taken as speculation, perhaps one coherent paraphrase of these final verses might be hazarded, using clues from the rest of this poem and from Merrill's other work.

Frossíni, in myth, is the "virginal and tense" Woman, the "incorruptible" one who said no to Ali and was drowned for her refusal. To *doff* is to take off or get rid of; what Merrill may be urging his friend to take off is a gloomy, disillusioned attitude toward "corrupt" womanhood, or a particular woman and his view of a relationship with her that might-have-been. In other words, he may need to get rid of his sea-greenness, the adamant idealism born of inexperience that believes one love should, and will, last forever. (According to Bergen Evans, Thomas Carlyle applied the epithet "seagreen Incorruptible" to Robespierre in *The French Revolution*, because of his "pallor and his uncompromising fanaticism.") Merrill's view as we know is that every green passion wilts and corrupts eventually, but that the proper approach—clinging single-mindedly to illusion, ignoring grimy reality—will keep it blooming longest. Just because a loved one leaves doesn't mean one should never try again, he seems to be implying—having had his share of trouble with his own advice. Still, to convince *him*, Merrill takes the friend to see how a woman sawn in two immediately "heals/ Like anybody's life. . . ." The convergence of the two versions of the Loved One symbolizes this healed life: bubble *and* smoke, in afterthought. What had seemed all bubble was smoke too all the time; but only afterwards need the smoke be thought of. One can choose *not* to be a grimy ragamuffin.

This reading leaves a few stray puzzle pieces unaccounted for, but makes a fairly plausible picture of the rest. The woman sawn in two provokes a wealth of interpretations: she might make sense as the Before and After sections of a life; as a heart broken and then healed by the same hand, Time's; as the Romantic and Realistic halves of a psyche; as the bubble and smoke of a life combined in art by memory; as the Total Woman (both versions complete in one); and on and on. Other pieces can more confidently be identified. The morning-glory image is turned about in "Glory of windless mornings"; the barge—and its afterthoughtful reflection—glides "outward and away," repeatedly shattering and reforming the images in the moving water just as the magician repeatedly cuts and heals the woman. If one thing does seem certain in all this uncertainty, it is the message that a life can be broken over and over by passion, and still be mended. And if the old man the barge *steers* away is Ali first of all, black beard (as painted on the "slapdash" postcard picture) turned "by then" to the snow white of passion spent and dead, he is also surely the poet himself—infertile, radiance wilted, yet somehow serene in his posture and gesture of renunciation and identified with his father at last. The narghilé he smokes, a water pipe, is the perfect emblem for the healing alchemy of Time the destroyer, whereby bubble and smoke converge, combining all the elements of experience—myth and reality, illusion and awful truth—into art, without giving pain ("Strato in Plaster"). As for Merrill, he is the mouthpiece of this exotic parable of healing, or else the poem is: an amber one, made to preserve and to last.

So much floundering guesswork, studded here and there with something firmer, is what comes of trying to interpret a poem at a level where, by the poem's own devising, no "correct" interpretation can be made. Nor "incorrect" one; asked in an interview about the underlying action in this poem, Merrill said:

> You mean it's implicit rather than presented as narrative? Yes. I'd wanted to let the scene, the succession of scenes, convey not meaning so much as a sense of it, a sense that something both is, and isn't, being said. I hoped that a reader's own experience would remind him that some things can go without saying. I was trying for an intimacy of tone, not of content. People are always asking, Was it real? Did it happen? . . . As if a yes-or-no answer would settle the question. Was it really Yánnina I went to? Was my companion real or imaginary? I can only say yes *and* no to questions like that.[3]

"Yánnina" survives its secrets because the touristy bits of its decorative outer structure work so well as simple narrative: Ali, Frossíni, Vassilikí, Byron's visit, the magician's trick, and the satisfactory structural placement of the "split" women—two Frossínis, two partners for Ali, two versions of the Feminine, two halves of the woman sawn in half—all mixed into a matrix of sights and local customs, presented in a delightful style, and leading to an obscurely moving conclusion. On a first reading one hardly notices the companion, and slides on past the more puzzling passages to another spot of sightseeing. The succession of scenes does, as Merrill intended, "convey the sense that something both is, and isn't, being said." The companion's difficulty, which careful readers will wonder about, is mirrored in the characters and details of these scenes, and can be partly inferred from them. But the complex dynamic between the travelers is deeply, deliberately submerged in private reference, and in parallels more obscure than those between the surface story and the friend's half-buried extra-poem situation; its nature cannot be known. And yet the emotion emanating from that shrouded inner core of privacy flows into every syllable and cell of the poem, which would be very much less tight and bright and entertaining were this not so.

4

"McKane's Falls" is notable both for its lyric excellence and for its inclusion of a metaphor Merrill has used elsewhere and will return to in *The Book of Ephraim*. There is more song than story to this, the sixth long poem from Part I, though it leads directly out of *Braving the Elements* and has a western setting where two "dirt-caked prospectors" pan for gold but only one turns up "In the casino mirrors of Cheyenne." A string of key words—"degenerate," "dirty-minded," "old sparkle"—belong to the emotional ambience of *Braving the Elements;* but the narrative content of the first sections matters less than a style whose puns and fresh clichés are wittier than ever before, a style that transforms "scentless violets" into "Senseless violence," calls currant berries "tiny redskins," and exclaims (in the voice of a creek tossing on the analyst's couch), "Doctor of locks and dams, the

delta's blinded,/ The mudfish grins, how do I reach the sea?"
Marvelous grinning mudfish! The old party line of "Yánnina"
notwithstanding, with *Divine Comedies* Merrill has begun to move
beyond his career-long commitment to the integrity of masks
and surfaces, of sparkling appearances. Urania's mother is
"Lovelier, I find, without make-up"; illusion is more appalling
than reality in "Chimes for Yahya" (where "Horrors twinkled
through the brain" at the "birth" of the white puppy to a
"mountain woman"), and when the woman is sawn in two by
the Yánnina magician. "McKane's Falls" marks the change another way.

In 1971 Merrill published a piece of nonfiction in *Prose*.
"Peru: The Landscape Game" lapses into couplets to describe an
"icy mountain stream" become a cataract: "The pounding in my
ears is after all/ Not so much terror as a WATERFALL/ Shaking
and shimmering till the blond/ Air has been atomized to diamond—" The waterfall puts Merrill in mind of "you whom I
am too old to love, yet love so intensely. No. From *within* intensity: a dry place, a niche behind the waterfall, yes."[4] *Divine
Comedies* expands this metaphor twice, first in the final section of
"McKane's Falls":

> Come live within me, said the waterfall.
> There is a chamber of black stone
> High and dry behind my stunning life.
> Stay here a year or two, a year or ten,
> Until you've heard it all,
> The inside story deafening but true.
>
> Or false—I'm not a fool.
> Moments of truth are moments only,
> Eyes burning on the brink of empty beds.
> The years wink past, the current changes course.
> Ruined by tin-pan blues
> The golden voice turns gravelly and hoarse.

> Now you've seen through me, sang the cataract,
> A fraying force, but unafraid,
> Plunge through my bath of plus and minus both,
> Acid and base,
> The mind that mirrors and the hands that act.
> Enter this inmost space . . .

"Now you've seen through me" is the same plea, almost the same words, as the one spoken in "Yánnina." *The Book of Ephraim* will take up again the image of a "brook that running slips into a shawl/ Of crystal noise—at last, the waterfall" behind which a character will find the skeleton of a young Pueblo Indian, "the dead self dressed in his own clothes." A dead young self within the rush of cool, sparkling water is a fit emblem for Merrill's view of his own sexual situation as the whole of *Divine Comedies* presents it (*The Book of Ephraim* will have a good deal more to say on the subject). The passion still troublesome in the early parts of "McKane's Falls" has weakened by "Verse for Urania," where Merrill mentions in passing that "A love I'd been taking nightly/ Readings of sets behind the foliage now;/[5] I wonder what will next rise from the sea—"

Had he known, nothing could have been better preparation for the expansions of his next major theme—the personal life projected upon or absorbed into a cosmic field—than the poems comprising the first part of this remarkable book. Full value has been given in "Yánnina," "Verse for Urania," "Chimes for Yahya," "Lost in Translation," even "The Will," to the sorts of love which transcend passion and outlast it. As a consequence, masks are insisted upon less. And, preoccupied as he is in all six poems with time's destructions, the Precession of the Equinoxes—a central subject and metaphor in "Verse for Urania"—helps keep the private mini-tragedy of human aging in perspective.

CHAPTER 8

The Changing Light at Sandover (Introduction)

> Then Sky alone is left, a hundred blue
> Fragments in revolution, with no clue
> To where a Niche will open. Quite a task,
> Putting together Heaven, yet we do.
> —"Lost in Translation"

> I have received from whom I do not know
> These letters. Show me, light, if they make sense.
> —"From the Cupola"

I

The Changing Light at Sandover is Merrill's grandest achievement. Into its more than five hundred pages has gone everything he knows about writing poetry, everything he believes about living among other people in the world, all his deepest-held values, fears, convictions, and prejudices, spread among passages of "revelation" spelled out on a Ouija board. Not everyone will wish, or know how, to approach that sort of book, and not everyone who approaches will feel welcome; the material takes getting used to. But many readers may well feel they have been waiting for this trilogy all their lives.

Beginning about 1955, when Merrill and his friend and lover David Jackson first moved to Stonington, they often diverted themselves with a Ouija board—a commercially manufactured one at first, later a larger one homemade from cardboard. A Ouija board, as described in *The Seraglio* (where Francis Tanning grew addicted to the use of one) is "a smooth wooden board on which had been printed the alphabet, the Arabic numerals, and the words YES and NO. At the top was the likeness of a female face, Oriental in spirit, lit from beneath: she peered down into a crystal ball wherein misty letters had materialized." The board is used to get in touch with the "spirit world"; the mortals below ask questions, the spirits reply by spelling out messages with a pointer on which each player allows the fingers of one hand to rest lightly. (Instead of the planchette that comes with a bought board, Merrill and Jackson preferred the handle of an inverted teacup.)

Some pairs of players, without consciously controlling the pointer, get very much livelier results than others do; and for a time JM and DJ (in the board's shorthand) made a regular parlor game of *their* extraordinary ability to summon the souls of the dead. Both the temporarily and permanently dead—for they were instructed in the rudiments of a cosmology whereby souls are reborn until advanced enough to embark upon the nine Stages of heavenly progression. The two grew ever more fascinated with the phenomenon; as to what it meant they remained in the dark. But the game had its disquieting, not to say sinister, aspects. Where in fact *were* these messages coming from? *Should* the whole affair have become so seductive that for a time DJ and JM found themselves living more within the spirit world than in their own? A poem in *The Country of a Thousand Years of Peace*, "Voices from the Other World" (written in 1955), describes how, finally, they began to call upon the spirits less often "Because, once looked at lit/ By the cold reflections of the dead . . ./ Our lives had never seemed more full, more real. . . ." But the board continued to play a background role in their lives, and eventually the substance of twenty years' irregular conversation with one favorite voice became the basis of "The Book of a Thousand and One Evenings Spent/ With David Jackson at the Ouija Board/ In Touch with Ephraim Our Familiar Spirit."

The Book of Ephraim appeared as the greater part of *Divine Comedies*, in 1976. *Mirabell* followed in 1978 and *Scripts for the Pageant* in 1980; these three Books, plus a Coda, make up the trilogy published in one volume in 1982 under the collective title *The Changing Light at Sandover*. *Ephraim* covers the decades between 1955 and 1974. The second and third Books and the Coda document another obsessive involvement with the board lasting roughly from June 1976 into late 1978, and need to be considered separately from *Ephraim* for several reasons. Not reasons of style: the entire trilogy displays the same wit, formal skills, economy, and lyric power as the very best of Merrill's previous work. Nor of overt theme: all were originally undertaken as a warning against nuclear disaster. But *Ephraim* was composed and published, in *Divine Comedies*, with no thought of anything to follow. In manner of composition it resembles the shorter narrative poems of that volume multiplied by ten or twelve. The varied experiences with the Ouija world have been thoroughly interpenetrated in *Ephraim* with the rich whole of the poet's life, and with the sea-changes of twenty years' unconscious ripening, to emerge in "timeskip and gadabout" form as a lengthier counterpart of "Lost in Translation" or "Chimes for Yahya." Time, and the material, had even allowed for a certain amount of manipulation and invention, improvements for the poem's sake on the literal truth.

Mirabell and *Scripts*, and the Coda, were composed very differently. A routine chat with the spirits, after Ephraim's book had been completed, was abruptly intruded upon one day by

dread powers bringing JM a daunting new assignment: "UN-
HEEDFUL ONE   3 OF YOUR YEARES MORE WE WANT   WE MUST
HAVE POEMS OF SCIENCE   THE WEORK FINISHT IS BUT A PRO-
LOGUE." Having impulsively accepted this charge, Merrill then
found himself obliged to give up enormous amounts of time—
his own and David Jackson's—to daily sessions of transcribing
dictation at the board, struggling to make sense of it, and later
tossing the messages lightly with details from his and DJ's ongoing lives as he drafted the POEMS OF SCIENCE he had been
commissioned to create. The result is that while *Ephraim* reads
like the rest of Merrill's work only more so, the other two Books
progress by fairly (*Mirabell*) or rigidly (*Scripts*) chronological
schemes to set forth material Merrill has not himself consciously
chosen: a bizarre creation myth involving, among other things,
Atlantan centaurs and huge radioactive bats which are at once
both "life-size" earthly creatures and subatomic particles; four
angels who conduct a seminar; and much gossip, often licen-
tious, about the famous dead.

   Though the assignment absorbs and enthralls the two mediums in time, Jackson initially reacts to it with fear and Merrill
with dismay ("Poems of *science?* Ugh."). The poet makes an effort, a successful one, to talk himself round:

> Not for nothing had the Impressionists
> Put subject-matter in its place, a mere
> Pretext for iridescent atmosphere.
> Why couldn't Science, in the long run, serve
> As well as one's uncleared lunch-table or
> *Mme X en Culotte de Matador?*

This is no new line of thought for Merrill, who had always liked
opera's emphasis on sound over sense, and that of French art
songs, and who quotes Andrew Marvell in *Scripts* (from Heaven)
as saying "THE LINE! LET IT RUN TAUT & FLEXIBLE/ BETWEEN
THE TWO POLES OF RHYTHM AND RHYME/ & WHAT YOU HANG

ON IT MAY BE AS DULL/ OR AS PROVOCATIVE AS LAUNDRY."
But the argument had always served *his* ends before—that is, he
could cite it when he wanted to safeguard a subject with lyrical
obscurity. Nowhere does *Mirabell* sound merely dutiful in the
writing, but parts—the bat's numerology, above all—are plainly
thrust upon a reluctant poet whose choice of material when
writing *Ephraim* had been free. And both *Mirabell* and *Scripts* tax
the mediums with doctrine that—at least at first—offends them:
the No Accident clause, the elitism clause, the prophecy of a
"thinning" to come. Two shades—W. H. Auden and Maria
Mitsotáki—are permitted to assist in their instruction, which
makes the project more appealing, and much of their resistance
eventually evaporates. Still, when Auden blandly urges Merrill
"ON WITH THE WORK! THRILLING FOR YOU JM," the younger
poet retorts:

> And maddening—it's all by someone else!
> In your voice, Wystan, or in Mirabell's.
> I want it mine, but cannot spare those twenty
> Years in a cool dark place that *Ephraim* took
> In order to be palatable wine.
> This book by contrast, immature, supine,
> Still kicks against its archetypal cradle . . .
>
> I'd set
> My whole heart, after *Ephraim*, on returning
> To private life, to my own words. Instead,
> Here I go again, a vehicle
> In this cosmic carpool. Mirabell once said
> He taps my word banks. I'd be happier
> If *I* were tapping them. Or thought I were.

But the case is easily overstated. While *Ephraim* has been
shaped at the center of Merrill's singular art and self in some
sense that the other two Books were not, these can hardly be
said to be *all* by someone else. The given subject matter determines the direction of the narrative; the daily transcriptions force

a structure upon it. But in and about these Lessons is ample room for Merrill to say how he feels about it all, to talk with David, pay calls, travel between Stonington and New York, Athens, California, and one way and another—shocked, alarmed, distressed, overjoyed, stimulated by what comes across the board—to reveal a great deal about his sense of the meanings of his life. Merrill has described "the way the material came" in an interview: "Not through flashes of insight, wordplay, trains of thought" in the ordinary manner of poetic composition (and, overall, of *Ephraim*), "More like what a friend, or stranger, might say over a telephone. DJ and I never knew until it had been spelled out letter by letter. What I felt about the material became a natural part of the poem, corresponding to those earlier poems written 'all by myself.' " [1]

It was expected that he edit the transcripts, recast the passages to be used into meters assigned to the various speakers, and polish the whole into something that would read smoothly. Sometimes this meant quite a lot of work, sometimes almost none; as DJ describes it:

> I was freer to enjoy the whole experience with the dictation than JM was. . . . great passages of it that I thought were just ravishingly beautiful, Jimmy was seeing as useless to the text, or a little too much of a good thing. And it must have been maddening for him to think that he couldn't, you know, improve upon something that was very nice; sometimes it already fitted into his syllabic scheme. [2]

But the sense of being driven to the task was unrelenting:

> They dictated it. All of the *Scripts*—it was very much a regimen. . . . We had to do it—it started in on this cycle talking about time and the series of moon cycles. We had to get this given amount done in them, and we had to come back at this given moment. They were precise about their schedules, as they were about when the poem would be finished, when it would be published, everything. [3]

Merrill's own sense of how he "Quarried murky blocks/ Of revelation" from the transcripts to build the second Book is described early in the third:

> *Mirabell*—by now more Tower of Babel
>
> Than Pyramid—groans upward, step by step.
> I think to make each Book's first word its number
> In a different language
> (Five is *go* in Japanese), then stop
>
> Sickened by these blunt stabs at "design."
> Another morning, Michael's very sun
> Glows from within the section
> I polish, whose deep grain is one with mine.

Of the three Books, *Mirabell* seems in one way to have been the most difficult to write. As the poet has described it:

> With "Ephraim," many of the transcripts I had made from Ouija board sessions had vanished, or hadn't been saved. So I mainly used whatever came to hand, except for the high points which I'd copied out over the years into a special notebook. Those years—time itself—did my winnowing for me. With *Mirabell* it was, to put it mildly, harder. The transcript was enormous. What you see in the poem might be half, or two-fifths, of the original. Most of the cuts were repetitions: things said a second or third time, in new ways often, to make sure we'd understood. Or further, unnecessary illustrations of a point. . . .
>
> With *Scripts*, there was no shaping to be done. Except for the minutest changes, and deciding about line-breaks and so forth, the Lessons you see on the page appear just as we took them down. The doggerel at the fêtes, everything. In between the Lessons—our chats with Wystan or Robert [Morse] or Uni [the trilogy's resident unicorn]—I still felt free to pick and choose; but even there, the design of the book just swept me along.[4]

Increasingly the great labor grew compatible, even joyous, till Merrill could acknowledge that while writing *Scripts* "I woke up day after day beaming with anticipation."[5]

Though he recoiled from the word, so mammoth a poem could not be managed without "design." The Ouija board itself provided the basic frame of each Book: one section for every letter of the alphabet in *Ephraim*, which covers a calendar year; one (with decimal subdivisions) for each number from 0 to 9 in the book of number-happy Mirabell; and a set of Lessons for the three major divisions—YES (ten), & (five), and NO (ten)—of *Scripts*, a fit scheme for that monument to ambiguity, corresponding to the plot's electric plusses and minuses, Whites and Blacks. A proliferation of voices from the Other World made further device imperative if the work were not to become hopelessly confusing. Merrill solved the principal problem (with help from WHA) in *Mirabell* 7.9: rough pentameter, "our virtual birthright," for the human characters living and dead; and for the bats, who think in fourteens, "WHY NOT MY BOY SYLLABICS? LET THE CASE/ REPRESENT A FALL FROM METRICAL GRACE." Five stresses by fourteen syllables, of course, borrows from the internal yardstick of the dyed-in-the-wool sonneteer. In *Scripts* a unicorn/centaur speaks a fair imitation of four-stress Anglo-Saxon alliterative meter. Greater powers—God, Nature, the angels—are bound to no metrical pattern and never use rhyme (apart from certain ceremonial occasions, and from Archangel Michael's clumsy couplet-making). Nor do the bats rhyme; but the humans often fall into couplets or stanzas as if for comfort. Tag phrases distingush the many upper-case human voices from one another: "MY BOYS" or "MY DEARS" for Auden, "MES ENFANTS" for Maria, "MES CHERS" for Ephraim, "LADS" (and baby talk) for Robert Morse, only George Cotzias calls DJ "DAVE," and so on. The variations of the effortlessly coalescing and dissolving lyric passages are too numerous to list; and if the middle distance of *Mirabell* does sometimes display what Helen Vendler tolerantly calls "a sheer willingness to bore,"[6] the verse of the trilogy's hundreds of pages consistently outdazzles everything critics can think to say about it.

2

As the foregoing should make clear, *Mirabell* and *Scripts* are the unforged record of a lived experience; for the nature of their "revelation" Merrill cannot, in the ordinary sense, be held accountable. By the terms of his commission he may—indeed must—paraphrase, condense, question, even criticize, as well as change prose to poetry. But he is not to decide which ideas to keep and which to exclude: is not to censor, embellish, nor in any way distort the *sense* of the revealed text. Thus restricted, he can take no more responsibility for its nature than John Constable could for the concepts of *cow* or *hundred-year-old oak* when he set out to paint the landscapes of East Anglia. Actually, the material revealed was such as to plague JM with skepticism (and DJ with fear) through much of the work. The first transcriptions strike them respectively as preposterous and terrifying; their harmless parlor game has changed character so drastically, in fact, that the question of *belief*—easily shrugged off in *Ephraim*—now reasserts itself again and again. To Auden's rhapsodizing in *Mirabell* 2, Merrill replies in exasperated couplets:

> Dear Wystan, VERY BEAUTIFUL all this
> Warmed-up Milton, Dante, Genesis?
> This great tradition that has come to grief
> In volumes by Blavatsky and Gurdjieff?
> Von and Torro in their Star Trek capes,
> Atlantis, UFO's, God's chosen apes—?
> Nobody could transfigure stuff like that
> Without first turning down the rheostat
> To Allegory, in whose gloom the whole
> Horror of Popthink fastens on the soul,
> Harder to scrape off than bubblegum. . . .
> *I* say we very much don't merit these
> Unverifiable epiphanies.

As the experience continues, appalling and ravishing him by turns, Merrill's doubts trouble him less and less, and near the end of *Scripts* his assent has become all but total:

Beneath my incredulity
   All at once is flowing
Joy, the flash of the unbaited hook—
Yes, yes, it fits, it's right, it had to be!
Intuition weightless and ongoing
   Like stanzas in a book
Or golden scales in the melodic brook—

Readers, of course, may more easily believe in Merrill's riveting experience than in the divine authenticity of its source, or the truth of its prophecy. "For me," Merrill has said himself (of *Mirabell*), "the talk and the tone—along with the elements of plot—are the candy coating. The pill itself"—the poem's apocalyptic message, its insistence on determinism and elitism—"is another matter. The reader who can't swallow it has my full sympathy. I've choked on it again and again."[7] His own sense, illustrated by the quotation, of his role of Poet as distinct from his role of Scribe is a distinction readers should bear in mind. Thinking of the two roles as Mind Conscious and Unconscious is one very workable way of reading the poem—as if all of *The Changing Light at Sandover* were an inexhaustibly elaborate dialogue between Merrill's waking intelligence and its own unconscious sources of feeling, myth, and dream, with David Jackson as essential catalyst (and supplemental unconscious story-trove).

DJ himself reports that, to the engrossed mediums, "Whether all that dictation came out of our collective subconscious or not finally became less and less of real interest. Rather as if a flying saucer were to land on one's front lawn, would one ask, 'Where's it *from?*' as one's first question?"[8] Readers unable or unwilling to fight clear of this question of source, or the related one "What does it mean?" risk spoiling their initial plunge into the trilogy's elemental weirdness—needlessly, because its Message and its meaning are not the same. Large tracts of Message—Mirabell's mathematical formulas, kernels of concept that refuse to crack, Lessons that often seem pure pretext for extravagant spectacle, parts of the System no sooner grasped at last than made pointless by revision—will certainly frustrate an approach to the poem which is too doggedly literal. *The Changing Light at Sandover* is, and expects to be read as, an immensely complex Overmetaphor packed more tightly with lesser metaphors within metaphors than a plutonium atom is with atomic particles. It's best to assume that what doesn't seem to make literal sense right away makes dramatic or metaphorical sense, or none that matters intellectually. "MAKE SENSE OF IT" Merrill is told and told in *Scripts;* but why should the sense wanted be merely verbal? As Vendler has noted, "Merrill's primary intuition is that of the absolute ravishment of the senses"[9]—those senses restored to the dead souls only at the highest heavenly Stage, and (in "YES" Lesson 7) identified one by one with the very angels. Musical and visual sense is the sort to look for in a baffling passage, like seeing a very fine operatic adaptation of *Dracula* sung in a foreign language.

Many years ago, Merrill wrote in "To a Butterfly," "Goodness, how tired one grows/ Just looking through a prism:/ Allegory, symbolism./ I've tried, Lord knows,// To keep from seeing double. . . ." Now in *Mirabell* he addresses the radioactive bats intemperately:

> How should you speak? Speak without metaphor.
> Help me to drown the double-entry book
> I've kept these fifty years. You want from me
> Science at last, instead of tapestry—
> Then tell round what brass tacks the old silk frays.
> Stop trying to have everything both ways.
> It's too much to be batwing angels *and*
> Inside the atom, don't you understand?

But truly the bats can speak no other way; "we get an effect of engines being/ Gunned in frustration, blasts of sheer exhaust." (This passage is one of those exceptionally easy to read as an argument between conscious Poet, who thinks he ought not to depend so heavily on metaphor, and unconscious Scribe, who knows himself unalterably addicted to it.) Only toward the end of *Scripts* does Merrill gratefully allow Auden to persuade him that metaphor-making can itself be a form of freedom, that (as WHA has already asserted, late in *Mirabell*) "FACT IS IS IS FABLE":

> But if it's all a fable
> Involving, oh, the stable and unstable
> Particles, mustn't we at last wipe clean
> The blackboard of these creatures and their talk,
> To render in a hieroglyph of chalk
> The formulas they stood for? U MY BOY
> ARE THE SCRIBE   YET WHY? WHY MAKE A JOYLESS THING
> OF IT THROUGH SUCH REDUCTIVE REASONING?
> ONCE HAVING TURNED A FLITTING SHAPE OF BLACK
> TO MIRABELL, WD YOU MAKE TIME FLOW BACK?
> SUBTRACT FROM HIS OBSESSION WITH 14
> THE SHINING/DIMMING PHASES OF OUR QUEEN?
> CONDEMN POOR UNI TO THE CYCLOTRON
> AFTER THE GREENS U'VE LET HIM GALLOP ON?
> Dear Wystan, thank you for reminding me
> The rock I'm chained to is a cloud; I'm free.

Like the elements of the sonnet form, metaphor is in Merrill's marrowbone. And to speak of it thus returns us full circle to the perceptions that took shape in his Amherst honors thesis and in *First Poems:* that earliest perception of metaphor as ice, sheeting the black abyss, making pain bearable, and of the thin blue eggshell of appearance with the tiny dead claw broken through. From that cracked robin's egg to "THE WHOLE FRAIL EGGSHELL" of the Earth "SIMPLY IMPLODING AS THE MONITOR'S/ BLACK FILLS THE VACUUM MOTHER N ABHORS" is but a step thirty years in length.

When it appeared as part of *Divine Comedies, The Book of Ephraim* had seemed about ready to put masks by, as if Merrill at last had found a way to make his peace symbolically with *this* world's reality by forswearing the spirit world for good. But Poet has a way of insisting on resolutions to which Scribe has not assented. The oedipal fire supposedly extinguished by Francis Tanning in *The Seraglio* blazed on, and metaphor has cheerfully persisted in doubling Merrill's vision despite the wish voiced twenty years before *Mirabell* in "To a Butterfly." And now, with the publication of *From the First Nine* and *The Changing Light at Sandover*, in two volumes, the import of *Ephraim* has been shifted; we are directed to consider it not as the last and most complex work along one line of development but as the first and simplest on another. It is, of course, both—and ought rightly to be printed last in the first volume as well as first in the second.

Renounce the Other World, spiritual metaphor and twin of this "one we feel is ours, and call the real . . ."? Strip the real world, never so loved as now, of her thin gold mask at last? Not if the Powers that decide such matters have anything to say about it—and in fact They have found all this to say.

3

And so the old themes whose conflicts *Divine Comedies* had seemed to resolve burst forth again, their vigor all restored, in *Mirabell* and *Scripts for the Pageant*. Literally, those resolutions were true enough. But some of the themes had shaped Merrill's outlook in profound psychological ways all his life, just as they had been shaped *by* his life. They are evidently not to be cast off merely because their actualizing source in life is neutralized. Now, though, the scale is grander and the mode transcendent, for none of them—masking and illusion, passion and sexuality, parents, aging, childlessness—need be life-size or earthbound any longer.

The spirits continually reaffirm that there are no appearances in Heaven; they can see JM and DJ in mirrors, and whatever their mortal "representatives" see, but never one another. The meaning of *mask* in such a realm cannot be literal, yet masking of many kinds, and the pretense of sparkling appearances, are perpetual; should this trilogy ever be adapted for the stage with skill it should play splendidly, but the costume budget would need to be generous beyond dreams. The whole poem is constructed of deceptions-for-a-purpose, successively unveiled as the mediums become able to tolerate what they will hear. Often the purpose is dramatic: quarrels between angels, rehearsed and staged to drive the Lesson home, or two characters finally revealed to be one and the same. Heavenly doctrine gets revised like drafts of a poem; Ephraim makes mistakes corrected by Mirabell, who must be corrected in his turn. The numerous pageants, fêtes, and masques overlay the revelation of "the Black" with imaginary spectacle as the schematic order of instruction overlays the revelation of Chaos—gilt or ice above the void. And much about Heaven remains permanently hidden, unfathomable.

But no secrecy now obtains between these mediums and us; and the sense of their shared life realized here forms a powerful chemical bond between reader and poem, tiding us over the "stretches of flats in the exposition of the mythology."[10] JM and DJ began together as lovers, and the "FORTUNATE CONJUNCTION" (as Ephraim calls their partnership) has withstood the stresses of Athens and Santa Fe. Passion was the keynote of Merrill's life and of his art when he and DJ first got through to Ephraim, or he to them, and continued to be its keynote for another twenty years. But, by the mid-seventies, radical social changes had affected that part of his life at the same time it was being reclaimed by trustier, less violent loves. *The Book of Ephraim* makes abundantly clear that their familiar shares, and rejoices in, his mediums' homosexuality. No more now of that sickness of self felt in "After the Fire"; nothing of the obsessive "dirt-caked" and "dirty-minded" talk New Mexico had produced. Strato himself is vividly evoked in *Ephraim*, in terms that recall that "animal nature" passage of "Chimes for Yahya":

> Strato squats within the brilliant zero,
> Craning at his bare shoulder where a spot
> Burns "like fire" invisible to me.
> Thinking what? he studies his fair skin
> So smooth, so hairless. . . .
>
>   Strato's qualities
> All are virtues back in '64.
> Humor that breaks into an easy lope
> Of evasion my two poor legs cannot hope
> To keep up with. Devotion absolute
> Moments on end, till some besetting itch
> Galvanizes him, or a stray bitch.
> (This being seldom in my line to feel,
> I most love those for whom the world is real.)
> Shine of light green eyes, enthusiasm
> Panting and warm across the kindly chasm.
> Also, when I claim a right not written
> Into our bond, that bristling snap of fear. . . .

Some of the funniest lines in *Mirabell* are "spoken" by Auden's widow Chester Kallman, who complains about how Auden treats him in Heaven, about a fickle heavenly lover, about the life in Johannesburg into which he is about to be reborn—all in a style suggesting that the subject of homosexuality and the gay world, off the leash at last, went slightly mad with unconfinement:

>   But you're coming back,
> It's too exciting!   PLEASE   TO SEE MY BLACK
> FACE IN A GLASS DARKLY? I WONT BE
> WHITE   WONT BE A POET   WONT BE QUEER
> CAN U CONCEIVE OF LIFE WITHOUT THOSE 3???

Well, frankly, yes. THE MORE FOOL U MY DEAR
You shock us, Chester. After months of idle,
Useless isolation—   ALL I HEAR
ARE THESE B MINOR HYMNS TO USEFULNESS:
LITTLE MISS BONAMI OOH SO GLAD
TO FIND ARCADIA IN A BRILLO PAD!
LAUGH CLONE LAUGH   AH LIFE   I FEEL THE LASH
OF THE NEW MASTER   NOTHING NOW BUT CRASH
COURSES   What does Wystan say? TO PLATO?
HAVING DROPPED ME LIKE A HOT   O SHIT
WHAT GOOD IS RHYME NOW

Extended passages like this one enliven *Mirabell* and *Scripts*, and
the trilogy is liberally salted throughout with witty camp chit-
chat. Willing at last to exploit this source, Merrill has drawn
upon it with a free hand.

But the subject of proclivity is not only a rich new well-
spring of comedy; the long-stoppered avowal will swell and swell,
and grant a still more deeply seated wish. "Why," wonders DJ
early in the *Mirabell* Lessons, "did They choose *us?*/ Are we
more usable than Yeats or Hugo,/ Doters on women . . .?" An
explanation ensues:

LOVE OF ONE MAN FOR ANOTHER OR LOVE BETWEEN WOMEN
IS A NEW DEVELOPMENT OF THE PAST 4000 YEARS
ENCOURAGING SUCH MIND VALUES AS PRODUCE THE BLOSSOMS
OF POETRY & MUSIC, THOSE 2 PRINCIPAL LIGHTS OF
GOD BIOLOGY. LESSER ARTS NEEDED NO EXEGETES:
ARCHITECTURE   SCULPTURE   THE MOSAICS & PAINTINGS THAT
FLOWERED IN GREECE & PERSIA CELEBRATED THE BODY.
POETRY   MUSIC   SONG INDWELL & CELEBRATE THE MIND . . .
HEART IF U WILL. . . .

NOW MIND IN ITS PURE FORM IS A NONSEXUAL PASSION
OR A UNISEXUAL ONE PRODUCING ONLY LIGHT.
FEW PAINTERS OR SCULPTORS CAN ENTER THIS LIFE OF THE MIND.
THEY (LIKE ALL SO-CALLED NORMAL LOVERS) MUST PRODUCE AT LAST
BODIES   THEY DO NOT EXIST FOR ANY OTHER PURPOSE

"Come now," the mediums demur, "admit that certain very great/ Poets and musicians have been straight." Self-despising homosexual behavior was displaced onto Panayioti in "After the Fire" and onto the Enfant Chic in *The (Diblos) Notebook;* in like manner this unblushing speech issues from Mirabell's mouth—or beak; Mirabell has turned, the instant before he makes it, from a bat named 741 into a peacock, in a kind of coming-out party of his own. The doctrine of homosexuals as evolution's crème-de-la-crème transforms the childlessness that once grieved JM into a trade-off beneficial, even essential, to his poetry. It also accounts for the gay-subculture ambience created in this poem by so much camp talk, and makes sense of a circumstance which would otherwise seem decidedly peculiar: that once they reach the formal-lesson stage, nearly all the poem's significant characters are male and gay. (The one who appears to be neither will ultimately reveal herself as both.) Two straight men added to the cast of *Scripts* are friends who died with *Mirabell* half-written and the "YES" dictations of *Scripts* completed; the poem fits them to a scheme whose shape is already fixed. Which cannot prevent JM from feeling, as he knows his readers must, that

> A sense comes late in life of too much death,
> Of standing wordless, with head bowed beneath
>
> The buffeting of losses which we see
> At once, no matter how reluctantly,
>
> As gains. Gains to the work. Ill-gotten gains . . .
>
> Well, Robert, we'll make room. Your elegy
> Can go in *Mirabell*, Book 8, to be
> Written during the hot weeks ahead;
> Its only fiction, that you're not yet dead.

The dead souls most important to the entire poem are two: W. H. Auden, and Maria Mitsotáki, an Athens friend who was the subject of a *Fire Screen* poem, "Words for Maria." JM's peace with his own mother has been ratified. His father died in 1956. The death of DJ's aged parents is the first major event of *Mirabell*; indeed, these impending deaths are what send them back to the Ouija board after an absence of more than a year ("As things were,/ Where else to look for sense, comfort, and wit?"). Helen Vendler, wise in this as in much else, writes:

> In the usual biological cycle, parents die after their children have become parents; the internalizing of the parental role, it is believed, enables the parents to be absorbed into the filial psyche. In the childless world of *Mirabell*, the disappearance of parents, or parental friends, is the disappearance of the parental and therefore of the filial; JM and DJ can no longer be "boys" but must put on the mortality of the survivor.[11]

Both childless like the mediums in (this) life, WHA and MM make idealized parent-figures, their two-sided humanity masked beyond the kindly chasm of death. As Merrill has said in an interview, "In life, there are no perfect affections. . . . Yet, once dead, overnight the shrewish wife becomes 'a saint,' frustrations vanish at cockcrow, and from the once fallible human mouth come words of blessed reassurance. . . . Given the power . . . would I bring any of these figures back to earth?"[12] Vendler amplifies: Auden and Maria "are the people who call JM and DJ 'MES ENFANTS' (Maria, known as 'Maman') or 'MY BOYS' (Auden). When these voices fall silent, there will be no one to whom the poet is a child."[13] A (twinned) only child: Maria, we learn in *Mirabell*, "Was hailed on arrival by "HORDES OF PO-LYGLOT/ SELFSTYLED ENFANTS . . . BUT NOW A DECENT/ VEIL IS DRAWN & I HAVE NONE BUT U."

These voices, even these, fall silent at poem's end—but only after the parents' and children's love has been perfected, like that of Dante and Beatrice, by its three-year ceremony of guidance, enlightenment, and farewell. Beyond this silence gleams the tantalizing hope of a rendezvous with Maria in 1991, Bombay, The World. And as the surrogate parents move inexorably toward their departures, behind them grow and fill out the personified figures of Mother Nature and God/Sultan Biology: all-powerful and capriciously destructive, even murderous, on the one hand, heartbreakingly loveable on the other, like parents as perceived by small children. By the terms of the myth, their "divorce" would destroy their third, last, human child and his green world; and the poet, struck by parallels between the broken home he grew up in and the present situation of all humanity, angry and afraid as no child of divorced parents is ever too old to be, evokes himself when young once more. "Between an often absent or abstracted/ (In mid-depression) father and still young/ Mother's wronged air of commonsense the child sat," he writes, and goes on to build the metaphor, cosmic by domestic detail, which will culminate in Earth-shattering divorce. "*That* was the summer my par—YR PARALLELS/ DIVERGE PRECISELY HERE," insists Maria. "HUSH ENFANT   FOR NO MAN'S MIND CAN REACH/ BEYOND THAT HIM & HER   THEIR SEPARATION/ REMAINS UNTHINKABLE." JM, if not entirely convinced, is convinced at least that Maria is right to stop this probing, terrifying line of thought. "Barbarity," he agrees, pulling himself together, "To serve uncooked one's bloody tranche de vie . . ./ Later, if the hero couldn't smile,/ Reader and author could; one called it style." Or called it metaphor, ever and always at work to make any new form of the oldest, most chronic pain bearable.

4

The *Prophetic Books* of William Blake and the *Vision* of Yeats come tentatively to mind when one considers all this, for *The Changing Light at Sandover* is a masterwork of great eccentricity. Unlike Dante's *Comedy* or *Paradise Lost*, those other major poems which purport to address man's role in the universal scheme, the value "system" given poetic expression here is not shared by an entire culture. Unlike them, it is not a morality tale. It substitutes yes-and-no ambiguities for moral absolutes. Sin is equated with the giving *and receiving* of pain, evil and good recognized on the cosmic level alone, outside the power of individual human beings (in a wholly deterministic universe) to choose, or to enact unless "cloned" to do so. Personal salvation then cannot be at issue; the issue is global survival. The poem accounts for the chief obstacles to survival—overpopulation and nuclear holocaust—in original ways, but does not propose, in the manner of science fiction, original ways of implementing the obvious solutions. Certain virtues—kindness, courtesy, devotion, affection, modesty, tolerance, tact, patience, plus intelligence, talent, and wit—are celebrated, many of these broadly shared with western religions; yet the values they embody are, lacking spiritual principles to back them up, social rather than spiritual values. ("LANGUAGE," says WHA, "IS THE POET'S CHURCH.") Neither deep religious sensibility, nor political savvy, nor philosophical inquiringness are at work in Merrill's poem, setting it off sharply in tone from Dante's and from Milton's.

The chief difficulty in viewing the trilogy as *western* religious myth is its insistence that innate class, on Earth as in Heaven, determines who can take steps to prevent the world from blowing up. Only elect "Lab souls" of sufficient "densities," preprogrammed or *cloned* in Heaven between lives, can do God's work on Earth to build an earthly Paradise; only they will read this poem's Message with comprehension:

A MERE 2 MILLION CLONED SOULS LISTEN TO EACH OTHER WHILE
OUTSIDE THEY HOWL & PRANCE SO RECENTLY OUT OF THE TREES.
& SO FOR U THE HARDEST RULE: THE RULE OF THE RULERS.
POLITICIANS HAVE LED MAN DOWN A ROAD WHERE HE BELIEVES
ALL IS FOR ALL   THIS IS THE FOOL'S PARADISE   ALL WILL BE
FOR ALL ONLY WHEN ALL IS UNDERSTOOD.

The absolute amount of "human soul densities" is finite, and has had to be pieced out in recent history with "animal densities" of dog and rat to cope with the glut of children. Holocaust is a present danger precisely because power has fallen into the hands of leaders with a high proportion of animal soul densities—"Rat souls"—who too easily lose control of their high-spirited but destructive impulses. And lately, therefore, accidents—slippages in the works—have infiltrated the realm of NO ACCIDENT. To restore balance, save the earth from utter destruction, and bring Paradise upon it, a thinning of the population is essential.

If the positive and negative charge within the atom is a metaphor for this global drama, the drama is in turn a metaphor for something vaster. The cosmic conflict of Good, or White, forces represented by God Biology—Earth is, so to speak, his representative, he Earth's patron, in a Galactic Pantheon—are at war with horrific forces called simply "the Black" (as in black holes), whose nature is utter nothingness: "The Black beyond black, past that eerie Wall—/ PAST MATTER   BLACK OF THOUGHT UNTHINKABLE," elsewhere defined as "ATOMIC BLACK/ COMPRESSED FROM TIME'S REVERSIBILITY," a phrase which resists conceptualization. Michael identifies it "IN MAN'S LIFE" with "THE DULLWITTED, THE MOB, THE IDIOT IN POWER, THE PURELY BLANK OF MIND"; perhaps these make time flow backward by reversing the evolutionary ascent of life through time toward the development of an ever larger, more convoluted brain. On his second visit Michael had stated resoundingly, "INTELLIGENCE, THAT IS THE SOURCE OF LIGHT. FEAR NOTHING WHEN YOU STAND IN IT." It follows that when the idiot rules you stand in darkness, and are afraid.

"Time's reversibility" remains a conundrum; but forward-flowing time is easy to see as Black in the context of Merrill's earlier work. "Why should Time be black?" he asks, having answered his own question through thirty years of poems wherein Time is the agent of aging, and of steadily diminishing beauty and passional capacity, and the destroyer of kindly masks and illusions. When Paradise comes upon Earth "THEN TIME WILL STOP": man will be immortal.

The poem's cryptic Message, however, is not identical with its meaning, as readers with any density of soul at all can see. Part of its meaning is its wit and style. The rest lies where the most meaning has always lain in Merrill's work: in the loves between human characters in life and beyond death, and in their losses; and especially in the evocation of twenty-five domestic years with David Jackson, which Thom Gunn has called "the most convincing description I know of a gay marriage":

> The men's life together is presented to us in detail which is al-
> most casual: we see them choosing wallpaper, keeping house,
> traveling, entertaining, and above all sitting at the Ouija board.
> It is not a minor triumph and it is not an incidental one because,
> after all, it is the two of them in their closeness who have evoked
> the whole spirit world of *Ephraim* and *Mirabell* [and *Scripts*], or
> perhaps even created it.[14]

Those "genre" glimpses of JM and DJ watering on the terrace, discussing the sense of a knotty transcript, going about their days together while *not* collaborating across the Board, are the most affecting, most authentic part of the entire story unstifled here, and the most human. *Have* they created the Other World, in its infinite richness and strangeness, between them? *The Book of Ephraim* includes an explanation suggested by JM's former psychiatrist: "what you and David do/ We call folie à deux"—a way of talking to one another from behind the mask of the Ouija board. The ex-shrink leads his ex-patient to speculate that Ephraim is an imaginary offspring produced in lieu of a real one to satisfy the biological urge to procreate, seeing that "Some-where a Father Figure shakes his rod/ At sons who have not sired a child." The explanation tidily foreshadows Mirabell's: homosexuals, being poorly suited to make children, are well-suited therefore to make poetry. *Ephraim*—and all that follows where he led—*makes sense* as the child of JM's and DJ's love and pro/creativity, conceived through their union at the Ouija board.

"Jung says—or if he doesn't, all but does—/That God and the Unconscious are one," we read in *Ephraim*, Section U. To theorize that in *The Changing Light at Sandover* two unconsciouses, linked skillfully by long practice, have played God by creating a cosmic vision still leaves a great deal unexplained. How, for instance, did DJ and JM know that Nabokov was dead—news that reached them first via the Board? More centrally, what is it these two do that others fail to do, which yields such astonishing results? When we leave JM at the close of the Coda, nervously preparing to read the completed trilogy to the heavenly host assembled (one auditor per letter of the alphabet), his situation is both so familiar in its Proustian stance and thematic preoccupations, and so outré in its total concept, as to baffle and defy any simple explanation. Even if the two did make all of it up unconsciously, an experience has befallen them scarcely less amazing and wonderful than if, like the prophets of old, they had heard God's voice address them aloud. And if God and the Unconscious are one—? As Merrill has observed, "if it's still *yourself* that you're drawing upon, then that self is much stranger and freer and more far-seeing than the one you thought you knew." [15] Put another way, in another place: "If the spirits aren't external, how astonishing the mediums become! Victor Hugo said of *his* voices that they were like his own mental powers multiplied by five." He adds that his time among the spirits has "made me think twice about the imagination," [16]—a reminder that Section S of *Ephraim* begins where this essay may properly conclude:

> Stevens imagined the imagination
> And God as one; the imagination, also,
> As that which presses back, in parlous times,
> Against "the pressure of reality."

CHAPTER 9

The Changing Light at Sandover: The Book of Ephraim

This suspension bridge joining the body of Merrill's earlier poetry to his *Sandover* trilogy may well be ultimately adjudged his finest single piece of writing. Though almost indescribably complex in reference and motif, and therefore in overall meaning, the surface is immensely readable. All Merrill's narrative, lyric, and structural strengths are showcased (as in the wonderful terza rima of Section W), the oedipal/erotic themes that have always powered his strongest work bind the material together, and the poem resolves itself at the end in a thoroughly satisfactory way. That its resolutions turn out to be less conclusive than they seemed detracts nothing from the dramatic satisfactions of *Ephraim*, which, though part of the trilogy, is self-contained.

Emotionally speaking, *The Fire Screen* was Strato's book and the focus of *Braving the Elements* was Santa Fe. *The Book of Ephraim* is at heart a sustained love poem to David Jackson, with whom Merrill has shared three homes (in Stonington, Athens, and Key West) since 1955. Their silver anniversary is celebrated in *Scripts for the Pageant*, and the trilogy's second and third Books were produced through their systematic cooperation; but, before *that* major commitment to the spirits, *Ephraim* takes a slow, clear, retrospective look at this marriage begun in passion and enduring in companionship.

At the start of their new life in the new house in Stonington, 1955, the two were idling away an evening at the Ouija board when all at once the cup began to spin about furiously:

> Was anybody there? As when a pike
> Strikes, and the line singing writes in lakeflesh
> Highstrung runes, and reel spins and mind reels
> YES a new and urgent power YES
> Seized the cup. It swerved, clung, hesitated,
> Darted off, a devil's darning needle
> Gyroscope our fingers rode bareback
> (But stopping dead the instant one lost touch)
> Here, there, swift handle pointing, letter upon
> Letter taken down blind by my free hand—

The "new and urgent power" of these superbly kinetic lines is Ephraim, "A Greek Jew/ Born AD 8 at XANTHOS . . . Died/ AD 36 on CAPRI throttled/ By the imperial guard for having LOVED/ THE MONSTERS NEPHEW (sic) CALIGULA." Who could resist such racy stuff? Not they. For many years after this First Contact, Ephraim comes eagerly to the board when called, bringing the spirits of the dead.

From the first he clearly approves of the liaison, even comparing DJ and JM flatteringly with the "orgy-fodder" recruited from five races by Tiberius. He can admire them in any reflecting surface—mirror, tidepool, telephone-booth glass, bronze gong—and one evening suggests hypnosis as a way (short of dying) for them to see *him*. DJ lets JM put him under, and the ensuing episode, charged with erotic tension, has been adapted for the poem (Section H) from notes David made on the morning after. Through an uncurtained window materialize

> *the limbs and torso muscled by long folds of*
> *an unemasculated Blake nude. Who then*
> *actually was in the room, at arm's length,*
> *glowing with strength, asking if he pleased me. I*
> *said yes. . . . As he stroked J's face & throat*
> *I felt a stab of the old possessiveness.*
> *Souls can't feel at E's level. He somehow was*
> *using me, my senses, to touch JM who*
> *this morning swears it was my hand stroking him. . . .*
>
> > *Now Ephraim tried to lead me*
> > *to the mirror and I held back. Putting his*
> > *hand on me then, my excitement, which he breathed*
> > *smiling, already fading, to keep secret*

DJ has confirmed elsewhere that Ephraim, in the trance, "was extremely seductive and charming . . . a great beauty," that a sense of danger made the experience all the more erotic, and that it was in some way part of or connected with the intense sexual bond between himself and JM.[1] To make effective use of this material, Merrill was clearly forced to let go even of the half-mask his homosexuality had until this point continued to wear—thus accounting for his reference, in the Coda, to Ephraim's "Having long since brought him out."

The Country of a Thousand Years of Peace is introduced and concluded by two emotionally unveiled yet finely restrained poems for Hans Lodeizen, a young Dutch poet who died of leukemia in 1950. Hans has a role to play in *The Book of Ephraim*, where his early death now seems less tragic (and the verse describing him more commonplace)—one can still communicate with him, or send messages through Ephraim, whose friend and tutor Hans has become. When the mediums are told that *power* on Earth, not "plain old virtue," is what carries weight in Heaven, their familiar illustrates his point by confiding that "YR HANS SAYS HE MIGHT/ WELL HAVE ATTAINED AT ONCE HIS PRESENT STAGE/ HAD HE BEEN LESS VIRTUOUS THAT SPRING

NIGHT." Now as if to compensate for that restraint we learn (in
G) how Hans has intervened, arranging for this present life of
JM's to be his last, whereas DJ still has "one or two, at most/
Three lives more" to live on Earth. JM immediately objects:

> Ephraim, this cannot be borne. We live
> Together. And if you are on the level
> Some consciousness survives—right? Right.
> Now tell me, what conceivable delight
> Lies for either of us in the prospect
> Of an eternity without the other?
> Why not *both* be reborn? Which at least spares one
> Dressing up as the Blessed Damozel
> At Heaven's Bar to intervene—oh hell,
> Stop *me*. You meant no harm. But, well, forgive
> My saying so, that was insensitive.

The skeptical reader will think what Merrill himself says a moment later, to David: that the cloud of his distress has proved to
be "Foreshadower of nothing, dearest heart,/ But the dull wish
of lives to drift apart." Yet JM and DJ, wedded for time if not
eternity, "live on, limbs thickening/ For better and worse in one
another's shade." The Haitian voodoo spell which their friend
Maya Deren had cast so many years ago by "laying down in
flour/ Erzulie's heart-emblem on the floor" of their new house
has worn, but not worn off or out:

> Times we've felt, returning to this house
> Together, separately, back from somewhere . . .
>
> Felt a ghost of roughness underfoot.
> There it was, the valentine that Maya
> Kneeling on our threshold, drew to bless us:
> Of white meal sprinkled then with rum and lit,
> Heart once intricate as birdsong, it
> Hardened on the spot. Much come-and-go
> Has blackened, pared the scabby curlicue
> Down to smatterings which, even so,
> Promise to last this lifetime. That will do.

Hans has intervened from his position at Stage One in Heaven. If most of Ephraim's communiqués are lighter entertainment, he also finds occasions to describe a cosmology whereby, after an unspecified number of incarnations and degree of development, each human soul is promoted to the first of nine Stages, thenceforth no longer to be reborn. At this point *he* becomes a "patron" with an earthly soul (called a "representative") to oversee, and the patron who has been overseeing *him* moves to a higher Stage. But Heaven in all its Stages (this is the crucial revelation of *Ephraim*, one withheld from DJ and JM for years) is dependent upon Earth for its very existence. When humanity destroys its world—only a question of time, it would appear—Heaven itself will vanish. As reported in "The Will," Ephraim has urged Merrill to warn mankind of the universal consequences of nuclear holocaust ("IF U DO NOT YR WORLD WILL BE UNDONE/ & HEAVEN ITSELF TURN TO ONE GRINNING SKULL"), and *The Book of Ephraim*, completed at length after false starts and bizarre mishaps, may be taken for the answer to this command. But by the time his alphabetical scheme has been brought as far as Section W, Merrill has quite abandoned (prematurely, as we now know) the idea of warning the world—is disinclined "in these sunset years . . ./ Mending my ways, breaking myself of rhyme/ To speak to multitudes and make it matter."

That "breaking myself of rhyme" refers to the fact that Merrill had first thought to use Ephraim's revelations as the basis of a novel, seeing that "The baldest prose/ Reportage was called for, that would reach/ The widest public in the shortest time." In a small way, Ephraim had already made his debut in fiction. A little simple collating shows how closely detail in *The Book of Ephraim* corresponds to detail in *The Seraglio*, where Francis and his Italian lover Marcello make contact with a spirit calling himself Meno. Now, however, an entire new novel's plot, setting, and theme come readily to mind; as for treatment:

> I yearned for the kind of unseasoned telling found
> In legends, fairy tales, a tone licked clean
> Over the centuries by mild old tongues,
> Grandam to cub, serene, anonymous.

To suit this tone, his characters were to be

> conventional stock figures
> Afflicted to a minimal degree
> With personality and past experience—
> A witch, a hermit, innocent young lovers,
> The kinds of being we recall from Grimm,
> Jung, Verdi, and the commedia dell' arte.

So far no surprises; *The Fire Screen* was clear about this preference for types. But the project evidently got on poorly ("My
downfall was 'word-painting' ") and had finally to be abandoned
when Merrill "accidentally" left the manuscript draft in a Geor-
gia taxi on a visit to his mother (see "The Will" for particulars).
Ephraim's doing, it afterwards emerges; he *wants* the warning
done as a poem despite an automatic diminishment in the size
of its potential audience.

Since the doctrines of No Accident and Lab Souls are still
veiled in the future, this preference is puzzling. Merrill com-
plies, but ingeniously finds a way to let the lost novel infiltrate
the poem; so that scattered through half a dozen sections we are
given a fair (and intriguing) sense of its characters, a rough plot
sketch, and lightly fictionalized highlights of JM's and DJ's own
experience with the Board. The hypnotism scene, for instance:
Ellen and Leo, the "innocent young lovers" from Merrill's cast
of types, are apparently living in Santa Fe, with or near Ellen's
grandparents Matt and Lucy Prentiss (modeled on DJ's father
and mother). A visitor, Joanna ("witch"), and a neighbor, Sergei
Markovich ("hermit"), " 'Recognize' each other, or I as author/
Recognize in them the plus and minus/ —Good and evil, let my
reader say—/ Vital to the psychic current's flow." Contact with

an Ephraim look-alike called Eros is achieved through the agency
of these two, both of whom find Leo extremely attractive:

> To Leo and Ellen, who presumably
> Love only one another, let me see . . .
> Let Leo rather, on the evening
> He lets himself be hypnotized, see Eros.
> Head fallen back, lips parted, and tongue flexed
> Glistening between small perfect teeth;
> Hands excitedly, while the others watch,
> Roving the to them invisible
> Shoulders, belly, crotch; a gasp, a moan—
> Ellen takes Lucy's arm and leaves the room.

Between them Joanna and Ellen create the contrast of Sexual Woman and Fair Maiden drawn in "Yánnina," while Sergei,
whose three labels read "old," "good," and "queer," stands in
for his author, or for what his author imagines time could make
of him—it was in the New Mexico poems of *Braving the Elements*
that the obsessive imagery of aging first appeared. "Joanna worries me. (Sergei I know.)" he writes, understanding that one reason Sergei so abhors smoking, predatory, evil Joanna is that she
has been imagined in the image ascribed, by himself at twelve,
to the Other Woman who "ENTICED MY FATHER FROM MY
MOTHERS BED." (According to Ephraim, Christ had this effect
on Ephraim's father.) Joanna in pursuit of "Old Matt's bank account" is unspeakable; Matt wakes to smoky "acrid nothings in
his ear,/ His knobby fingers gripped between her thighs" while
Lucy stirs wakefully in the other twin bed. In Section J, Joanna's "sun-scabbed brow [and]/ Thin hair dyed setter-auburn"
are turned into "this entire/ Parched landscape" of the Southwestern desert city where the novel is set. In effect, Merrill's
oldest, most fundamental trauma forms the very ground of the
lost novel, and emotions attending it undergird both the more
"unmasked" autobiography of the poem and the parts masked

by fiction. "Since it had never truly fit, why wear/ The shoe of prose? In verse the feet went bare," he says in Section A. The statement passes too quickly over what Stephen Yenser has called "The deft persistence with which reality and fiction are woven together in *The Book of Ephraim*";[2] but soon enough, with Auden's reassurance that "FACT IS IS IS FABLE," shod and unshod will be seen to come to the same thing.

The first break in communications between the Real and Other worlds follows upon DJ's and JM's having suggested human mothers for the representatives of Ephraim and of Hans. A mistake at which "THE POWERS ARE FURIOUS" occurs, and the flippancies of the two earthly meddlers are not to be borne in Heaven: the cup goes dead. In the ensuing panic over losing Ephraim—exactly what Francis Tanning had felt when he knew Meno was out of reach—Merrill consults his former psychiatrist and is provided with a plausible explanation for the entire Ouija phenomenon. As the doctor puts it, "what you and David do/ We call folie à deux": use Ephraim and the Board, by unspoken mutual consent, as a way of telling each other home truths from behind a mask. That same evening their familiar spirit returns, and the delighted friends put aside for another day the question of exactly who Ephraim may be. What matters to both is "never to forego, in favor of/ Plain dull proof, the marvelous nightly pudding."

Accordingly, on the trip round the world commenced soon after, they feel an odd lethargy, a reluctance to put him to the proof. In the first session at the Board, Ephraim had told of documents buried on Capri that Tiberius wanted destroyed, had described an underground chamber to which he could direct them. Now DJ and JM cut Capri out of their itinerary. They are in the Far East when Merrill's father dies. Soon Ephraim reports that CEM has been reborn, in Kew, furnishing a name and address. They plan to look him up when they get to England, but in the event

> at the mere notion of Kew—
> Ten thousand baby-carriages each maybe
> Wheeling You Know Who—
> NOTHING is exactly what we do.

While this might be taken as characteristic fear of probing beneath the mask—at odds perhaps with the unconscious wish to *know*, since the means of probing are so unreservedly provided by Ephraim—it seems also to indicate the first signs of dwindling interest in the other world, confronted as they are by so many of *this* world's wonders. In the light of subsequent events this section, K, appears as a divide, the point past which the attractions of the other world began to pall. After Section O the strong narrative thread is broken repeatedly by more isolated topics, discursive passages, and passages of dense language. Besides putting greater distance between us and the spirits, these indicate greater lapses of attention to Heaven on the part of the protagonists.

The major theme of *Ephraim*, as announced in Section A, was to have been "an old, exalted one:/ The incarnation and withdrawal of/ A god." In fact, the "god" seems less to withdraw than to be gradually abandoned, as JM's preference for the earthly world intensifies through the poem's twenty years of time. In Section P he has to admit that

> This (1970) was the one extended
> Session with Ephraim in two years.
> (Why? No reason—we'd been busy living,
> Had meant to call, but never quite got round . . .)
> The cup at first moved awkwardly, as after
> An illness or estrangement. Had he missed us?
> YES YES emphatically.

Busy living in what Section K calls the "Simmering mulligatawny of the Real," then—hence the sense of estrangement, and of Ephraim's urgency. As if to renew his grip on their attention, P also strikes the first truly ominous note and the first prophetic one, foreshadowing the "heavy" revelations of *Mirabell* and *Scripts for the Pageant:*

> NO SOULS CAME FROM HIROSHIMA U KNOW
> EARTH WORE A STRANGE NEW ZONE OF ENERGY
> Caused by? SMASHED ATOMS OF THE DEAD MY DEARS . . .
>
> CLEARANCE HAS COME TO SAY I HAVE ENCOUNTERED
> SOULS OF A FORM I NEVER SAW B4
> SOULS FROM B4 THE FLOOD B4 THE LEGENDARY
> & BY THE WAY NUCLEAR IN ORIGIN
> FIRE OF CHINA   MEN B4 MANKIND . . .
>
> What do they look like? SOME HAVE WINGS TO WHICH
> THE TRAILING SLEEVES OF PALACE ROBES ALLUDE
> New types, you mean, like phoenixes will fly
> Up from *our* conflagration? How sci-fi!
> (Observe the easy, grateful way we swim
> Back to his shallows. We've no friend like him.)

This only appears to make light of what had been, by Mirabell's account, a dreadful shock ("YR EPHRAIM 6 YEARS AGO CAME/ WEEPING TO US   'THEY ARE IN ANGUISH' "); nevertheless it will take Mirabell himself to make a reluctant JM over into—as he puts it at the end of R—"the good gray medium/ Blankly uttering someone else's threat."

By W, in fact, when Merrill runs into his young artist-nephew Wendell (an invented character) by chance in Venice, he remembers only after the evening spent together has ended that "Wendell was Ephraim's representative!" and that an opportunity to "Guide Wendell's theme (this world's grim truths) around/ To mine (his otherworldly guardian)" and so enlist Wendell's talents in his assigned enterprise of warning the world, has been lost. Section Z, finally, describes the carton of Ephraim's transcripts in Stonington which now might as well be burned, for surely no one will ever read them again. In fact, the wish to burn them accords with Tiberius's wish for his own manuscript buried in its bronze box, and with Auden's for *his* box of papers in Oxford "that must QUICKLY BE/ QUICKLY BURNED":

> And in the final
> Analysis, who didn't have at heart
> Both a buried book and a voice that said
> Destroy it? How sensible had *we* been
> To dig up this material of ours?
> What if BURN THE BOX had been demotic
> For *Children, while you can, let some last flame*
> *Coat these walls, the lives you lived, relive them?*

Ephraim's transcripts are spared, though a door is shut upon them with a sound of finality. Life itself, the Real, intervenes to save them, demonstrating again the other world's dependency upon this one:

> So, do we burn the—   Wait, the phone is ringing:
> Bad connection; babble of distant talk;
> No getting through. We must improve the line
> In every sense, for life.

The reader is left believing that the affair with Ephraim, whether or not it has entirely ended, will never again seduce Merrill away from the life he means to improve the line—the telephone line, the life-line of verse—for. The impression is false, in a sense; yet when he turns again to the other world, against all desire and expectation to resume the role of Jeremiah, the summons comes not from frivolous Ephraim but from a voice more difficult to ignore.

We were introduced, in the "Dramatis Personae" of Section D, to "Smith, Rosamund, character in the novel," enigmatically described as

> Perennially youthful, worldly, rich,
> And out of sight until the close, at which
> Point—but no matter, now. By degrees grows . . .

> A twilight presence. *I* may need her still
> But Ephraim shoulders her aside.

Rosamund—the Marchesa Santofior, Sergei's (earthly) patroness—represents the "woman of the world" mentioned on the poem's last page, as her name indicates; when Merrill calls Time "the very attar of the Rose" in Section A, this is one rose he means. Ephraim shoulders her aside quite understandably; she is his rival. But Merrill notes that he himself may still have need of her, and in the end she triumphs:

> And look, the stars have wound in filigree
> The ancient, ageless woman of the world.
> She's seen us. She is not particular—
> Everyone gets her injured, musical
> "Why do you no longer come to me?"
> To which there's no reply. For here we are.

The real world is conceived to be a woman in the tradition of earth-mother and Mother Earth, the other world approached via the spirit of a homosexual youth. This coming to terms with the world, then, marks an acceptance with implications more far-reaching even than a decision in favor of the Real. Merrill's own contrived quotation under Q (purporting to have been taken from a novel entitled *Time Was*), combines these two guardians of opposing portals into a single high-camp character:

One evening late in the war he was at the crowded bar of the then smart Pyramid Club, in uniform, and behaving quite outrageously. Among the observers an elderly American admiral had been growing more and more incensed. He now went over and tapped Teddie on the shoulder: "Lieutenant, you are a disgrace to the Service. I must insist on having your name and squadron." An awful silence fell. Teddie's newly-won wings glinted. He snapped shut his thin gold compact (from Hermès) and narrowed his eyes at the admiral. "My *name*," he said distinctly, "is *Mrs Smith.*"

This little scene is a piece of alchemy. Teddie has angelic flyer's wings and is associated with the god who wears winged sandals, as well as with the ancient winged souls of the "MEN B4 MANKIND" in the previous section, P. A reference to St. Theodore in X will broaden the base of his identity. When he calls himself "Mrs Smith," he stands for Ephraim—who stands in this poem for so much—on his way to becoming Rosamund Smith, or for Rosamund about to take Ephraim's place in Merrill's affections. All this must mean, if it's to mean anything, at least a qualified reconciliation with the female principle in the world: Mother Nature, in fact, as she will appear in *Scripts*. Section X sheds some light on this point—though mostly it's left implicit—through Merrill's remarks upon

> the absence from these pages
> Of my own mother. Because of course she's here
> Throughout, the breath drawn after every line,
> Essential to its making as to mine;
> Here no less in Maya's prodigality
> Than in Joanna's fuming—or is *she*
> The last gasp of my dragon? I think so;
> My mother gave up cigarettes years ago. . . .

The dragon image is taken from a painting, revealed by X-rays beneath the mask of Giorgione's *Tempest*, of St. Theodore "at ease here after rescuing/ His mother from a dragon—'her beauty such,/ The youth desired to kiss her,' as the quaint/ Byzantine legend puts it." So elemental an oedipal tableau requires no comment. Maya is a white witch, a loved friend, thoroughly female. That Merrill's mother is represented in her as much as in dragonlike, cigarette-consuming Joanna—the wicked-step-mother figure whose "evil" charge opposes that of "good" Sergei within the psychic atom of the poet's life—is more than a re-statement of the contradictions in the mother of "The Broken Home." Even at those deep levels no one can command, it seems that his oedipal demon has been truly exorcised—or, perhaps, simply outlived. In retrospect, Merrill's work to this point can be seen to embody, in its entirety, a progression through time from the passionate and transitory toward the domestic, from illusion toward reality, and especially from oedipal hobgoblins toward acceptance of the principle personified here as the woman of the world.

The Book of Ephraim gathers these skeins and makes one patiently achieved reconciliation do for all. In Section T, thoughts of the twenty years through which these losses and gains were accomplished—years so busy and full in the living, so fleet in memory—condense into one of dozens of lyric passages set like stars in the firmament of this text. Merrill, leading Sergei toward the lost novel's close and empathizing with him deeply, locates both in the remembered New Mexico landscape where he sees

> Stones named on a picnic with DJ
> Summers ago, or only yesterday . . .
>
> Only yesterday! Too violent
> I once thought, that foreshortening in Proust—
> A world abruptly old, whitehaired, a reader
> Looking up in puzzlement to fathom
> Whether ten years or forty have gone by.
> Young, I mistook it for an unconvincing
> Trick of the teller. It was truth instead,
> Babbling through his own astonishment.

CHAPTER 10

The Changing Light at Sandover: Summaries and Highlights

> When it comes to atoms, language can be used only as in poetry.
> —Nils Bohr to Werner Heisenberg

> What lies below the visible world is always imaginary, in the literal sense: a play of images. There is no other way to talk about the invisible—in nature, in art, or in science.
> —J. Bronowski

This concluding chapter is intended primarily for reference: a preview or masterplot of the trilogy's often bewildering second and third volumes. It supplements the material presented in chapter 8, which should be read first, and condenses the content of *Mirabell* and *Scripts for the Pageant*. Critical commentary has been kept light, but the summary of *Scripts* incorporates interpretation of difficult "doctrine" where called for.

1. MIRABELL: BOOKS OF NUMBER

The choice James Merrill and David Jackson made in *Ephraim,* to return and belong to this world, had been reinforced

by a scare: powerful forces which had "nailed DJ's free hand to
the Board's edge" in Section U. But no terrifying powers in-
trude to mar the session held on behalf of the old Jacksons, and
the two enjoy renewing contact with Ephraim, and with Chester
Kallman and Maria Mitsotáki, both dead within the past year.
After the anticipated deaths have occurred, talks with David's
parents and others increase in frequency. Almost unawares, as
the months pass Merrill and Jackson are drawn back within the
frame of the other world, and a day comes when they have again
grown edgy—when censorship increases—when they are caught
and possessed by the forces that had so unnerved them once
before.

And for a purpose. These powers now command JM to
write "POEMS OF SCIENCE," to "MAKE GOD OF SCIENCE." They
intend him for a kind of Gospel Scribe, recording after his own
fashion the truths they mean to reveal. Early assumptions that
these revelations will flow through him "Outright, with no re-
course to the Board," prove unfounded; months of glumly reading scientific texts like homework, waiting for the lightning to
strike, seem to get JM nowhere. Finally he faces up to the obvious in a letter to DJ: "We *may have to approach* Them/ *for those
lights to turn green.*" This guess turns out to be correct.

The scene, then: Ouija board on a round milk-glass table in
a domed, round, red room in Stonington, in the summer of 1976.
(The adjacent room is a small square parlor papered in a blue
pattern of bat-shapes.) Visible are only JM and DJ, each with
the fingers of one hand balanced on an inverted cup. Unseen,
however, is a crowd of spirits: the souls of friends from various
Stages, and others between lives, who ring the room to insulate
the mediums with their affection from the lethal power of fifteen
other "beings" also present. These friends are crucial to the *poem*
as well: the human interest they provide comes, again and again,

as providential relief from a bout of heavy slogging through pages
of offbeat "science" and "theology."

The pupils are first informed that God is Biology: Life, this
will be seen to mean, rather than the science of life. Two cosmic
forces are locked in combat: Biology, which uses mind and reason, and Chaos, which employs feeling. Chaos must not be allowed to win. We may expect it to take a while for this notion
to sink in, and that it will encounter resistance, since all Merrill's previous work has been more than clear about whose side
he chooses between reason and emotion; yet this will be the
central message JM is charged to deliver, elaborated with codicils and corollaries. The teachers who have commissioned him
are black, and "look" (according to Maria) "QUITE LIKE BATS,/
HUGE SQUEAKING ONES WITH LITTLE HOT RED EYES." They
have numbers for names, and are, metaphorically, the rebellious
angels; they are also the negative electrical charge within the
atom, *and* antimatter itself, "A DISAPPEARANCE   AN ABSO-
LUTE VOID   ASTRONOMERS/ HAVE AT LAST SEEN OUR BE-
NIGHTED WORK   THE BLACK HOLES   THEY GROW." It seems
impossible for the bats to describe themselves, or the world they
say they made and then destroyed by an arrogant misuse of
power, except by metaphor; and thus early the confusions are
intense, both for JM—whose patience is taxed to the limit (he,
after all, is expected to make poetry out of this poppycock)—
and for the reader. The bats, for instance, cannot experience
emotion, or so they say—yet they seem to. But if they dwell at
the heart of Chaos, and if Chaos employs feeling . . .?

At any rate the story must be kept going at both levels,
literal and subatomic. In one sense the batwing angels rose above
the surface of the Earth and built a crust world, "WEIGHTLESS
AND SELF-SUSTAINING," in the ozone layer, anchoring it with
stones and cables at fourteen sites, one at Avebury in England,

one near LA, and so forth; in another sense this crust world seems to be "the evolving cortex of the brain." The crust was destroyed when these beings despised and abandoned it, moving on outward into space; there was a nuclear explosion and their world fell, and they with it. There had been two Edens before humanity's: Atlantis, or "CERTAIN ANCIENTS WHOM/ BIOLOGY ABANDOND" and "A VAST CIVILIZATION IN CHINA." So much, no more, is set forth in Book 1; yet at its close JM and DJ promise to give all they can to receiving (and JM to expressing, somehow) what the bats offer; and W. H. Auden, forswearing the "DREARY DREARY DEAD BANG WRONG/ CHURCH," receives permission to join Maria and the two mortals in the seminar at the Ouija board. The covenant is made.

The mediums, having found it difficult to work with their maddeningly figurative first teacher, are happy (in Book 2) to meet his somehow more youthful- and eager-seeming replacement, name of 741. The Board is equipped with punctuation symbols, another improvement. Class convenes nearly every afternoon, DJ and JM questioning and transcribing, Maria and WHA standing by to contribute as they may, talk it all over afterwards, and generally lighten the tone with wit and affection; and now the lessons go on much better. To a degree, these are intertwined with lessons from the mediums' experiences in life, for life in the world does proceed—yet increasingly at a distance, save for a few major events with a specific gravity of their own, such as DJ's operation.

Time goes by. DJ and JM learn (this sort of fact-dispensing is inevitably a lower grade of entertainment than the likes of the bats' Gothic drama, though evidently necessary): that the moon was formed by the materials of the crust world when it broke away; that the good (white, positively-charged) angels spoke directly to: Dante, the writers of the four Gospels, Buddha, and Mohammed; that "88%/ Of us is Chemistry, Environment,/ Et

al. (*The 12%* becomes a dry/ Euphemism" for our angelic properties of soul; and that—one early hint of an elitism about which
the bats are adamant—only souls of a higher "density," "At most
two million relatively fleet/ Achievers," matter in the cosmic
scheme. What else? That salt is "Fuel and stabilizer/ Of the body
electric (thank you, Walt)." That there are five "immortals"—
five souls retaining through each rebirth a perfect knowledge of
all their previous lives; the twins Akhnaton and Nefertiti *together*
were the first such soul, other incarnations of the Five having
been in one life or another: Montezuma, Galileo, Mozart, Dag
Hammarskjöld, Einstein. The greatest densities are theirs. (The
souls of both JM and DJ are quite dense, those of Maria and
Auden still denser.)

Soul densities in the significant two million are determined
and implanted or "cloned" by the bats in what 741 calls "THE
RESEARCH LAB," both before and after rebirth—cloned increasingly, due to the population explosion and a consequent short-
age of human densities, with admixtures of dog and rat, animals
that have lived close to humans for millenia. The Lab worries
about "A CONCERTED USE OF ATOMIC/ WEAPONRY NOW FALL-
ING INTO HANDS OF ANIMAL SOULS" who are by nature too
given to high "animal spirits" and *joie de vivre*, too little to reason
and restraint. Through such souls Chaos can gain ground. Dry
lecture or no, by this point the "real" world has dimmed for JM
and DJ and the Board world become realer than real:

> About us, these bright afternoons, we come
> To draw shades of an auditorium
> In darkness. An imagined dark, a stage
> Convention: domed red room, cup and blank page
> Standing for darkness where our table's white
> Theatre in the round fills, dims . . . Crosslight
> From YES and NO dramatically picks
> Four figures out. And now the twenty-six
> Footlights, arranged in semicircle, glow.

What might be seen as her "petit noyau"
By Mme Verdurin assembles at
Stage center. A by now familiar bat
Begins to lecture. Each of us divines
Through the dark house like fourteen Exit signs
The eyes of certain others glowing red.
And the outside-world, crayon-book life we led,
White or white-trimmed canary clapboard homes
Set in the rustling shade of monochromes;
Lighthouse and clock tower, Village Green and neat
Roseblush factory which makes, upstreet,
Exactly what, one once knew but forgets—
Something plastic found in luncheonettes;
The Sound's quick sapphire that each day recurs
Aflock with pouter-pigeon spinnakers
—This outside world, our fictive darkness more
And more belittles to a safety door
Left open onto light. Too small, too far
To help. The blind bright spot of where we are.

And so to 3, where we are told that experiments using plant
soul densities have taken place and that the Lab workers are not
unhopeful of the results. Burbank and Muir were given plant
densities; indeed "U JM HAVE THIS COMPONENT AS MANY POETS
DO:/ THE GREAT AGE OF FRENCH & ENGLISH PASTORAL PO-
ETRY/ & FROM ITS ORIGIN ALL JAPANESE POETRY WAS/ THE
RESULT OF OUR EXPERIMENTS IN VEGETABLE/ CLONING" (*clone*,
by the way, often seems to signify not that, or that alone, but
something more like modify or program). At the end of Book 3
will come a hint that a pinch of *mineral* densities may help calm
the vegetable world's unfortunately fervent fertility. And now
abruptly 741 reveals that Maria, whose recently-ended life should
have been her last, will after all be sent back to "JOIN THIS
WORLD OF PLANT LIFE"—a completely unprecedented phenomenon so far as the mediums know. The news upsets them badly
("We're losing her? They can foreclose/ All that humor, that

humanity . . . And she won't be/ A *person* even, next time?
Why? How soon?") Ephraim joins forces with Auden and Maria
herself to console them, and the tone turns comic; yet the grief,
and mystery, persist.

Soon 741, who ought to be unable to feel, admits that he
has come to love his pupils, who have taught him courtesy. His
metamorphosis from bat to peacock transpires forthwith, and in
his new guise he propounds the theory about homosexuals making the best poets and musicians because they make no progeny.
DJ and JM are skeptical, but when 741 begins to explain, the
censors sweep the cup off the Board and send in WHA to dis-
tract them: "What's Plato *like?* O YOU KNOW   TATTLETALE
GRAY/ NIGHTGOWN OFF ONE SHOULDER   DECLASSEE. . . ."

This recess of wit in Chester's vein is welcome, for the next
day is to be the most intense thus far. 741 tells his mortals and
spirits that "OUR 5 SOULS MUST BEGIN TO BE A SINGLE POWER,"
four representing one material element each and "DJ THE SHAP-
ING HAND OF NATURE." Invoked by a complex lyric poem, in a
form Merrill used more than once in *First Poems* and will use
again here, the five elements acknowledge identities between
themselves and these five souls, and lastly say:

THE MATTER WHICH IS NOT WAS EVER OURS
    TO GUARD AGAINST. ITS POWERS
ARE MAGNETIZED BY FOREIGN BEACONS, BLACK
HANDS TESTING THE GREENHOUSE PANE BY PANE
CLING TO YOUR UNION: 5   THROUGH THE DARK HOURS
    WE KEEP WATCH   WE PRESS BACK.
    AT ZERO SUMMON US AGAIN.

The experience releases an ecstatic 741 from his negativeness.
All are being prepared for something more shattering; metaphorically, their five elemental faces are to form together the
faces of a perfect pyramid, whose power will be "Such as to lift

the weight of the whole world" and build Paradise. Work toward this end is known henceforth as V Work.

Book 4, an agreeable respite from straight instruction, elaborates the legend of Atlantis. We are asked to imagine a featureless world of green grassy plains whereon are nurtured a race of immortal centaurlike creatures, who in turn breed small green radioactive flies—by feeding them uranium—to carry messages between centaur herds as trees sprang up and separated these. In time the centaurs developed stubby fingers and the winged things grew into great black creatures, large as they yet still their servants, and still radioactive. Eventually the centaurs' immortality made the planet crowded, so the bats were charged with the task of "RIDDING THEM OF THEIR RELICS" (the oldest, most primitive centaurs) by atomic means. In the event, atomic power gave the bats dominion; they destroyed all the centaur civilization but fourteen sites, the anchor points for the crust world whose antigravitational lattice platforms the centaurs were forced to build.

The centaurs lived on, tending the anchor stones and moorings and accepting grain from the bats, but in a thousand years they had mutated into dinosaurs, the bats had grown too proud to do their own upkeep or descend to reconfront their humbler past, the jungle encroached steadily, and their whole world toppled in a vast cataclysm that sank Atlantis and hurled the crust into space. Damned in the egg by their makers, obedient to the murder of immortals, that fall was the bats' punishment; and their destiny was to become fossil fuel: "WE JOIND OUR BONES TO OUR OLD HORSEMASTERS IN THE CRUSH OF/ THEIR GREENERY & NOW AFTER 5 MILLION YEARS EMERGE/ TO POWER YR MACHINES & DRESS YR HOSTESSES IN MAUVE."

DJ must go to Boston for a pre-surgery exam; when he returns the lessons resume with "A BASIC PRECEPT U WILL NEED

TO TAKE ON FAITH: THERE IS NO ACCIDENT." The precept is a codicil to God Biology's one law: survive. A second codicil reads: "THE SCRIBE SHALL SUPPLANT RELIGION."

Book 5 is one of the most interesting. 741 explains that gamma rays destroy human soul densities, so that those of anyone exposed to the rays are not recyclable—though, as we've learned already, "NOTHING IS EVER EVER LOST" and 741 assures JM and DJ that "THESE UNACCOUNTABLE LOSSES ARE SOMEWHERE A GAIN" ("BUT WHERE" he adds). The foreshadowing slips past them. Other topics touched on earlier are now taken up and further clarified. God Biology *is* history *is* the Earth ("THE GREENHOUSE") *is*, in effect, on the side of the positive charge within the atom and implacably opposed to antimatter, radioactivity, the black hands that press and press against the greenhouse panes. "THE SCRIBE'S DAY IS AT HAND" says 741 again. Yet, JM reflects, there are so few serious readers—how can books do more than a little good? The reply—"THE MASSES WE NEED NEVER CONSIDER   THEY REMAIN IN AN ANIMAL STATE"—disturbs them, as do all references to heavenly elitism, but 741 replies simply, "MILK TO CREAM TO BUTTER."

The No Accident clause is a fairly new device of God Biology's dating from the time when Akhnaton and Nefertiti built an almost-perfect pyramid whose true perfection would have destroyed the whole world instead of a small piece of it; references to this recur and recur, and relate to the metaphorical pyramid the five of them are to build together. (Many of Biology's present tools and policies, in fact, seem to date from very recent history—particularly from changes in the greenhouse, and in how people live, brought about by the Industrial Revolution.) 741's account of how and why the Survival law evolved its codicils resists paraphrase, like most such explanations, but JM's musing villanelle is plain as plain:

It sinks in gradually, all that's meant
By this wry motto governing things here
Below and there above: *No Accident.*

Patrons? Parents? Healthy achievers, bent
On moving up, not liable to queer
The Lab work. It sinks in, what had been meant

By the adorable dumb omen sent
TO TEST EXALT & HUMBLE U MY DEAR
Strato? ET AL   Maisie? NO ACCIDENT . . .

The clause is self-enacting; the intent,
Like air, inscrutable if crystal-clear.
Keep breathing it. One dark day, what is meant
Will have sunk in past words. *No Accident.*

Apparently the No Accident clause means that what happens to
Lab souls is planned and purposeful to the minutest detail. Two
sets of parents are brought together so that DJ and JM can be
born, and meet, and enter upon the present experience. Life,
events, are the complete opposite of random, even among non-
Lab souls, since their doings affect the elite. This clause helps
explain why so many of the people JM and DJ have loved and/or
lost to death are revealed as important not only to them but in
the universal plan, and far from accidentally brought into the
orbits of their lives. Book 5 ends on a hopeful note. The Lab
workers can see a limited distance into the future, and report
that "THREE DECADES HENCE WE GLIMPSE FAIR GREEN AT-
LANTAN FIELDS." JM wonders how problems so immense can
be solved so quickly, short of disaster, but 741 assures him (with
mildly ambiguous qualifications) that Biology will defeat Chaos,
or won't yet have been defeated by it in 2006. Presumably the
effects of JM's poems of science have been factored into this
foretelling.

David's operation is a success. But the direst revelation thus
far now bursts upon them in Book 6: 741 and Co. not only

supervised the surgery but might have forestalled the need for it altogether had they not been unwilling to bring their radioactivity, which destroys the soul, to bear. Though the mediums have known since Ephraim told them in 1970 that no souls rose from Hiroshima, only now do they realize that Maria has been admitted to the seminar because "SHE IS ONE OF US": radium treatments for cancer have destroyed *her* soul, she is no longer human. Both living friends are utterly devastated, far more so by this ultimate annihilation of Maria's humanity than by her physical death. Now they understand at last why she must return to Earth as a plant.

Reconciliation follows upon horror and grief, and after a bit the seminar continues. A more frightening bat arrives to speak of colors: blue of reason, red of power; 741 adds yellow, the "SWEET JOYOUS LIGHT." The mediums are then asked to close their eyes. In a moment a sense of cool "whiteness" bathes JM's left side (cheek, forearm) and DJ's right, like alcohol: color of the good/positive angels they are to meet when this series of lessons is over. Auden later describes what he "saw": "ABSOLUTE RED BLINDNESS/ WITH AT ONE POINT A BAR OF WHITE/ SLICING DOWNWARD LIKE A KNIFE." As JM comments, "Nothing quite this strange/ Has happened up to now." Nothing quite this medicine-showy, either; it's probably as well for the poem that the spirits rarely try to reach thus literally out of their world into the other. In an interlude, DJ voices again his growing sense of isolation from the world while this V Work is ongoing, and his fears of not being able to care for or belong to it again when the work is done. JM agrees that it may be so: all quests are completed only at dear cost to the hero, who survives but cannot be thereafter what he was.

Merrill's task in ordering, condensing, and stylishly presenting this welter of material, under the guns of urgency and haste, staggers the imagination; and never more than in Book 7, where he must somehow make palatable the bats' mania for numbers and numerical formulas. Just one example of how he manages this: *Rachel* was a neutral, place-holding "name" provided, early on, for one of the Five immortals. Now she is conjured from the R/Lab where God B deposited her formula:

> Thus "Rachel" stirs, whom we had left asleep
> Dumbly, wrapped in Hebrew burlap. Deep
> Past consonant and vowel, a hushed din,
> The formulaic race beneath her skin,
> Her digits twitch, her eyes' unpupilled amber
> Gleams with crazy logic: she's a number!

Such passages, rising well above their occasion, may show why the bats picked Merrill to tell their wacky tale; who else would even try to make poetry of this "science," let alone do it with flair and humor? Much space in 7 is devoted to the Five, and especially to the Akhnaton-Nefertiti-pyramid story. Some of what follows that story is discomfiting, however. JM has absorbed the heavenly viewpoint by now to the extent that he can describe the case histories recounted in *Life After Life* as "interviews with people/ 'Brought back alive,' as to some local zoo,/ From the Beyond. All no doubt true, but what/ People! Not a Lab soul in the lot." 741 endorses the suicides of minds that "OUTLIVE THEIR USEFULNESS" so as to get them recycled again as quickly as possible. That sort of thing goes down with difficulty, despite the sugar-coat of style.

But the lessons go on, and on. Man and Nature are in conflict: "GOD WANTS BOTH HIS CHILD & HIS SLAVE TO GET ON TOGETHER/ BUT MAN WANTS IMMORTALITY & NATURE WANTS MANURE." The statement contains a notion only JM resists: "she's not a slave . . . Why is everyone so anti-Nature?" (Later, he will draft "my starstruck hymn to Mother N"—and telephone his own mother.) Following some byplay about the magic number 5, and references to earlier Merrill poems now seen as foreshadowing this present one, 741 gets overexcited and indiscreet—"IN NATURE YES IS VIOLENCE . . . AS U YRSELVES WILL SEE WHEN SHE COMES TO U"—and is whisked away, returning sobered and dimmed to promise a review of the lessons to date, one each day for the next ten days. He is pleased with the name JM has thought up (out of Congreve) to give him: Mirabell.

Most of the review covers old ground, though from time to time a concept comes finally into focus or a brand new bit of information gets presented (example: the first soul "WE SLIPPED INTO AN APE FETUS   THAT RARE SINGLE CREATURE/ AFTER 1 MORE VISIT COVERD IN BLINDING LIGHT CAME FORTH./ THE APES SCREAMD IN FEAR   FOR EVEN AS HE SUCKLED HE STARED/ ABOUT AND TERRIFIED THEM WITH THE 00 OF HIS EYES. . ."). Somewhere along the way, WHA and JM determine the metrical scheme for the planned poem. Book 8 continues the review: the peacock says flatly that language is man's greatest work, and greatest of all in three areas: science (whose language is formula), music (notation), and poetry (metaphor). A hurricane then forcibly demonstrates the violence of Nature, which Mirabell was punished for alluding to prematurely. A week later Robert Morse drops in, to express doubts about the poem (" 'Molecular structures'—cup and hand—obey/ 'Electric waves'? Don't *dream* of saying so!") which Heaven will revise when he appears there to take his part in *Scripts for the Pageant*. Book 8 concludes with an especially clear statement of the bats' warning to humanity, worth quoting at some length:

THE NUMBERS OF
MAN IN PARADISE WILL BE DETERMIND BY THE LIMITS
HE SETS ON HIS OWN NUMBERS, & WHEN THE RULE OF NUMBER
IS OBEYD BEYOND THE SMALL CIRCLE OF THE 2 MILLION.
2 CHILDREN PER COUPLE: IS IT NOT A SIMPLE RULE? YES.
IS IT UNDERSTOOD? NO. & NOW U SEE HOW RAPIDLY
& INTENTLY WE MUST WORK IN OUR FRIENDLY RIVALRY

WITH NATURE   FOR NATURE IS IMPATIENT: CLEAR OUT THE TREES!
KNOCK DOWN THE FLIMSY CITIES   KILL OFF THE EXCESS MILLIONS
START FRESH! BUT GOD B'S CHILD IS UNAWARE OF HIS FATHER'S
GRAND DESIGN. IMAGINING ONLY THAT THE GAP MUST BE
FILLD, HE RESPONDS TO NATURE'S OTHER SIGNAL: REPRODUCE!
SO GOD B ORDERS US: CORRECT THE SIGNAL.

From the end of Book 8 throughout Book 9 the sessions
grow increasingly lyrical and clear, the penultimate one perhaps
most of all. The subject—again—is belief. "THAT U DO NOT
DOUBT US IS WONDER ENOUGH   THAT OTHERS/ DO IS NONE"
says Mirabell, without fear of contradiction. JM and DJ have
comported themselves well, have not spoiled the sessions with
selfishness in the manner of

> OTHER FIELDS WE HAVE SETTLED INTO:
> CRIES OF HURRAH HURRAH THEY HAVE COME! & HARDLY HAD WE
> FOLDED OUR MANY WINGS THAN SMALL GREEDY HANDS PLUCKED AT
>   US
> SAYING: WHAT OF TOMORROW? WHAT OF AUNT MIN? WHERE IS THE
> BURIED TREASURE? & O LEAVE BEHIND THE FEATHER OF PROOF!

> You overestimate us. I at least have
> Longed for that feather on occasion, knowing
> Deep down that one must never ask for it.

WELL WE HAVE GIVEN FEATHERS B4, OR LEFT THEM BEHIND
IN OUR HASTE TO LEAVE   & LEFT ALSO MANY A MIRROR
SHATTERD & MIND WRECKD   DULLD WIT   THE CHEAP NOTO-
     RIETY
BUT WE & YOU   WE & YOU MOVE IN OUR FIELD TOGETHER . . .
WITH WHAT REGRET THAT WE CAN NEVER SAY: CAREFUL DEAR
     FRIENDS
DO NOT TAKE THAT FALSE STEP! OR IN ANY WAY PROTECT U
WHO ARE OUR LOVED ONES   WD THAT WE CD LEAD U TO THAT
     LOST
VERMEER THAT MANUSCRIPT OF MOZART OR LEAVE U SIMPLY
A LITTLE GLOWING MEDAL STRUCK IN HEAVEN SAYING: TRUE

Selfless to the end, they do not ask why the feather of proof
must be denied. The final lesson consists of instructions for how

to prepare and purify oneself for a visit from the Archangel Michael. On the day, or suncycle rather, to follow, DJ and JM must abstain from meat, alcohol, and tobacco; they are to "DRESS THE MIND" in the four colors and elements and think of one another. The interminable day (its tensions and dragging slowness beautifully described) subsides at last to sunset, and the angel appears—to conclude the cycle of lessons, and this volume, and prefigure the next: "WE WILL MEET AGAIN/ I AM MICHAEL/ I HAVE ESTABLISHED YOUR ACQUAINTANCE AND ACCEPT YOU."

2. SCRIPTS FOR THE PAGEANT

(Note: the Heaven of *Scripts* is altogether vaster and richer than that of *Ephraim*, or even of *Mirabell*. Its pronouncements sound more plausible, yet are at the same time more equivocal and insubstantial. Most of the texts and elaborations of doctrine quoted by the angels and spirits are fancy-dress aspects or versions of the one fearful idea which has pursued JM from childhood: that whenever a person probes beneath the surface appearance of any "idea"—gift horse, loved one, atom of uranium—destruction will follow. When the revelation can be understood rationally, it can usually be understood in some relation to this fundamental belief, though no doubt there are other ways to view the messages from Heaven as well. But, however they are viewed, it's the fancy dress that best rewards attention. Interpretive material, appearing within parentheses below, may help sort out the concepts of which the poem is built; but the true value of *Scripts* is not so much of substance as of style, and the best use of this summary will be to let it direct the reader, as speedily as possible, back into the poem.)

YES

Auden and Maria describe Michael's "appearance": an immense shining presence with a "FACE OF THE IDEAL/ PARENT CONFESSOR LOVER READER FRIEND." The experience reduces Mirabell to a heap of feathers; but the next day, revived, he imparts new information about Nature: that matter is hers to shape and control, but is only 88% of what is ("THE DIVINE RATIO 88:12" is a constant from volume II). When DJ notices that Mirabell seems suddenly servile, Maria explains that the four of them—since Michael's coming, probably—now outrank their peacock. Random observations of this sort bring us to the angel's second visit, when he tells the creation myth of *Mirabell* from another perspective:

God Biology created the world; then, aware of enemies— dark sucking forces that had bested him before—he created also out of his intelligence four powers or "sons" to help him: the four angels. The green earth was prepared and divided by seas, for God "HELD IN HIS INTELLIGENCE SEVERAL CHILDREN HE WISHED TO KEEP APART." He instructed the angels to fashion some forms from earth, and two of these were approved: the centaurs and (in reserve) man, made in the angels' image. After the first creature failed and the world had been reshaped, and made more arduous with mountains and seasons, then man came into his own: the ape was stunned with intelligence and God claimed and loved him. Michael's memorable exit line: "INTELLIGENCE, THAT IS THE SOURCE OF LIGHT. FEAR NOTHING WHEN YOU STAND IN IT."

David sails for Athens at summer's end; JM stays on alone in Stonington to work through the fall on *Mirabell*. The sense of months blurred and foreshortened by this absorbing labor comes across beautifully, and an evening with the ailing Greek-American scientist George Cotzias gives occasion to protract the flow of top-quality writing. Then JM joins DJ in Athens for the New

Year, 1977, and dictation briefly resumes. (*Scripts* will be transcribed in Athens, as *Mirabell* was in Stonington.) A first flurry of callers—Hans Lodeizen, Wallace Stevens, Mirabell, WHA, MM, Mademoiselle—is swept apart by Mirabell's old teacher oo and by Michael, who alert them to expect another angelic visitor: Elias the "Water Brother." Their second angel is "A GIANT ALL HOAR & SPIKY ICE" but the third, his twin Elijah, the "Earth Brother," is better still: he assumes the shape of Mount Lykabettos, across the street from the house, "ALL MASSIVE ROCK & GREEN WITH BOUGHS FOR LASHES," like an illustration by Arthur Rackham. Made of cosmic dust, Elijah contains not only topsoil but also irradiated metals: an *essential* yes-and-no. Unlike Elias, who has spoken only of himself, Elijah sounds the sober overpopulation theme from *Mirabell*. (The twins, we will learn later, are also called Raphael and Emmanuel and are usually known by those names.)

Between visitations the mediums have learned an astonishing thing: that Auden will return to Earth in *mineral* form. Mirabell is reassuring: the vegetable and mineral futures of WHA and Maria should be seen as "NOT/ SAD OR SINISTER BUT . . . A NEAR-MIRACULOUS REPLENISHMENT." They go to join the dominions of earth and water, there to make, alas, the famines that will help to bring Earth's ecosystem back into balance. Nor are DJ and JM to worry about George Cotzias, though radium treatments have destroyed his soul as well. Just before JM is to return to Stonington, Auden introduces a theme destined to preoccupy the trilogy's third volume:

> It's as we were told at the outset—every grain
> Of dust, each waterdrop, to be suffused
> With mind, with *our* minds. This will be Paradise.
> PRECISELY JM & TO GO ON: THAT RACE
> USING US, EVOLVING FROM US IN
> THAT PARADISE, ASK THEM ABOUT THAT RACE.
> IT IS I THINK NOW BEING READIED . . .

Back home, JM hard at the V Work, time passes in another
blur; and four months later JM is in Athens again to meet "the
shy brother" Gabriel (*shy* is Gabriel's epithet as *witty* is Elijah's,
though neither seems to fit). He speaks through flame, in the
absence of sunlight (curtains drawn, candles lit in the house in
Athens). He is Death and Destruction, created to wipe out God's
first creature, and then his second, as God could not have brought
himself to do: charged forever to be the unmaker of God's V
Work, its other side; as he says, "I AM THE SHADOW OF MY
FATHER . . . A NEUTRAL ELEMENT."

Now the four Angels of Air/Light, Water, Earth, and Fire
assume responsibility for instructing the Scribe. (1) The lessons
take place in a "schoolroom" which we are to visualize as the
former nursery at Sandover, the imaginary English estate mentioned in *Mirabell*, Book 9, whose name is an hourglass emblem.
This from the spirits' and angels' point of view; the mediums
are in the entrance hall of their house on Athenaion Efivon. In
Heaven a hedge encircles the estate: spirits without clearance are
kept outside. Michael dominates the cycle of ten "lessons that
say Yes." In the first he declares his text (as in a sermon) to be:
"THE MOST INNOCENT OF IDEAS IS THE IDEA THAT INNO-
CENCE IS DESTROYED BY IDEAS." A round-robin elaboration of
this assertion consists entirely of questions, as does most of the
ensuing discussion, and fails to clarify it or reduce its abstract-
ness; the establishment of a scale and a particular rhetorical tone,
rather than clarity, is the point of these pages:

Emm. AND I THE EXTINGUISHER OF THE FIRST BURNING IDEA FLUNG
     FROM THE PANTHEON OF SPACE
    WAS SUMMONED BY A VOICE: 'COOL THIS ROUNDED IDEA!' . . .
Gabr. I AM GOD'S SCION AND HIS NATURE. HE, BALANCER OF CHAOS
     & CREATION.
    THESE, O EASILY MAY THEY NOT BE
    CHAOS: INNOCENCE? CREATION: IDEA?

FIRSTBORN WAS CHAOS, THAT I KNOW!
& WHEN THE STEAMING BALL PEERD THROUGH IT I FELL BACK
   ONE STEP AS OUR FATHER CALLD LIGHT! LIGHT!
AND MY BROTHER MICHAEL SHOWD US THE WORLD. SAY, SLY
   MICHAEL
His red glow whitening with intensity.
WHY DID YOU TAKE AS TEXT THIS?

Auden asks about *sin*—whether innocence is lost to guilt or experience—but goes unanswered. As in *Mirabell*, discussion among
the mortals and shades follows the withdrawal of the Instruc-
tors, but enlightenment will have to wait for a later day. They
wonder, but cannot tell, whether Gabriel is Chaos and whether
Chaos is dispelled by creation.

(2) Raphael speaks first, of *thought*. His metaphor for the
human cranium is the cave with painted walls. At this point the
sense of his lecture is enigmatic, yet he is often eloquent as he
enlarges upon "CAVE AFTER CAVE STACKED UPON EACH OTHER,
SKULL PILE AND SKYSCRAPER,/ THE BONE OF HUMAN THOUGHT
THRUSTING UP. . . ." Emmanuel's turn is next, and his metaphor is the stilted houses of the lakedwellers who, he believes—
having encountered their "FIRST SHOCKING IDEA: FEAR OF EACH
OTHER" in the caves—tried to return to the "innocent" water
they had emerged from, to escape "THAT FEARFUL FORWARD
MARCH." Then it is Michael's turn: "EARTH & WATER, THESE
ARE INNOCENT NATURE,/ WHILE I, OH I, MUST BEAR THE
BURDEN OF IDEAS." (The source of confusion is that *thought* and
ideas, which look identical in this second lesson, will shortly be
seen to oppose one another within the myth. "Idea" is used here
in the limited sense of "concept" or "belief," identified with intelligence but not with reasoning. The distinction is a useful one
to bear in mind.)

The next day the four friends voice their consternation; the
tenor of the second lesson seemed to bode ill for the future of

mankind. Auden suggests giving the poem-to-be the *Yes & No* structure of the Ouija board; then (3) he and Maria—as class begins—in turn implore the angel of death to "SPARE OUR WORLD." Gabriel seems willing to listen; in a kind of torment he rails at Michael for bathing man in the light of ideas, thus fostering in him pride, ambition, a false "SENSE OF SENSE IN ALL HIS SENSELESSNESS." Gabriel, one now gathers, is full of feeling—suitable in a candidate for the role of Chaos—and would far rather spare worlds than destroy them. (In fact, he follows orders; the decision to destroy a creature of God's is God's, not Gabriel's.) Yet, as Auden suspects, Gabriel's kneeling and weeping—"AH CHILDREN, CONVINCE ME, CONVINCE!"—is a mask of melodrama; for the next day they learn (4) that an old pact between Gabriel and Emmanuel, to wipe out God's failed experiments, was later altered as Gabriel began to crave destruction for destruction's own sake. When the Death Angel says that the suicide alone reverts to pure innocence at the moment of death, "STRIPT OF IDEA AS MORTALITY IS SHED" unresistingly, Maria's own death is abruptly revealed as a suicide. The two mortals are shocked and distressed. DJ has recently been to tidy up the grave, weeding, planting, mulching; "It looked so really nice when we were through./ And now . . . . JM: And now, you mean, beneath it/ Somebody's lying whom we never knew?"

But words of comfort from Maria begin the next session: "DJ: DEAR ENFANT LEAVE MY PLOT/ TO THICKEN NICELY BY ITSELF. ALIVE/ & WELL (& IN FULL FIG TO MEET THE F I V E)/ I'M HERE WITH U, NO? ALL THE REST IS ROT." And now the Five Immortals, each representing one of God's five senses, pass in review. Plato is currently between lives but is about to be reborn; we also hear that one of the Five is someone the mediums have known personally. (George Cotzias, guesses JM.) The following session (6) sets forth the duties, natures, and elements associated with each of the angels. (In the process it makes the essential clarification. Michael—light, intelligence, idea—opposes Gabriel, who serves Chaos in the dark and is called (in 7) "THINKER ON IDEAS. RESTLESS URGER-ON OF MAN'S MIND" by God himself. If intelligence and thought are combatants, then a probing, analytical mind like Auden's must be allied with Gabriel. Michael represents the sensitive, perceptive intelligence that does not investigate or evaluate ideas but ignores them or takes them in entire, the sort revealed in Merrill's poetry as his own. So the tree of the knowledge of good and evil is still proscribed; but the role of Serpent is played by Gabriel in this version of the myth. The meaning of Michael's text now comes clear: Innocence is not destroyed by Ideas, but both Innocence and Ideas are destroyed by Thought.)

In (7), when God's own voice suddenly breaks into transcription, the mediums feel uncomfortable:

> Why should God speak? How humdrum what he *says*
> Next to His works: out of a black sleeve, lo!
> Sun, Earth, and Stars in eloquent dumb show.
> Our human words are weakest, I would urge,
> When He resorts to them.

But distrust fades to amazement, as it increasingly will do before the unexpected in this Volume, as Auden describes the experience from his vantage point; and now (8) the angels, as if nothing unusual had happened, proceed to identify themselves with God's senses as the Five have done. God has other senses numbered beyond five, however: intuition, judgment, command, pronouncement; "AND THEN THE ZEROETH WE DO NOT KNOW/ FOR THAT HE EXERCISES OUTWARD/ . . . OUR FATHER SINGS,/ SINGS, ALONE, INTO THE UNIVERSE." They are to hear the exercising of that zeroeth sense at (10).

Now JM and DJ prepare to celebrate the twenty-fifth anniversary (by Greek reckoning; twenty-fourth by ours) of their companionship. By coincidence ("NO ACCIDENT" corrects MM) it's the Queen's Silver Jubilee as well. Their instructions are to bring to the table "SALT. A SPICE OF YR OWN CHOICE./ A SCENT. ICE IN A BOWL. A CANDLE LIT/ & A LIVE FLOWER." While *Rosenkavalier* plays on the turntable, Strauss, Homer, Kirsten Flagstad, Montezuma, Akhnaton and Nefertiti, and Plato troop in. Section (9) is not a lesson, but the party's planned entertainment. The live flower chosen was a lily; here, from among a multitude of the poem's small perfect details, comes this from one important guest:

> *Enter a plumed Splendor:*
>   OUR SCULPTORS CARVED
> THAT FLOWER BY THE THOUSAND & WHEN MY PALACE
> FELL INTO THE MOAT (It's Montezuma!)
> ONE BLOSSOM, ONE STONE LILY FLOATED FREE
> THE LIGHT VOLCANIC ROCK YOU SEE

A stagy bit with the ice and spice and the other stimuli now brings the mediums through to WHA and MM sensually, and unreversed by the mirror, for the first time. (The moment also strengthens the thematic force of so much protracted attention to the senses of God Biology. And how Merrill glories in his own senses can only now be fully appreciated—even Helen Vendler's word "ravishment" seems scarcely strong enough.) Flagstad sings an aria: Michael's formal invocation, addressed to the four humans, welcoming them into "THIS HEAVEN IT IS GIVEN YOU TO WIN." Though all present have made the utmost effort to transcend the Divide, and though the spirits say their senses were restored, even that they were able to touch the two mortals, DJ and JM see nothing (David "felt . . . a chill?")

Last of all in this cycle of lessons (10) the four are permitted to hear God singing eerily, in a black void:

> . . . ALONE IN MY NIGHT BROTHERS I AND MINE
> SURVIVE BROTHERS DO YOU WELL I AND MINE
> IN MY NIGHT I HOLD IT BACK I AND MINE

SURVIVE BROTHERS SIGNAL ME IN MY NIGHT
I AND MINE HOLD IT BACK AND WE SURVIVE

Only they have ever heard that song; Dante heard *something* but, as JM rather chillingly observes, "The lyrics may be changing." Humanity's survival still seems anything but certain. (The idea that its survival depends on action that will be taken as a result of JM's poem seems to have quietly atomized and vanished, somewhere along the line, though no one has said so.) To complete the grimness, DJ and JM are told now that at the end of fifteen more lessons *they* will be called upon to unforge the four-way bond, letting Maria and Auden return to the world: "THAT DAY/ ENFANTS TAKE OUT A SMALL EXPENDABLE MIRROR/ ONTO THE FRONT STEP   KISS & WITH ONE WISE/ CRACK SET US FREE." DJ wants to refuse, Maria suggests a bowl of reflecting water instead of a mirror (as less violent a severing), but JM sees that the logic of the poem requires the shattering of a glass. Mirror and bowl as well, proposes DJ; and session and section end with a little lyric, dictated by Auden, on God B's song:

> . . . ONE SAILOR'S CLEAR
> YOUNG TENOR FILLS THE HOUSE, HOMESICK, HEARTSICK.
>   THE MAST NEEDS COMFORT. GALES
>   HAVE TATTERED THE MOONBELLIED SAILS.
>   MAY HIS GREEN SHORES O QUICKLY
> SAFELY NOW FROM RAGING FOAM APPEAR.

&

The ampersand section, bridge from YES to NO, begins with an already justly famous canzone, "Samos," the repeated end-words sense, water, fire, land, and light. George Cotzias dies on June 13, 1977, while DJ and JM are on the island of Samos, and he promptly joins the seminar. Having undergone years of radiation therapy, he too will be gathered to the elements. He finds the cosmic scheme compatible with his research into the living cell, and alludes cheerfully to the superman whose development is currently underway in the R/Lab—George, of course, had instant access to the Lab.

Then news arrives that Robert Morse is dead. Though the seminar will not admit him, he immediately makes friends with Maria ("RM ENCHANTING"), looks ahead hopefully to a new life, and begins adjusting to Heaven. One more new character shyly introduces himself: a centaur, the very last to die, Mirabell's servant and messenger, whom Maria describes as a hornless long-necked unicorn. He seems childish and goodhearted, and the mediums think him enchanting. It is his task to guard the "gate" in the "hedge," to see that no one unauthorized gets into the seminar. Robert bestows a name on him: Unice; and Unice (Uni for short) reports on Robert's phenomenal social success in Heaven, saying how unusual it is for a "BETWEENER" to receive so much attention—no surprise to Robert's old friends, however.

And now the Middle Lessons begin. Formal presentations by the human spirits distinguish this section from the first, and Maria begins now (1) with an account of how the cooling world was seeded by God Biology: Michael/sun/generative force/ "RADIATION TO THE BILLIONTH POWER/ OF EXPLODING ATOMS" called to God in the Pantheon, and he gave Emmanuel seeds— "COSMIC DUST/ LADEN WITH PARTICLES OF INERT MATTER"— to rain upon the Earth, which sprouted vegetation. The plant world, besides providing food and oxygen, is "THE RESTING PLACE OF SOUL"; as it prospers, so does man. (2) Auden is next, but his lecture is enigmatic and he contests with Gabriel for every advance. The Pantheon allowed God B materials with which to shape his world, but required him also "TO TAKE THIS ONE,/ OUR M O N I T O R, TO DWELL WITHIN YOUR BALL." Monitor?? WHA, sinking into Earth's substance, encountered something infernal and terrifying: "HARD AT ITS HEART THE

MONITOR'S RAGING WILL." After letting slip a hint about the superman to come, for which Gabriel rebukes him, he pleads with all the angels to save the world. When school is over he tells the two mortals that he, Maria, and George "HAVE MADE A PACT: TO PRY IT OUT OF THEM! . . . THEY'VE 'ASKED' JM/ FOR A PIECE OF WORK. THEY CAN'T JUST GO ON SPILLING/ HERE A BEAN THERE A BEAN, IF & AS THEY PLEASE:/ A L L MUST MAKE SENSE."

(Throughout the poem, Auden's is the mind that pushes and probes. In YES/3, after Gabriel's grand performance, Auden alone refuses to be taken in:

MY BOY DON'T QUOTE THIS OLD STICKLER FOR FORM.
WHERE IN ALL THIS IS THE AFFIRMATION?
In the surrender, in the forward motion—
POWER BLAZING ON SHUT LIDS? MIND LAPPED IN WARM

PRIMORDIAL WATERS? Yes, yes! NO NO   THIS
INGENUE'S TRUST IN FEELING: NEVER TO THINK?
CHECK UP? ASK QUESTIONS? ONWARD TO THE BRINK,
ANCHOR CUT LOOSE? THAT WAY LIES NEMESIS

But Gabriel was kneeling, he was weeping!
YES, AS THE UNIVERSE'S GREATEST ACTOR . . .

No sparkling appearance is safe with Auden; Gabriel will have to take responsibility for that mind. George Cotzias, a well-known specialist in neurological disorders in life, and Scientist-in-Residence of *Scripts*, also harbors a powerful desire to understand the meaning of things, and consistently forces the discussions into grim areas—following out implications, refusing to be placated or gulled. Together, WHA and George resist and balance the mediums' faith in feeling and their willingness to be reassured, as Gabriel balances Michael and electron, proton.)

George has the floor next (3), and his text is "MATTER"; he speaks also of matter's opposite, "NOTHING." Each resists the

other, like the subatomic particles. Where matter ends is "NOT
VOID BUT/ SOLID EMPTINESS. AS WHO SHOULD FLING/ A WIN-
DOW UP ONTO A WALL OF GRAY CEMENT." (Perhaps this is the
other 12%, the antimatter which Nature does not control.) GK—
C becomes K in the Greek spelling of George's name—suspects
now that the force behind the angels may be evil: did God's
energy, he wonders, "COME/ FROM A TRIUMPH OVER, OR A
COMPROMISE WITH, BLACK MATTER?" Was that window "THE
DEATH BEYOND DEATH?" He confides to JM, when the angels
have gone, his fear that the sense which must soon be made of
all this may be devastating. JM responds with some lines which
restate more clearly what went obliquely past before.

> Back to your speech. See if we've understood:
> Even immobilized by powerful chains
> Of molecules, our very table strains
> Obscurely toward oblivion—or would
> Save that the switch of matter stays at Good.
> Now, does your question also touch that spin
> Of antiparticles our Lord of Light
> Darts promptly forward to annihilate
> —But which keep coming, don't they? and are kin
> Both to the Monitor and the insane
> Presence beyond our furthest greenhouse pane?

GK neither confirms nor denies JM's paraphrase. Privately, all
wonder whether Gabriel serves the Monitor, a truly awful
thought.

And now the slide toward NO begins. (4) Michael opens the
next lesson by bringing on the nine Muses, prompting each in
turn to speak of her function. Their presentation is dismaying.
Memory and History appear wholly unreliable, Terpsichore calls
herself "FORMALIZED DISTRACTION, STEP/ DAUGHTER OF
CHAOS," Urania is "ICY RATIONALITY," and so on. Afterwards
the mediums are more upset, and if possible more bewildered,

than ever; they experience the lesson as a general sinking into nastiness. The muse Calypso speaks of "P S Y C H E - C H A O S OUR IMMORTAL MOTHER"; they suddenly wonder whether the cast may not be much smaller than it seems, whether—for instance—Michael and Ephraim may have shared the same voice all along. And so many powers have been called Chaos! They rather dread the next lesson, in which they will have to *meet* this mother of the Muses; but (5) the power Michael ushers in is wearing "THE THIRD/ AND FAIREST FACE OF NATURE" (who is also Psyche, and who—and *not* Gabriel—*is* also Chaos!):

> *Enter—in a smart white summer dress,*
> *Ca. 1900, discreetly bustled,*
> *Trimmed if at all with a fluttering black bow;*
> *Black ribbon round her throat; a cameo;*
> *Gloved but hatless, almost hurrying*
> *—At last! the chatelaine of Sandover—*
> *A woman instantly adorable.*

Nature takes as her text, of all things, an "ENTWINING" of "BLAKE'S FAITH" and "THE FIRST LAW OF PHYSICS: MOTION KNOWS ONLY RESISTANCE." Nature and God B are twins, and the two are always in accord; just as proton and electron resist one another yet together made the "FIRST/ MINUTE PASTE" of matter, so Biology and Chaos. When God was about to begin the creation, he said to Nature:

'SISTER, BEFORE I CALL FORTH INHABITANTS OF THIS PLACE,
    LET US PLAN.
WHAT POINT IS THERE IN AN IMMORTAL BEING (THOUGH LESS,
    MUCH LIKE OURSELVES) IF HE CONTAINS NOTHING NEW, NO
    SURPRISE, TO CALL HIS OWN?
LET US DIVIDE THE FORCE OF HIS NATURE, JUST AS WE WILL
    MAKE TWO SIDES TO ALL NATURE,
FOR IN DUALITY IS DIMENSION, TENSION, ALL THE TRUE
    GRANDEUR WANTING IN A PERFECT THING.
SISTER, TAKE COMMAND OF HIS . . . RESISTANCE? HIS "UN-

GODLY" SIDE. MAKE HIM KNOW DARK AS WELL AS LIGHT,
GIVE HIM PUZZLEMENT, MAKE HIM QUESTION,
FOR WOULD WE NOT LIKE COMPANY?' I AGREED.

(Harmony within resistance, already established as a key concept to the poem, will be constant to its end.) The first consequences of the freedom to resist—the saga of the centaurs and
bats told in *Mirabell*—were tragic. God's next creature was the
ape transmogrified to man, and his uses of resistance (thanks to
the enfeeblement of the No Accident Clause?) are such that Nature is often tempted to destroy him too. "BUT THEN THE APE
SINGS, HE TOUCHES MY HEART . . . I CLOSE THE LID AND
SMILE."

There is general relief at this—so man is safe! But death
still resists the forward motion of life. The formula GK had
been working on when he died, a way to prevent the degenera-
tive process in cells, is correct; but man will not be ready for
immortality until he can "IMPROVE THE STRAIN AND LIMIT ITS
NUMBERS . . ." Passing compliments all round, Mother Nature
exits with a charge to Gabriel: that he explain, in the ten semi-
nars of NO, "ALL DEEP AND 'DIRE' THINGS." Michael follows
her out and the Middle Lessons are over. (The story has taken on
overtones of Miltonic paradox, though no one here tries to justify
the double-handedness of giving a creature thought, then threatening to destroy him for using it.) Everyone is pleased to learn
that Nature herself has given Robert clearance to join the class
for NO. And now after the fact, MM and WHA reveal how-
much *they* had to do with the first ten lessons, helping the angels
to remember "THE IMAGE-THWARTED PATHS BY WHICH WE
THINK," nudging them from abstract to concrete, *becoming* a lex-
icon for their use. The dissension between Gabriel and the others was only an act, rehearsed on the principle that "ALL GOOD
DISCOURSE MUST, LIKE FORWARD MOTION,/ KNOW RESIS-
TANCE." Then, afterwards, they had forgotten what they learned

and did until the five "&" lessons were ended. RM and GK, at work even now on the last ten, are similarly to forget and remember.

Dark thoughts, however, crowd back in as the four have time to think over what they have been told. The shifting and doubling of characters, for instance, disturbs the mediums. Then George suddenly wonders whether they aren't all being unduly optimistic about Mother Nature: "GABRIEL IS HER SPOILED DARLING,/ SHE A 'PERMISSIVE MAW.'" Both Nature and Gabriel have been called Chaos; might Gabriel *be* the Monitor? The revived notion that things may not yet be settled in favor of man's survival badly upsets DJ. On the other hand, in Plato's new V life he is to be a biochemist due, 27 years hence, to invent "A POLLUTION-EATING ANTIGAS"—*that* seems to bode well. The signals continue to flash Yes and No. But JM, while in awe of Nature's power, is inclined to trust her still. Her emblem is the moon; at this juncture eight lines coalesce out of the moonlit blue, slant-rhymes purifying to a perfect couplet in imitation of the poet's hopefulness:

> New moon this evening. Rim of plate.
> Forbodings luminous if incomplete.
>
> A moon we shiver to see wax
> —What will our portion be in two more weeks?
>
> MM to Gabriel: AH LORD, THAT MEAL.
> But spoken gently, spoken with a smile . . . ?
>
> Ripen, Huntress, into matron. Light
> Come full circle through unclouded night.

The newest report on Plato says he will be reborn in "BOMBAY   A RICH/ PUNJABI FAMILY   FATHER A MATHEMATICIAN/ AND BANKER   MOTHER A DOCTOR OF MEDICINE." Now speaks OO, that once-dread power: "I SALUTE YOU AS MY MASTERS."

The following day begin "the lessons that say No"; but before they do JM explicitly settles the crucial "intellectual" question hanging fire since YES/2. Maria is speaking:

> ALL THE RELIGIONS
> WE NOW THINK WERE MICH'S V WORK. HIS REALM, IDEAS
> And Gabriel's thought. Does thought destroy ideas?
> WHAT ELSE? Well, *our* faith came to be in Feeling.
> Feelings for one another, love, trust, need,
> Daily harrowing the mini-hells
> They breed— DON'T TALK TO YR MAMAN OF FEELINGS
> TOO FEW WERE STARS   TOO MANY WERE BLACK HOLES

This brief passage is a kind of Rosetta Stone for much of what has gone before it. Finally, the House in Athens—Hill Cumorah of these dictations—is described in a sweet lyric interlude, just before the new school term gets underway.

NO

For these Last Lessons a larger group assembles: two mortals, four shades, and four angels. Nature, and God Biology himself, will also erratically attend. (1) Gabriel, who will be in charge of these sessions, announces his theme—Time—and his text: "OF ALL DESTRUCTIVE IDEAS THE MOST DESTRUCTIVE IS THE IDEA OF DESTRUCTION." George rises to speak, is overcome, is encouraged by Nature/Psyche: "TAKE GABRIEL'S TEXT AND REMEMBER:/ THE MOST DESTRUCTIVE OF ALL IDEAS IS THAT FEELING SETS IT RIGHT!" Pulling himself together GK speaks of immortality, the subject of his research, "A BANISHMENT OF TIME." Immortality destroyed the centaurs; and he, having found the secret, was whisked back to Heaven before he could reveal it. But immortality will be offered again, after the thinning which is now imminent. George pleads with Gabriel to thin gently and sparingly; Gabriel replies that GK can judge the kindness for himself when he returns to Earth "AS ONE OF THIS NEW GENERATION, AN ALPHA MAN."

Whew. The ensuing discussion (gods and angels having withdrawn) touches fleetingly on a number of points, none dull. JM: "Why should Time be black?/ Why is it Gabriel's?" Because, says Auden, the original pact was between God and the Black beyond black, the solid emptiness of anti-matter and black holes. (Here, as often throughout both *Mirabell* and *Scripts*, the bats and spirits reply to questions without actually answering them, or by distracting the questioner, or by censorship; the best answer to this particular question is given in chapter 8. Another instance of the reply that raises more questions than it answers concerns the "thinning" which now begins to sound inevitable:

> DJ: It's true? They wash their hands of us?
> Of people? After going to such lengths—
> WE TOO ONCE DOTED FONDLY (EH CONFRERE?)
> ON EARLY WORKS WE RATHER SQUIRM AT NOW
> JM: We've threatened—therefore we must go—
> Earth and Sea and Air. JIMMY   NO NO
> It's only a "thinning process," George? THE KEY
> WORD IS ALPHA   Yes, yes—"Brave New World".
> MY BOY U GOT IT   WHAT OF THE OMEGAS?
> 3 BILLION OF EM UP IN SMOKE POOR BEGGARS?
> Wystan, how *can* you? COURAGE: GABRIEL
> KNOWS WHAT HE'S UP TO & (LIKE TIME) WILL TELL

By implication the thinning will be done according to the Lab's elitism: the denser souls saved, the inferior majority destroyed by Gabriel's fire. But the signals still flash Yes and No; we can't be sure.)

Early in the first lesson, Auden said something interesting: "SUNUP TO SUNDOWN, HUMANKIND/ HAS SET IDEA TO INNOCENCE, TO ALLAY/ ITS FEARS & HOARD ITS HOPE AGAINST THE NIGHT." The second lesson (2) demonstrates one sort of idea man has set to innocence (in the sense of "set to music"): religion. Gabriel calls forth Gautama, Jesus, Wagner (for the Norse gods), and Mercury (for the Greek ones) (but no Hindu gods), and we hear their common lament: the slackened force of their teachings in the lives of men. As we know from *Mirabell*, and are reminded here, the new religion will be literature, "THE FLAT WHITE PRINTED PAGE." This day's discussion reveals how uncertain the mediums have become about whom to trust. The Monitor can't be Gabriel, says GK, but—are they sure it was God B they heard singing? But "the Brothers told us—DO THEY KNOW?" Are things all backwards, a negative of themselves, and much worse than anyone supposed? What if there were a Black God—the Monitor—who resists a "WHITE OF MIND/ UNLIMITED . . . IMAGINATION METAPHOR/ SHATTERED BY WHITE REASON!" George seems to be applying something like scare tactics, which work extraordinarily well; he might almost be describing himself.

(3) Mohammed is the third lesson's featured attraction. He alone of these religious leaders is of the Five; his is the only faith still thriving. He is scornful of Jesus and Buddha, asserting that Islam had a more practical appeal to his constituency of fighters "READY FOR A KILL & A PLUMP WOMAN." But, when called to order by a sternly feminist Nature, he stops swaggering and talks fearfully about the Black: horrific, irresistible, a sucking, a rising of sand. Gabriel relentlessly confirms that Mohammed "DOES OUR WORK . . . BY PREPARING [EARTH'S] LAST, HOLY WAR." The three lines punctuating the poem just here are an exquisite emblem of dread:

> *Night, windless, clear. Beneath a crescent moon*
> *Thousands of little whetted scythes appear*
> *With each slow forward breath of the great dune.*

Robert's aria, sung next, and of no relief to the doom-laden atmosphere, concerns the two powerful souls of Caligula and Hitler, distorted by a black whispery seepage through a "crack." The song continues: we "LIVE IN TIME'S FORWARD RUN. THE

BLACK/ BEYOND BLACK IS OF TIME SET RUNNING BACK . . . /
THEIR LEADERSHIP INSTRUCTION (THIN! KEEP CLEAR!)/ SPEEDS
UP, BECOMING: TERMINATE! THEY HEAR/ ANOTHER SIREN
SINGING. PITY THEM." Gabriel finishes his day's work by saying
there is no punishment, no mercy, no right and wrong, no sin,
no hell. Outside time, these are meaningless; vagrant souls are
condemned only to idleness ("IN HEAVEN NOT TO BE USED IS
HELL," said Ephraim long ago).

"Won't someone please explain the Black?" asks JM desperately, and an "explanation" does accordingly follow:

> NOW (GEORGE HERE) IN AMONG EARTH'S TREASURES ARE
> THE INFRA-TREASURES OF THE MONITOR:
> NOT FORWARD TIME COMPRESSED (COMBUSTIBLE
> OILCAN OF 'THINNER') BUT ATOMIC BLACK
> COMPRESSED FROM TIME'S REVERSIBILITY,
> THAT IDEA OF DESTRUCTION WHICH RESIDES
> BOTH IN MAN & IN THE ACTINIDES.
> PART OF THE GREENHOUSE, FOR (THO MATTER HOLDS)
> THESE FORKED TONGUES FLICKER FROM ITS OILS & GOLDS.

But this is the mad, plausible voice of a fever-dream; GK goes
on, but there is little point in struggling to make sense of what
he says. JM, who *must* try to, blames the murk on the limita-
tions of language (and language's limitation, rather than the Black,
becomes the point of the passage):

> It all fits. But the ins and outs deplete us.
> Minding the thread, losing the maze, we curse
> Language's misleading apparatus. . . .
>
> My characters, this motley alphabet,
> Engagingly evade the cul-de-sac
> Of the Whole Point, dimensionless and black,
>
> While, deep in bulging notebooks, drawn by it,
> I skim lost heavens for that inky star.

That inky star—the Black—will remain one more unanswered question, unless he can discover an answer somewhere in the vastness of accumulated transcription.

(4) Gabriel responds to a question of Auden's, brushed aside in YES/I, by naming "THE ONE SIN:/ PAIN. PAIN GIVEN, PAIN RECEIVED . . . THE ONLY CHILD OF TIME AND FEELING." Maria, tackling now the difficulty raised in NO/I, argues in defense of man's "UNWRITTEN SIN": dabbling in nuclear physics. She claims that since the powers have nourished the "AVID WEED CALLED CURIOSITY" in man, they deliberately invite the consequences of thought: the unveiling of Nature's secrets, including the secret of atomic fission. But Gabriel conducts their descent into a place where an underground nuclear test is going on. Maria describes the experience later: "A PURE/ WHITE LIGHT, THE NEGATIVE OR 'EYE' OF BLACK/ BURST ON US   The *bad* white, the metaphor-/ Shattering light? AMORAL   YES MY DEARS." But even this powerful, unanswerable argument against too much snooping and meddling cannot exonerate God B and Nature for their gift; and in (5) a further explanation is attempted.

The *very* first of God's creatures, hinted about before but never taken up until now, was a wingèd man in China, who destroyed himself and half the world in the nuclear explosion alluded to by Ephraim in his own book, Section P. When the centaurs bred their radioactive messengers, the green flies they used were the winged men remade. These eventually grew huge and built the crust world, which also self-destructed. And now a third time the fatal secret is out; no wonder God and Nature are worried. (And no wonder the No Accident clause was devised. It sounds from this as if the discoveries of twentieth-century atomic physics, as well as their fateful misuse in weaponry, should be laid at the door of overpopulation, the necessary use of animal soul densities, and the beginning of accidents. JM loves GK; but he has not perhaps forgotten or forgiven that "congenitally slug-/ Pale boy at school, with his precipitates,/ His fruit-flies and his slide rule"—a prejudice confessed to in *Mirabell*.)

Section (6) is devoted wholly to the unveiling of Maria; for it is she—not Auden, not George—who has been Plato all the time. She is about to re-enter the world, not as a plant after all! but to take up a new life in Bombay, as a male biochemist. She is, of course, of the Five, and part of her mission in her life as Maria was to recruit somebody to do the V Work this trilogy has become; another was to dispose of Edward VIII so Elizabeth could become Queen of England. (In other lives—see YES/5—Plato was Genghis Khan and John Muir, though this last is subject to revision: Muir died in 1914; Maria was born in 1907.) In spite of this dizzying revelation school goes on. (7) Raphael tells of how he buried the luckless wingèd men in China, and Emmanuel how he drowned Atlantis and seeded the Sargasso Sea above it: but this is a light workday before the last hard lesson, (8).

Everyone is present to hear Gabriel's explanation of the "IT" which gods, spirits, immortals, and JM are supposed to make sense of. He starts from what we know: God made his creature man and commanded: Let it survive, and Let there be No Accident. JM is then instructed to draw a tall X representing man, and place the X upright on a curved line representing the Earth and its resistance. Emmanuel fills his arms with sand—any source of energy—from the "TIMELESS SHORE," and Presto! an hourglass, much like Yeats's double cone. But then the figure becomes stranger: Gabriel says to draw his shadow, or mirror image, below, which gives

TIME'S MAN BECOME TIME AGAINST MAN:
SAND RUNNING UP, DEEP FUELS TAPPD, MAN STRADDLING
 HEAVEN, HEAVEN RECEIVING TIME
WHICH RUNNING OUT THROUGH A MINOAN WAIST
STOPS HERE WHERE WE ARE:

WE WHO (M) LIVING IN THIS RISING DUNE HOLD IT BACK, HOLD
   BACK A RESERVOIR OF SPENT TIME,
FEEL AT OUR FEET & LIKEN TO ATOMIC WASTE THIS WASTE,
   THIS UPWARD VOLATILE FORCE,
AND KNOW THE TWO MINDS OF MATTER.

POET, YOU WISELY MADE US STAND ON RISING GROUND, FOR
   BENEATH US, MORTALS, SHADES AND GODS, IS THE CAPPD
   VOLCANO.

The rest of this riveting lesson is Michael's apocalyptic Jere-
miad: the angels see all the old signs of impending doom, signs
of the Monitor's activity, the first accidents, "THE IDIOT IN
POWER." When he is done, the mortals are allowed a Question
Period. Some of the questions are good: Why the Ouija board?
(Michael: because dreams and "inspiration" didn't work.) About
scale: "When we suppose that history's great worm/ Turns and
turns as it does because of twin/ Forces balanced and alert within/
Any least atom, are we getting warm?" (This is the theme of
Harmony Within Resistance, and Gabriel's answer is Yes.) How
did Maria (and George) escape destruction? (They "WERE GIVEN
MEANS TO PUT OUR SOULS BEYOND/ THE RAYS.") But the grief
and horror JM felt when first told of Maria's "fate" were instruc-
tive: it "REMAINS WITH YOU TO FEEL/ FOR ALL CREATION" on
the brink of atomic disaster; with this feeling he is charged to
charge his poem.

A Spenserian stanza introduces, and others will advance,
the masque (9) in celebration of man—a showier occasion than
Michael's party at YES/9. Nature herself is in charge, bringing
in people—Maria-as-Plato, Yeats, Ephraim, Mirabell—and dis-
missing them; pronouncing; distributing gifts. She quenches the
nuclear fire-ache in Mirabell's eyes; she restores to Ephraim his
senses for a day, and one—vision—for keeps. Robert, in Stra-
vinsky's place, conducts Auden's and Chester's opera *The Rake's
Progress* (record playing in Athens). Yeats is instructed to plead

for DJ on Judgment Day, that he and JM never be parted; thus is a clause in *Ephraim* overthrown. The most unusual guest is Feeling, embodied in an unrolled windowblind "Daubed in poison-sugar tints by *Blake,/* A poster figure, not of humankind." Nature, knowing Feeling of old as a "SEVENFOLD SIN," as "CHAOS" (she who has herself been called Chaos, yet is offended by tears?—well, one more paradox), nevertheless has invited this odd guest for the sake of the two mortals who cherish her:

NOW LISTEN, JEZEBEL!
& WHEN WITH CRIPPLING TIME THEY ARE BROUGHT LOW,
WISH THEM WELL, WISH THEM WELL
FOR TOO LONG HAVE YOU SPENT ON AGE
YOUR PENT-UP RAGE.
Snap! As the blind rolls shut two mortals melt.

These mortals have been waiting from lesson to lesson, hopes alternately raised and dashed, to learn the fate of humankind. With Nature's exit line—"BUT LET ME CRY A LAST RESOUNDING YES/ TO MAN, MAN IN HIS BLESSEDNESS!"—they seem again to know; yet again WHA shadows their relief: what exactly did she mean by "last"?—that "man won't be hearing Yes much more?" Auden seems to feel that man's fate still hangs in the balance, an impression strengthened when God speaks again, at (10)—so briefly that we may as well hear him in full:

MY SON MICHAEL LIT UP YOUR MINDS   MY SON
GABRIEL TURNED THEM TO THE DARK FORCE WE
CONTAIN   POET FROM THIS MAKE A V WORK
GIVING BOTH PAUSE AND HOPE TO THIS FIGURE
I SEE EMBLAZONED HERE

[the cup traces an X on the Board, YES to NO to A to Z to YES]

MY UPRIGHT MAN
FULL OF TIME   HE STRUGGLES TO HOLD IT BACK
AND CREATE FOR ME A PARADISE I
IN MY OWN UPSTRETCHED ARMS WILL SHOW CRYING

SEE BROTHERS WE HAVE HELD IT BACK SEE SEE
I AND MINE BROTHERS IN OUR DAY SURVIVE

And thus, leaving both pause and hope to the Scribe, God B
signs out and the lessons are complete.

Though school's over, JM and DJ stay in touch with Maria
and Auden while they still can—passing the time, before the
separation, with travel and with random low-key conversations.
Robert, George, and Uni look in often. Again, as the climax
approaches, JM's writing grows positively luminescent. GK and
WHA describe their unusual destinations: George will be sub-
divided by eighteen, to hex or safeguard that many labs world-
wide; Auden will enter the sphere of minerals, perhaps to contribute to the coming thinning—about which Nature now begins
to sound obsessive—as a desert. All are waiting for the word
which Maria finally passes: on September 16, 1977, DJ's 55th
birthday, the mirror must be broken. But, to ease the pain of
parting, the mediums propose and Maria agrees to a naughty
scheme: they will visit Bombay in 1991 to rendezvous with "A
SCRUBBED 14 YEAR OLD PUNJABI LAD/ CARRYING SOMETHING
U WILL KNOW ME BY."

Flash-forward now: 00, the Senior Bat, promises a visit,
just before JM leaves Athens, with someone who can answer
leftover questions. What to ask? JM doesn't want to know much
about the Alpha Men, but he does have one question, difficult
to frame: What form will Resistance (our humanizing wilfulness,
God's idea, Nature's gift) take in Paradise? At this final fore-
gathering, news of their departed friends is conveyed by Nature, who addresses their other questions as well. WHA has
surfaced off Alaska as a vein of pure radium, and George begun
with an electrical experiment over Russia; Maria is 19 days old
in Bombay. In spite of his resistance, JM is told something of
the new man, for whom—when his ideal numbers have been

reached—time will stop. As JM must have feared, there will be *no* Resistance; Alpha Man will be "A SIMPLER, LESS WILFUL BEING. DULLER TOO?/ IF SO, IS THAT SHARP EDGE NOT WELL LOST/ WHICH HAS SO VARIOUSLY CUT AND COST?" (JM's answer to this would be Yes and No, had he given one.) Alpha Man is to be "A CREATURE MUCH LIKE DARLING MAN," but he will *not* be man: he will produce no Einsteins and make neither bombs nor brilliant breakthroughs, though gods will walk among these beings out of whom the passion for knowledge about the physical universe will have been bred. "Yes and no" is the real answer to the poem's question *Does man survive?*, not a slick evasion.

Flashback, finally, to the sendoff day, which is described last for dramatic reasons. The ritual of farewell dictated in YES becomes reality: quick goodbyes are said, a marble doorstop shatters a souvenir mirror, the shards go into a ricebowl of water and then water and shards together into a blooming Cassia once dug up wild and potted by a living Maria. At that moment the souls of their three friends pass out of Heaven into "EARTH WORK   LIFE," and the curtain is rung down on a final chorus of God Biology's song.

3. CODA: THE HIGHER KEYS

The *Coda* (July 1978) describes Robert Morse's eventful final week in Heaven. He is to be reborn in Minnesota as a flautist and composer named Tom, will write operas, will see the thinning through and write "THE SWEET REVEILLE/ FOR THOSE STILL LEFT TO WAKE." RM will be crippled but wealthy in this new life, with a devoted sister. Day by day he is readied in the womb, his senses bestowed upon him one by one; finally he is born. Meanwhile in Bombay Maria (as a baby boy) is performing miracles. DJ and JM worry:

Too much publicity won't sabotage
Maria's—Plato's—V Work? AU CONTRAIRE.
GAME PLAN: VAST CHILDHOOD FAME FOLLOWED BY SPELL
OF GREAT QUIET BARGAINING   THEN THE CAREER:
MONEYLENDERS DRIVEN FROM THE TEMPLE,
OUR FRIEND EMERGING AS A SCIENTIST
WILL GRADUATE IN LONDON AGE 19
THUS (HELPED BY GK & WHA) BEGINNING
A SAGA OF DISCOVERY & INVENTION
STARTLING THE WORLD AT FIRST, THEN SLOWLY THINNING

While plans are afoot for JM to read his poem—all 500 pages—
to a select heavenly audience, other news events crowd in from
both sides of the Divide. Mimí Vassilikos, another old friend,
dies unexpectedly. Ephraim has his own unveiling—as Michael,
a notion the mediums entertained in &/4. A moment before the
reading is to commence, Vassilikos himself appears at their door,
grief-stunned, desperate for distraction, and insists that they
proceed; he on their side, Mimí in the "bleachers," are an unexpected fresh bond clenched between Earth and Heaven:

> So in the hopelessness
> Of more directly helping we resume.
> Out come cup, notebook, the green-glowing room,
> And my worst fear—that, written for the dead,
> This poem leave a living reader cold—
> But there's no turning back. . . .
> > Both rooms are waiting.
> DJ bright-eyed (but see how wrinkled!) lends
> His copy of the score to our poor friend's
> Somber regard—captive like Gulliver
> Or like the mortal in an elfin court
> Pining for wife and cottage on this shore
> Beyond whose depthless dazzle he can't see.
> For *their* ears I begin: "Admittedly . . ."

—the first word of *The Book of Ephraim*.

Appendix: "The Parrot"

I am impatient of the myth that numbs
    A spinster as she hums
Sweet nothings to her parrot in its cage.
The haggard eye set in white crinkled paint
Meeting her eye over the cracker crumbs
    Tells much about old age
    Beyond what is serene or quaint.

Our revels now are ended, pretty Poll,
    For midnight bells extol
The individual face behind the mask.
Each dancer seeks his partner to embrace
As if he had seen deep into her soul
    And gave what it dared ask,
    While knowing but a woman's face.

As she grew older, old, it was to sense
    A sad irrelevance
About the Moment she had so long wanted,
When mask *did* matter least, and face *did* tell
More than it knew of private riches, whence
    Came surely the enchanted
    Eye, the enchanting syllable.

Think how the parrot masked always not young,
    Selecting as from dung
The oaths and greetings she let fall when most
She suffered or felt joy was possible,
Destroys the personal with its gray tongue,
    That frail and talkative ghost
    A bird of utterance can dispel;

Speaks with no human voice, which is pretense
    Of gentleness and sense.
Against such masks, its ancient cry awoke
Jungles within her, sunsets of its flight,
Being the music that informed her dance
    Until all music shook
    To stillness in the bestial night.

Notes

CHAPTER 1. INTRODUCTION: MASKING AND PASSION

1. Hannah Arendt, *The Life of the Mind: One / Thinking* (New York: Harcourt Brace Jovanovich, 1977), pp. 42, 59.

2. George Santayana, *Skepticism and Animal Faith* (New York: Dover, 1955), p. 11.

3. Arendt, *Thinking*, p. 27.

4. Vladimir Nabokov, *Nikolai Gogol* (Norfolk, Connecticut: New Directions, 1944), p. 148; *The Annotated Lolita by Vladimir Nabokov*, ed. Alfred Appel, Jr. (New York: McGraw-Hill, 1970), p. 314.

5. Howard Moss, *The Magic Lantern of Marcel Proust* (New York: Macmillan, 1962), p. 3.

6. Peter Davison, "New Poetry," *The Atlantic Monthly*, 204 (July 1959), p. 74.

7. Helen Vendler, *Part of Nature*, p. 206.

8. Letter to the author, November 5, 1974.

9. David Kalstone, "The Poet: Private," p. 45.

10. Donald Sheehan, "An Interview," p. 5.

11. Letter to the author, August 14, 1976.

12. James Merrill, "Object Lessons," p. 31.

13. Arendt, *Thinking*, p. 36.

14. Letter to the author, November 5, 1974.

15. Sheehan, "An Interview," pp. 10–11.

CHAPTER 2. *JIM'S BOOK, FIRST POEMS, THE COUNTRY OF A THOUSAND YEARS OF PEACE*

1. Louise Bogan, "Verse" [omnibus review], *The New Yorker*, 27 (June 9, 1951), p. 110.

2. Ashley Brown, "An Interview," p. 7.

3. The Stevens poems quoted from here are, respectively, "The Emperor of Ice Cream" and "Academic Discourse at Havana"; Merrill's are "Accumulations of the Sea" and "Variations: The Air is Sweetest That a Thistle Guards." Other first poems with a heavy Stevens accent are "The Flint Eye," "Dancing, Joyously Dancing," and "Entrance from Sleep."

4. Sheehan, "An Interview," p. 3.

5. Richard Howard, *Alone with America*, p. 329.

6. Brown, "An Interview," p. 9.

7. Ibid., p. 10.

8. Paul Engle and Joseph Langland, eds., *Poet's Choice* (New York: Delta, 1962), p. 241.

CHAPTER 3. *WATER STREET*

1. Vendler, *Part of Nature*, p. 206.

2. M. L. Rosenthal, *The New Poets: American and British Poetry Since World War II* (New York: Oxford University Press, 1967), p. 40.

3. David Kalstone, *Five Temperaments*, p. 77.

4. Sheehan, "An Interview," p. 10.

5. Kalstone, *Five Temperaments*, p. 89.

6. Brown, "An Interview," p. 12.

CHAPTER 4. *NIGHTS AND DAYS*

1. Kalstone, *Five Temperaments*, p. 93.

2. James Merrill, "Marvelous Poet," pp. 12, 14.

3. Kalstone, *Five Temperaments*, pp. 103–4.

4. Ibid., p. 104.

5. Merrill, *The Immortal Husband*, p. 183.

6. Sheehan, "An Interview," p. 8.

CHAPTER 5. *THE FIRE SCREEN*

1. Merrill, "Marvelous Poet," p. 12.
2. Richard Saez, "Oedipal Fire," p. 170.
3. Merrill, *The Seraglio*, p. 139.

CHAPTER 6. *BRAVING THE ELEMENTS*

1. Vendler, *Part of Nature*, pp. 205–6.
2. From *Webster's Seventh New Collegiate Dictionary:* "a nodule of stone having a cavity lined with crystals or mineral matter."
3. Merrill, "Object Lessons," p. 32.
4. William K. Wimsatt, Jr. and Cleanth Brooks, *Literary Criticism, A Short History, Vol. 4: Modern Criticism* (London: Routledge & Kegan Paul, 1970), p. 719. The authors are discussing Jung's views on "visionary" art, but to cite the statement in this context does not distort their meaning. The subject is treated more fully in my article "Sound without Sense: Willful Obscurity in Poetry," *New England Review*, 3 (Winter 1980), pp. 294–312.
5. Merrill, *The Seraglio*, p. 47.

CHAPTER 7. *DIVINE COMEDIES*, PART I

1. "Palme" by Paul Valéry, trans. James Merrill, *The New York Review of Books*, 29 (March 18, 1982), p. 10.
2. Letter to the author, December 30, 1974.
3. Kalstone, "The Poet: Private," p. 45.
4. Merrill, "Peru: The Landscape Game," pp. 112–13.
5. Cf. "desire sinks/ Red upon piercing stubble" from "Flèche d'Or" in *Braving the Elements*.

CHAPTER 8. *THE CHANGING LIGHT AT SANDOVER* (INTRODUCTION)

1. Vendler, "James Merrill's Myth," p. 12.
2. J.D. McClatchy, "DJ," p. 37.
3. McClatchy, "DJ," p. 35.
4. McClatchy, "The Art of Poetry," pp. 190–91.
5. Vendler, "James Merrill's Myth," p. 13.
6. Vendler, *Part of Nature*, p. 230.

7. Vendler, "James Merrill's Myth," p. 12.

8. McClatchy, "DJ," p. 38.

9. Vendler, *Part of Nature*, p. 227.

10. Ibid., p. 230.

11. Ibid., p. 225.

12. Vendler, "James Merrill's Myth," p. 12.

13. Vendler, *Part of Nature*, p. 225.

14. Thom Gunn, "A Heroic Enterprise" [review of *Divine Comedies* and *Mirabell*], *San Francisco Review of Books* (August 1979), p. 4.

15. McClatchy, "The Art of Poetry," p. 194.

16. Vendler, "James Merrill's Myth," p. 13.

CHAPTER 9. *THE CHANGING LIGHT AT SANDOVER: THE BOOK OF EPHRAIM*

1. McClatchy, "DJ," pp. 30–31.

2. Stephen Yenser, "The Fullness of Time: James Merrill's *Book of Ephraim*," *Canto*, 3 (May 1980), p. 136. Readers interested in a detailed explication of *Ephraim*'s intricacies cannot do better than to consult Yenser's sensitive, painstaking, and thorough essay.

Selected Bibliography

I. BY JAMES MERRILL

POETRY
First Poems. New York: Alfred A. Knopf, 1951.
The Country of a Thousand Years of Peace. New York: Atheneum, 1959.
Water Street. New York: Atheneum, 1962.
Nights and Days. New York: Atheneum, 1966.
The Fire Screen. New York: Atheneum, 1969.
Braving the Elements. New York: Atheneum, 1972.
The Yellow Pages. Cambridge, Mass.: Temple Bar, 1974.
Divine Comedies. New York: Atheneum, 1976.
Mirabell: Books of Number. New York: Atheneum, 1978.
Scripts for the Pageant. New York: Atheneum, 1980.
From the First Nine. New York: Atheneum, 1982.
The Changing Light at Sandover. New York: Atheneum, 1982.

FICTION
The Seraglio. New York: Knopf, 1957.
"Driver." In *The Poet's Story*, ed. Howard Moss. New York: Simon and
     Schuster, 1973.
The (Diblos) Notebook. New York: Atheneum, 1965.

PLAYS

The Immortal Husband. In *Playbook: Five Plays for a New Theatre,* pp. 161–240, 1956. New York: New Directions, 1956.

The Bait. In *Artists' Theatre: Four Plays,* ed. Herbert Machiz, pp. 79–124, 1960. New York: Grove Press, 1960.

NON-FICTION

"Peru: The Landscape Game." In *Prose* (Spring 1971), pp. 105–14.

"Object Lessons" [review of *The Voice of Things* and *Things,* by Francis Ponge]. In *The New York Review of Books,* 19 (November 30, 1972), pp. 31–34.

"Marvelous Poet" [review of *Cavafy, A Critical Biography,* by Robert Liddell, and *C. P. Cavafy: Collected Poems,* trans. Edmund Keeley and Philip Sherrard, ed. George Savidis]. In *The New York Review of Books,* 22 (July 17, 1975), pp. 12–17.

"Divine Poem" [review essay on the *Inferno,* Vol. I of *The California Dante,* trans. and ed. Allen Mandelbaum]. In *The New Republic,* 183 (November 29, 1980), pp. 29–34.

"Condemned to Write About Real Things" [autobiographical sketch in "The Making of a Writer" series]. In *The New York Times Book Review,* 87 (February 21, 1982), pp. 11, 33.

II. BY OTHERS

BOOKS ON MERRILL

Lehman, David, and Charles Berger, eds. *James Merrill: Essays in Criticism.* Ithaca, N.Y.: Cornell University Press, 1982.

BOOKS CONTAINING CHAPTERS ON MERRILL

Howard, Richard. *Alone with America.* New York: Atheneum, 1969.

Kalstone, David. *Five Temperaments.* New York: Oxford University Press, 1977.

Vendler, Helen. *Part of Nature, Part of Us: Modern American Poets.* Cambridge, Mass.: Harvard University Press, 1980.

IMPORTANT ARTICLES

Moffett, Judith. "Sound without Sense: Willful Obscurity in Poetry." *New England Review*, 3 (Winter 1980), pp. 294–312.

Saez, Richard. "James Merrill's Oedipal Fire." *Parnassus*, 3 (Fall/Winter 1974), pp. 159–84.

Yenser, Stephen. "The Fullness of Time: James Merrill's *Book of Ephraim*." *Canto*, 3 (May 1980), pp. 130–59.

INTERVIEWS

Brown, Ashley. "An Interview with James Merrill." *Shenandoah*, 19 (Summer 1968), pp. 3–15.

Kalstone, David. "The Poet: Private." *Saturday Review*, 55 (December 2, 1972), pp. 43–45.

McClatchy, J.D. "The Art of Poetry, XXXI: James Merrill." *The Paris Review*, 24 (Summer 1982), pp. 184–219.

Sheehan, Donald. "An Interview with James Merrill." *Contemporary Literature*, 9 (Winter 1968), pp. 1–14.

Vendler, Helen. "James Merrill's Myth: An Interview." *The New York Review of Books*, 26 (May 3, 1979), pp. 12–13.

with David Jackson:

McClatchy, J.D. "DJ: A Conversation with David Jackson." *Shenandoah*, 30, no. 4 (1979), pp. 23–44.

Index